Robert Blackburn Knigł
with Mark Falstein

A Man's Recovery
from Traumatic
Childhood Abuse
The Insiders

Pre-publication
REVIEWS,
COMMENTARIES,
EVALUATIONS . . .

"**R**ead this book twice! The shock, horror, courage, and healing journey of the author simply cannot be encompassed with one reading. The author describes a midlife reckoning with the gradual disclosure in therapy of unimaginable childhood abuse and incest by both parents. Here, we have an honest account of the difficult work of recovery, insights into the dissociative response to trauma, and the redemptive possibilities that exist within the soul. This book is a must-read for clinicians and laypersons interested in trauma, dissociation, and recovery from severe childhood abuse."

Donald L. Davies
Psychiatrist
in Private Practice,
Aptos, California

"**T**his is an important book on many counts. It fills a gap in the literature about healing from childhood sexual abuse by allowing us to hear from a man, in undiluted terms, about his history and journey of recovery. For men who may be struggling to give voice to their experience, the explicit language used by the author gives permission and validation. For anyone who wants to understand more about dissociation and the kinds of therapeutic work that addresses ego states, this book will be enlightening. Included as well is an interesting and concise critique of a number of theories and theorists working in the field. Though painful to read, this is ultimately a story of the courage and determination of the author to reclaim his wholeness."

Amy Pine, MA, LMFT
Psychotherapist
and Co-Founder,
Survivors Healing Center,
Santa Cruz, California

A Man's Recovery from Traumatic Childhood Abuse
The Insiders

A Man's Recovery from Traumatic Childhood Abuse
The Insiders

Robert Blackburn Knight
with Mark Falstein

HMTP

The Haworth Maltreatment and Trauma Press®
An Imprint of The Haworth Press, Inc.
New York • London • Oxford

Published by

The Haworth Maltreatment and Trauma Press®, an imprint of the Haworth Press, Inc., 10 Alice Street, Binghamton, NY 13904-1580

PUBLISHER'S NOTE
Identities and circumstances of individuals discussed in this book have been changed to protect confidentiality.

Cover design by Marylouise E. Doyle.

Library of Congress Cataloging-in-Publication Data

Knight, Robert Blackburn.
 A man's recovery from traumatic childhood abuse : the insiders / Robert Blackburn Knight.
    p. cm.
 Includes bibliographical references and index.
 ISBN 0-7890-1064-X (alk. paper)—ISBN 0-7890-1065-8 (alk. paper)
 1. Knight, Robert Blackburn. 2. Psychotherapy patients—United States—Biography. 3. Adult child abuse victims—United States—Biography. 4. Adult child sexual abuse victims—United States—Biography. I. Title.

RC464.K646 A3 2002
616.85'8369'0092—dc21
 [B]
                                                                              2001039106

CONTENTS

Foreword   xi
     Michael Jarvis, PhD

Preface   xiii

Chapter 1. Robert: A Proposition from My Inner Child   1
   June-October 1987

My Experiences with Hypnotherapy   2
I Awaken the First Monster   6
More Family Skeletons   10
Splits, Ego States, and Multiple Personalities   13

Chapter 2. Young One, Honey, Dream Woman, and Bear:
    Memories Are Made of This   19
   November 1987-February 1988

Struggling to Believe the Memories   22
Young One: A Second Child Within and a Second Monster   24
Block That Fantasy!—Or Not?   27
The Insiders   29
More Splitting   32

Chapter 3. Child Abuse and Its Discontents   35
   March-May 1988

The Rewards and Frustrations of Amnesia   37
Coping with Wine and Weed   40
"The Courage to Heal," the Cowardice of Denial   42
100 Ways to Kill My Father, Give or Take 85   45
Trying to Show Kindness to the Inner Children   47

Chapter 4. Anger, Despair, Self-Hate, Binges   53
   June-November 1988

I Try to Hide, but They Still Find Me   56
Eddie and How He Died   61

This Is Not What's Meant by a Rich Inner Life 63
Feeling Abandoned 65

Chapter 5. My Man-of-Anger Takes Charge 69
November 1988-April 1989

Massaging the Feelings Loose 71
A Child Molester in a Survivors' Group 75
The Insiders and I Deal with Betrayal 78
The Return of Red: That's What You Get for Theorizing 81
Trauma, Ego States, and Why I'm Not a Multiple 85

Chapter 6. Sex Rears Several of Its Heads 91
April-August 1989

Working It Out with Linda 95
Remembering Abuse, Reading About Recovery 98
Big Honey, the Champion 103
Grace, the Sexually Needy 106

Chapter 7. Earthquakes, Within and Without 111
September-November 1989

Another Group, Another Perp 114
Torture 117
Loma Prieta 119
Listening to the Insiders . . . and a Few Bureaucrats 122

Chapter 8. Q: The Memory of Pain 129
December 1989-April 1990

Looking for Structure Among the Insiders 132
Memories in and out of Time 135
Hitting Bottom with Linda 140
Feeling Q's Pain 144

Chapter 9. Frankie: Befriending the Monster 147
May-October 1990

Talking About Sex—and Enjoying Some 149
A Workshop on Ego-State Therapy 152
Confront My Mother? The Insiders Say No 154

All Ego States Have a Positive Function 156
Working with Jack and Helen Watkins 160
The Dad Introject Becomes Frankie 164

Chapter 10. Male at Risk **169**
October 1990-April 1991

Grace's Sexuality—and Mine 171
More Depression, More Theory, More Denial . . . Less Sex 174
Choosing to Confront Mom 182
Shut Down 186

Chapter 11. The "Oh, No!" Experience **191**
May-November 1991

Couples Therapy 193
Me and My Shadow 197
The Inner Pervert: Crystallizing My Sexual Conflict 199
Q's Sexuality—and Linda's 201

Chapter 12. The Cost of Denial **209**
December 1991-May 1992

Being OK Sexually: Therapy for Christmas Haters 211
Linda and I Deep in Each Other's Stuff 214
Pain, Screams, and Other Unfinished Business 217
The Cost of Ignoring Mom 221
Memoirs of a Child Prostitute 225

Chapter 13. Disintegration **229**
June-September 1992

Bobby and Red: The Insiders Prepare for War 230
Oedipus and I 234
"Moments of Healing": Working with Mariah Gladis 238
Die Soon, Mommy 240
Night of Horrors 244

Chapter 14. Healing **249**
September-December 1992

"The Mother Wound Is Always Deepest" 252

Breaking the Fantasy Bonds   255
Another Christmas with the Insiders   260

Chapter 15. Burning Mom   265
    January-May 1993

Gestalt at Esalen   267
The Insiders Are Healing One Another   270
Putting the Anger Where It Belongs   273
Trusting the Process   277
Letting Mom Die   281
The Pyre   284

Postscript   291

Bibliography   297

ABOUT THE AUTHORS

Robert Blackburn Knight holds a master's degree in psychology.

Mark Falstein is an educational writer and product-development consultant. He has ghostwritten, co-authored, and/or edited numerous books in the business, professional, and self-help fields, including *They Shoot Managers, Don't They?* by Terry L. Paulson, PhD; *Psycho-Cybernetics 2000* by Bobbe L. Sommer, PhD; and *Children of Character* by Stephen Carr Reuben, PhD. He lives in Seattle, Washington.

Foreword

I have had the privilege of knowing Bob for the last five years as he scratched his way out of the terrible quagmire of his past. Betrayed by the very people who were supposed to nurture and protect him, Bob is a living tribute to the resiliency of children. He survived horrendous parental abuse to become a successful businessman, crusading philanthropist, and loving friend, but not before undertaking decades of self-healing personal growth work.

This journey has been a fearless undertaking in and of itself. We all owe Bob a debt of gratitude for having the courage to share his story with us.

In this sensitive testimony to his courageous pursuit of the truth and his own healing, he has woven a fascinating story about the bits of seemingly unrelated evidence which emerged in fits and starts during many years of painfully intense personal growth. His memories formed a frightening mosaic of sadistic torture, presenting a bold challenge to the false memory syndrome believers.

For anyone who wants to understand child abuse from the victim's perspective, this book offers valuable insight. It also provides hope, inspiration, and affirmation to those who have survived an abusive childhood and are trying to make sense of their experience.

This is a difficult book to read, not because the author uses big words or arcane concepts. This book is difficult to read because it tells the truth about one of the "dirty little secrets" of American culture. Behind those closed doors, whether they front a neatly trimmed lawn in suburbia, a dirt road in rural America, or a drug-infested tenement hallway, more child abuse occurs than most of us are willing to admit. This abuse most commonly takes the form of a slight, such as a parent ignoring the child's accomplishment or denigrating the child's personhood ("You're worthless!"). However, as we see in this hauntingly moving autobiography, child abuse can reach down to the lowest depths of "man's inhumanity to man." Bob spells out just how perverted and convoluted this ordeal can be by explaining how desperately dependent he was on his abusers. He *needed* them to love him. He *needed* them to take care of him and protect him. Not only did they fail to perform any of these basic parental functions, they subjected him to a most perverse quid pro quo: In order to survive, Bob had to submit to an unimaginable level of psychological, physical, and sexual abuse, all for the amusement and pleasure of his "caretakers."

Michael Jarvis, PhD
Orange County, California

Preface

This is a book about healing. Although it contains recollections of violence and sadism, the thread of healing is always present. Follow the thread, even where it may seem tangled or invisible. I often lost sight of it myself as I underwent the process of recovery from childhood sexual abuse, but it was ever present, a lifeline through a dark terrain.

I have a unique advantage in writing this book: I am both an incest survivor and a trained psychotherapist. I began keeping a detailed record of my experience in therapy to help me evaluate, digest, and integrate what was happening to me. During this process I read dozens of books and articles about incest, trauma, personality dissociation, memory, and related subjects. I attended numerous workshops, conferences, and training sessions; I listened to hundreds of hours of taped lectures. Much of this material was addressed to mental health professionals, but I did find many books written for sexual abuse survivors to aid their own recovery. In general, I found self-help books written by therapists to be of little help. They tend to talk down to the reader, and they are often more about the authors' need to showcase their knowledge than about healing. Autobiographical accounts by survivors are generally much more powerful, inspirational, and instructive. Virtually all such books, however, have been written by and for women. Although some have been of unquestionable value to me, they contain little that is specific to male survivors. Despite estimates that one in seven American men has been a victim of childhood sexual abuse, few have come forward to bear witness.

I had the wish that my personal story might help others through the difficult and anguished process of recovery. My healing has come at a tremendous cost in effort, time, and money. It is my hope that this work and my painfully won understandings should do more than make one individual less neurotic. This book is one component in a continuing effort to turn my shit into gold.

M. Scott Peck has discussed the idea that mental health is committing to reality at all costs (see Peck, 1978, pp. 44-46). While writing this book, I had a strong desire to censor the material, to gloss over the intensely shameful, humiliating, and disgusting parts of my life. I also felt that these parts might be the most important to record with unflinching candor. I resolved this dilemma by promising myself I would never attach my real name to this account. Choosing to hide my name felt cowardly at first, but one woman's comments in her own anonymous memoir of childhood abuse made me feel clean about the decision. She said she chose not to give strangers the power to throw these intimate and painful facts in her face when she was unprepared; and so have I.

The raw material for this book was my journal and research notes, some 2,400 pages in all, which I edited to 880 typewritten pages. At this point Mark Falstein joined the project. He helped me shape my account into readable form by cutting, consolidating, rearranging, questioning, and clarifying the material. Amazingly, Mark accomplished this draconian task without sacrificing anything of major significance or wounding my ego.

Here and there throughout the book, I set aside my personal narrative to assume a professional role, interpreting and evaluating various theories on trauma and recovery, memory, and personality. I do this to provide readers with information that I wish I'd had; to highlight ideas that might further their recovery; and to caution them against victim-blaming notions that might actually sabotage healing.

One such notion, the so-called false memory syndrome, merits comment up front. Because survivors in psychotherapy often recover memories that have been lost to amnesia, some people would have us believe that such memories are invalid, imagined, or even manufactured by incompetent or unscrupulous therapists. Denial, as they say in Alcoholics Anonymous, is more than just a river in Egypt. In denying the evidence of the reality and prevalence of child abuse, these theorists carry on a destructive, often self-serving tradition that began with Sigmund Freud. I, too, had to grapple with denial and shame as my amnesia was broken and my childhood experiences were revealed to consciousness. If such memories were true, I asked myself, how could I possibly have forgotten them? Likewise, I suspect, many readers will respond with disbelief to some aspects of my story. No one wants to believe that people would victimize children in such a way; it's more comforting and reassuring to deny the validity of memory.

The fact, however, is that amnesia is not only common among victims of trauma, it is typical among them. This was first documented in studies of combat veterans of World War I. Several recent studies focusing on sexual abuse found that between 40 and 64 percent of subjects had experienced partial or total memory deficits. A fascinating finding of this research is that frequently repeated traumas are actually more likely to be forgotten than one-time events. As many therapists observe, trauma affects memory, and severe trauma affects memory severely.

The most telling study was published in 1995 by Linda Meyer Williams. She obtained hospital records of female children who were examined after sexual assault in the early 1970s. Nearly two decades later Williams was able to locate and interview 129 of these now-adult victims. Thirty-eight percent of them had no recollection of the sexual abuse documented in the hospital records. An additional 16 percent reported that at some point in their lives they had been unable to remember the abuse.

A biologist once remarked that the mind, like tooth and claw, is an instrument designed for survival, not for the pursuit of truth. It is only when survival is subjectively assured, and there is an internal sense of safety, that determining truth becomes a priority. I suppose I had reached that place of safety at the time I entered therapy. Truth, as it emerged, initially sent me running for cover, but it was safety and trust that allowed me to begin to heal.

Chapter 1

Robert: A Proposition
from My Inner Child

June-October 1987

"Your conscious mind is very smart," Milton Erickson said, "but your unconscious mind is a hell of a lot smarter" (Carol Erickson, personal communication). I have an MA in psychology and have worked with many of the leading Ericksonian hypnotherapists, but I didn't find out how smart my unconscious was until I entered psychotherapy in the summer of 1987.

Why did I feel I needed a therapist? The primary reason was a serious lower-back problem. I was thirty-nine years old. For years I had kept myself in shape to play tournament tennis and do heavy hands-on construction work, but that Christmas my back had been so bad I'd had difficulty walking. Despite regular physical therapy, I'd been forced to make major changes in the way I lived. For ten years I had been investing in real estate, remodeling houses, and renting them out. I was building the equity I would need to acquire and operate a small, rural tennis resort near the northern California community where I live. Now this was no longer a reasonable goal. My social life, too, had centered on tennis, and I could no longer be a part of that world. My back problems were, and are, real: two partially herniated disks, a malformed vertebra—the list goes on. Yet I suspected there might be a psychogenic component as well. Somatizing—releasing emotion as physical symptoms—was my mother's way of expressing herself, and I despised her hypochondria.

I had other, less immediate reasons for seeking therapy. One was excessive use of alcohol and drugs. As a teenager I went through a typically adolescent heavy-drinking phase. When I went to college in the 1960s, I did a lot of LSD and other psychedelics and gave up alcohol entirely. After college I drank moderately and continued to smoke pot regularly. Now and then I would quit, sometimes for months, usually as part of a diet program for athletic conditioning. Since my back injury, booze (mainly wine) and pot seemed less benign. I had battled flab all my life, but now it had become a more pressing problem.

Sex was another issue. For ten months I had been in a solid, monogamous relationship with a woman I'll call Linda. The only reason we weren't living together was the incompatibility of our pets; her dog would have killed mine. Yet in the past whenever I established a stable relationship with a woman, I'd lose interest in her sexually. Since my divorce six years earlier, I'd had many such relationships: serial monogamy with some lapses of promiscuity, my sex drive for my partner vanishing while my head was constantly being turned by other women, young women in particular. I'd also had a few homosexual encounters, and although intellectually I thought bisexuality was ideal, I didn't feel good about being gay.

Pain and fear, alcohol and pot, teenage pussy and perverted stimulation—add to these falseness about money. I come from an upper-middle class family; I'm well educated and I'd inherited a small income from a trust fund. I had worked hard and made lucky and/or wise investments. I owned two duplexes and four houses and was financially secure. Yet I looked like a self-made, blue-collar man; I wore old clothes and drove a pickup truck. My finances were a closely guarded secret, more private than my sex life.

I had chosen work where I could be my own boss and did not have to dress up or impress anyone. I prided myself on my intelligence and independence. I was an outsider. I had a few good friends but didn't enjoy groups. I hated phonies, hypocrisy, status-seekers, and the government. I was Scottish and frugal in my personal habits and style. Typically, I would do things intensely, become involved in some project and work very hard at it.

MY EXPERIENCES WITH HYPNOTHERAPY

Such was my assessment of my personality at the time I entered therapy. It was Linda, my sweetheart, who introduced me to the therapist I chose to work with. I'll call her Nan. Nan had, at one time, been Linda's therapist.

Nan's office was next to her home. It was a strange but comfortable room. You walked down a few steps to an exposed aggregate concrete floor, like a fancy patio. The walls were partially covered with wooden wainscoting. Above ground level, windows looked out in all directions onto semirural countryside. One wall was all sloping windows.

Nan appeared to be in her midforties. She had a youthful complexion, but her hair was graying. She was tall and solidly built—solid psychologically, too, I would learn. She was an MFCC, a marriage, family, and child counselor. This is a master's-level credential which in California and some other states legally qualifies a practitioner to use the title "psychotherapist."

I chose to work with Nan not because of the specifics of her credential, but because of her experience with hypnosis. I was a student of hypnotherapy, particularly of the work of the late Milton Erickson, who had done so much to deepen psychology's understanding of hypnotic trance and its uses in therapy. I knew how to go into trance and how to induce trance in others.

There is a lingering mythology about hypnosis. It is neither a hoax nor a sinister tool for manipulation. In fact, each of us goes in and out of light trance states several times each day. Consciousness does not simply switch on when we wake up and remain at the same level of intensity until we fall asleep again. When we head for work feeling vague and unfocused, when we become so lost in daydreams that we tune out conversation, when we concentrate so hard on a task that we lose track of time and surroundings, we're in a hypnotic trance. Clinical hypnotherapists guide people in using this innate ability to alter their consciousness. It can be a powerful tool for such diverse purposes as reducing stress, overcoming phobias, lowering blood pressure, controlling pain, improving athletic performance, and curing warts.

In our first few sessions Nan and I did no trance work. We talked, mainly about my problems, my goals, and my background. I thought of my life as falling into three major periods. As an adolescent growing up in New York City, I wanted to be a shrink or a minister. I read a great deal about religion, both Eastern and Western, but I had no faith in any organized church. These goals vanished in the psychedelic haze of my college years.

When I got out of college I had no idea what I wanted to do. I decided that until I found a worthwhile goal, I would keep my body athletically healthy and have fun. One reason for my lack of long-term goals was that both my older brother and my father had died at an early age. My brother Eddie drove his car off the road on the way to his eighteenth birthday party. Five years later my father died as the result of a street beating in San Juan, Puerto Rico. His murder was never solved. His money wasn't taken, and the cops guessed that the beating was about a romantic affair.

In my late twenties, I began my disciplined and organized effort to get that tennis resort of my dreams through investment in real estate. I worked at this program with reasonable success until my back problems put an end to it.

That was when I began to work on the MA. Initially, I considered taking a long trip to Asia but decided instead to go back to school. I had a BA in cultural anthropology and long-term interests in non-Western religion, meditation, Jungian studies, and transpersonal psychology. I chose an independent-study program focusing on hypnotherapy and dreams. I attended workshops and seminars almost every weekend. Many of them were held at Esalen, the famous human-potential center and hot spring overlooking the ocean at Big Sur. The topics and approaches ranged from Jungian stuff to neurolinguistic programming to clinical training. I dove headfirst into the human-potential movement. I kept a record of my dreams, about 400 in all, filling several notebooks. I also earned the California hypnotherapist certificate through the local, somewhat flaky College of the Healing Arts.

I had taken my first course in self-hypnosis in 1977 out of curiosity and a desire to improve my athletic performance. I had an experience then which probably led to my studying hypnotherapy. The instructor got us to go into trance and suggested we visit a room in our imagination, a place in which we felt completely safe. He led us to imagine ourselves descending a staircase and opening a door. He had us slowly examine the room behind the door in great detail, then find our safe place there.

I found the exercise tedious and somewhat silly. I was growing restless and bored. I had imagined a room down a flight of stone steps with a heavy arched doorway, but it seemed pointless. Suddenly, in this imaginal room, I sensed my father come up from behind me. He put his arm around my shoulders and mutely tried to establish contact.

This unexpected event stunned me. My father had been dead for some time then, and we had not been on good terms when he died. I felt that he was asking for forgiveness. I was not confused about reality. I knew that this was just an image, but it still gave me gooseflesh. For several days I mulled it over and finally decided not to forgive him. I didn't know why I made this decision and had no idea of its significance.

After this class, I got involved in real estate and didn't do anything with hypnosis or imagery for years. But when I started working on the MA I often went into trance and visited this room. My father never reappeared, but several interesting characters did: a cynical, angry, funny, red dwarf who was called Red; a thin, puritanical preacher dressed in black; a large, silent bear; a little girl who stayed with the bear; and a sexy, whiskey-drinking black woman named Honey.

These dramatis personae changed and interacted over time. Two of them seemed to have antecedents going back to my childhood; As a young boy I'd had raging, out-of-control tantrums. I remember someone telling me there was a little man-of-anger inside me and that every time I gave in and got mad, it fed him and he got bigger. This man-of-anger seemed to be Red.

When I was in high school I had a dream that made a deep impression on me. In the dream I was at a gathering in our family home, a wake perhaps. All my relatives were there. Everyone was drinking. I drank too much. I was going to be sick. I struggled woozily to my parents' bathroom, tripped over the threshold, and fell headlong into the room. As I pulled myself up on the sink, I stared into the mirror. Instead of my own reflection, a beautiful, sexy black woman was smiling back at me. This, seemingly, was the first appearance of Honey.

Another experience that touched me happened in a seminar on Ericksonian hypnotherapy given at Esalen by Paul Carter. I volunteered to work with him in front of the group. He had been talking about the use of metaphors in hypnosis, and after hypnotizing me he told me the following story: For years hunters in Africa had been aware that they rarely saw elephant skeletons, and rumors circulated about an elephant burial ground with a vast fortune in ivory. No such place was ever found, of course. When a herd of elephants finds an elephant's skeleton they gather around it, touch it with their trunks, and trumpet loudly. Then they crush the bones in the dirt by walking repeatedly over them.

At one time, the story continued, the entire elephant herd in the San Diego Zoo seemed ill. They were moody, off their feed, and losing weight. Vets were consulted, but the animals kept getting worse. The keepers feared that the whole herd would die. In desperation they consulted an alleged psychic. She stood near the animals and began weeping. She wept and wept. Finally she asked if any of the herd had died recently. The keepers told her yes, a young male. She asked about the bones, and the keepers told her they had saved only the skull. She told them to place it in the elephants' cage.

The leader of the herd, an old female, was the first to notice the skull. She went over to it, placed her trunk on it, and began to trumpet. The other elephants gathered. They picked up the skull with their trunks and passed it around, trumpeting and bellowing. After they had all touched it, the bellowing died down. Then, slowly and purposefully, they walked on the skull until it was crushed into dust. After this the herd's behavior slowly returned to normal.

This story did not have an immediate effect on me. I asked for explanations and was given none. But a half hour later when we went to lunch, I felt a wave of intense, bittersweet sadness. Every few minutes for the next half hour or so, these waves of feeling were accompanied by silent tears. I finally had to lie down, amazed at my reaction.

I AWAKEN THE FIRST MONSTER

After such experiences I found Nan's technique to be straightforward. When she wanted a trance she simply asked me to go inside and waited while I did. It was easy and undramatic—no flashy induction or complex, embedded metaphors, no fun stuff. I would lie down, relax, breathe deeply, and enter trance. This established a pattern for our therapeutic relationship: She would walk beside me and support me, but choice and responsibility were mine.

In one of our first trance sessions, Nan asked me to go back to a time in my childhood and reestablish contact with my childhood self. I (or my unconscious) chose a time when I was about twelve. I found myself sitting in my favorite porch swing at our country house at Lake George, in upstate New York. . . .

The child is singing "Swing Low, Sweet Chariot." I ask him if he wants anything. He says, "Yes, sex. A lover." I'm a little taken aback and fumble for a response. Then the kid says, "Why don't you suck my dick, or bend over and I'll fuck you?" He's horny and hostile.

Nan insisted that I draw a clear boundary—no sex with the child, not even in fantasy. I felt shame. My inner child wanted a blow job, and if not for Nan's warning I probably would have given it to him. I (we) continued working with him, asking: "Well, what else would you like? What would you like to be called?" He didn't respond at once, but eventually he decided he wanted to be called Robert. Nan and I continued to talk about my background, problems, dreams, relationships, trance experiences, and fantasies during the first half hour of our weekly sessions; but I began to spend the second half hour of almost every session in trance contact with Robert. With Nan's help, we established some basic rules for our relationship: no sex, no violence, no force. Robert was often angry and difficult, but gradually we got to know each other a little.

Then, in mid-September, I had a strange dream. Inside a shop, three Frankenstein-like monsters were sleeping on tables. I poked at them and ran, then returned and poked some more. Outside hung three beautiful oriental rugs, covering the shop's window and concealing the monsters. I stole the rugs and ran. I felt mischievous. Some homosexual images seemed to be mixed in, but they may have been from another dream.

After telling Nan this dream, I entered trance and made contact with Robert. Nan asked if I was ready to meet the monsters. "Maybe just one of them," I said.

I try to wake one monster and pull it off its table. Suddenly I see, quite clearly, that the monster has my father's face. It is precise and unmistakable, and it has a strange expression. My father's right hand reaches out, palm down, to grasp my shoulder. He starts pulling me toward him and down. He wants me to suck his cock. . . .

The trance imagery stopped. I didn't see my father's genitals—they were blacked out—but I knew what was happening.

I'd had strange physical reactions during the trance: dizziness, gooseflesh, and melting sensations. I must have had an erection because later I noticed seminal fluid in my pants. I was stunned and dazed. I felt both intense shame *(I wanted the contact. I was turned on)* and disbelief *(This could not be real)*.

That week I thought a lot about Dad's sexuality. I'd consciously known he was bisexual since I was a high-school freshman, when I came home unexpectedly one day and found a naked man in his bed. Many of his friends were pretty blatantly gay—and some of them lived with us off and on throughout my childhood—but Dad's homosexuality was never acknowledged. Once, shortly after this discovery, I yelled at him and called him a "faggot." The next day he told me severely never to say that word again and, surprisingly, I didn't. Afterward, my brother assured me that Dad couldn't be gay because my brother had "seen him in action" seducing women.

That was typical of Dad. He loved to party and drink, and he involved us kids in it. I admired his social skills. He had an incredible gift of gab and was a skillful manipulator of people. As a teenager, I had watched him win the trust and friendship of business associates. As soon as they were gone, he'd gloat about how he'd "scored points with that clown." He didn't seem at all bothered by conscience, guilt, or shame.

Often he would go cruising Saturday nights. We lived on West 87th Street, within easy walking distance of a part of Central Park West that was known as "fag row." My father would drink a six-pack before dinner and fall asleep in his chair. Later, when the rest of the family were going to bed, he'd "walk the dog," often staying out most of the night. The next morning he'd show up in the big Presbyterian church where he was a deacon and trustee.

The only other time his homosexuality was discussed in our family occurred several years later. I told my mother that I knew Dad was gay. It was like pulling teeth to get her to nod her head in agreement. We never discussed it again, not even after Dad started spending almost all his time in Puerto Rico with Hugh, one of his long-term lovers, and his marriage with my mother became a complete sham.

I did not believe the trance image, but it had a strong effect on me. I wondered if the abuser could have been one of Dad's friends. Also, if I had been molested, when did it happen? How could I have had such total amnesia? Yet if it didn't happen, why would I (or my unconscious) fantasize it?

All that week I was irritable and uptight. I obsessively reviewed all the kinky, shame-producing sex acts I'd ever done and fantasies I'd ever had. I had a hard time believing the amnesia because I remembered so much I'd rather have forgotten. In seventh grade I spent an afternoon in sexual play with another boy. Later that year I chickened out of an assignation with a gay boy and humiliated him in front of our class by denouncing him as a "faggot." I still feel very guilty about this. I remembered as an adolescent having strange, somewhat erotic fantasies of being drowned in a septic tank. I also clearly remembered the sensation of being forcibly bent over the side of a bed face down with my arms spread, my head turned to the side. This posture memory seemed imbued with the same strange shame and excitement as the image of Dad's hand pulling me down toward his crotch.

I wondered about my own conflicted homosexual urges. I would express desires to men who would not, or could not, satisfy them. When I was around men who were willing and able (and there were plenty of them), I would retreat. I tried to have sex with a half-dozen men, and all but one were impotent. The exception was David, my most recent male lover. He could get an erection, but he literally had no balls, and though he experienced climax, he did not come.

What conflict could have produced this self-defeating behavior against my conscious wishes? It is being on the passive end of gay sex that seemed (and seems) shameful to me; enjoying and wanting to be fucked and to suck dick. Although I had an intense desire to be the passive object, to be a victim, this fantasy carried equally intense humiliation and shame. Except for those two weeks with David, I prevented myself from acting it out. I liked sucking David's dick at first. I liked the tightness of his ass when I fucked him, though the sight of shit on my dick bothered me. I was sure he had fucked me at least once, maybe twice—it was odd I couldn't remember this clearly—but I'd been disappointed. There was excitement and shame and energy, but the act itself provided no release. It didn't satisfy the fantasy. Or maybe I really liked it, but my defenses made me deny the pleasure because I didn't want to be gay. When I'm in a crowd, it's the women that catch my eye, the women I feel drawn toward. The weirdest sex I ever had was with a woman named Jennifer. We would gamble, and the winner would be master and the loser a slave for an hour.

The only limit was no injuries, no scars. These memories were a favorite masturbatory fantasy.

The next session with Nan was hard. I told her all these dirty little secrets, not looking at her face until I was done. Her response was sympathetic and dryly humorous: "When you decide to tell the truth, you really do." She made no judgment and assured me I was entitled to some secrets. However, I felt it was important to tell her all this stuff. These were the most shameful things I knew about myself, and I felt that telling them cleared the decks and allowed us to go deeper.

I was feeling a lot of anger toward my mother. I was angry at her weakness in allowing Dad's male lovers to live with the family. How could she have let something like that happen?

MORE FAMILY SKELETONS

Mom lived next door to me in a home I owned and was renting to her. She'd had a successful career as an educator, but after she retired she was no longer happy living alone in New York. Having her next door was not entirely selfless on my part. She had loaned me money for my business. She also did occasional motherly things such as making me clothes and food, though we almost never ate together. I felt very ambivalent toward Mom. Sometimes when I would see her at a distance, bent and old, sad and worried, my heart would go out to her. Yet in day-to-day living I could barely tolerate her, and there was almost no real contact or support. She was a hypochondriac. She responded to problems by developing migraine headaches or other physical symptoms. Once, when we were children, my brother and I caught her faking a temperature by putting the thermometer under hot water.

She'd also had several psychotic episodes. Once we found her in the street, dressed in her nightgown and looking for formula for her (nonexistent) babies. She was institutionalized for another incident; it happened while I was away at college and was kept a secret from me until I accidentally learned of it decades later. Dad frequently ridiculed her irrationality and her neurosis to us kids, poisoning our minds against her. "Just do what she wants; it's easier than talking with her," he'd say. She, on the other hand, never denounced him.

The memories of Dad reaching out for me, of being bent and held over a bed, stayed strong and charged with energy. When I approached them in trance, my heart would pound and I'd get sexually excited. On the heels of these sensations would come a mixture of shame and fear. During a session in October, I remembered a little more about that bent-over position. I felt a hand pushing me down, sometimes between my shoulder blades and sometimes on the back of my neck. I didn't seem to be able to turn around and look. There were fleeting images of a man moving around, a shape in the darkness. I was reminded of the eyes of a panicked, young horse I'd seen at a race track. They were wide open, rolling, and straining, trying to look around while his head was held by the bridle.

Nan and I tried to let these memories expand in trance. I would try to sense my whole body. At first I was aware only of my eyes, face, and cheek. Then the block moved down a little, and I got a sense of the hand on my back. Frustratingly, this was all that I could see when we had to quit for the day. Other images came to me during the session and later, but they didn't have the same riveting and scary fascination; I saw the tip of a penis pushing at an asshole, a large hand playing with an ass, a thumb being shoved up an ass. These images were dissociated from emotion. I hoped they were speculation or fantasy and not memory.

The issue of spanking came up. I remembered my parents' pride in being "disciplinarians" and "not permissive," but I could not remember a single spanking. Dad did drink a lot. Did unrecalled drunken spankings turn into sexual abuse? Was punishment the only interpretation a young child could put on incestuous sex?

I had been a discipline problem from first grade on. I was thrown out of several schools for fighting. I would steal with no concern about being caught. I stole money from my parents and ostentatiously wasted it. I stole knives from the kitchen and kept them in my room. I matured physically at an early age. By sixth grade I was nearly six feet tall and weighed 170 pounds, and I became the school bully. Once I chased my father out of the house with a knife, screaming that I would kill him, but I remembered no repercussions, no punishment. He ran from me. The happiest period of my childhood was third through fifth grades, when I went to a progressive private school. I was a bed wetter, and I saw a psychologist there, Dr. Bixby. I stopped wetting the bed and was socializing a bit. I was taken out of that school against my will. I was told that the school had insisted my whole family see the shrink and my parents had refused.

Compared to me, my brother was an angel. Eddie was older by a year and nine months. He was never thrown out of school. He got straight As and once was moved up a grade. When he died he had completed a year of an accelerated premed program at Cornell. As any family systems therapist would recognize, we had both adopted stereotypic roles for children of a dysfunctional or alcoholic family. While healthy families tend to produce children who are individuals, dysfunctional families tend to produce children who fill certain prescribed roles. There's the star child who does everything right and makes everyone proud—that was Eddie. Then there's the scapegoat or rebel who's always in trouble and forces the family to deal with his problems—that was me. If we'd had more brothers or sisters, one of them would probably have been the family clown who makes everyone laugh and thereby hides the pain and conflict; another would have been the lost, quiet child who's all but ignored.

The therapy sessions were having an impact on my day-to-day life. My emotions were unbelievably intense. I vacillated between periods of irritability and anger and periods of sadness and depression. I was drinking more and smoking pot regularly. One Friday night I told Linda what I was experiencing in therapy. I just blurted it out. She held me, and I cried intermittently. The crying felt incomplete, restrained.

Real or not, the memories had shaken me up. I felt sorrow for that isolated, lonely child whose best times were spent sitting in the porch swing and singing to himself or playing with his dog. He was caught between a father who molested him and a mother who coped by denial and somaticizing. In one session with Nan I recalled that there used to be wrestling mats in the basement of our home. I remembered once asking Dad why they were there. He said that he, my brother, and I used to go down there and wrestle, but he quit when we boys got big enough to beat him. I had no memory of the wrestling. Finding the hole in my memory during therapy was chilling.

Even though each session yielded details, there were times I didn't buy any of it. For one thing, I couldn't pin down the time that these events occurred. Could it have been when I was twelve or thirteen? I remembered playing homosexually with other boys by then and already seemed to have been damaged. I'd had two serious accidents when I was in kindergarten. One was a fall from a wrought-iron fence outside the school. A pointed iron post caught under my chin and penetrated deeply, leaving me hanging. The other accident happened in an elevator. As the door slid open my left arm somehow got caught and pulled into the mechanism. I was stuck there until a man came and yanked my arm out. Both these accidents required stitches and left small but permanent scars. Were they a mute cry for help? Could I have been abused as a preschooler?

What was my evidence? Trance images and sensations charged with a special energy? A few free-floating, dissociated homosexual images? Yet the emotional intensity indicated that I was on to something psychologically important, whether or not the memories were real.

I started reading the literature on child abuse and incest. Much of it had a preachy, feminist, "politically correct" tone that turned my stomach. They called people who were abused "survivors," not victims. This was supposed to make them feel better about themselves, but to me it seemed like dishonest, mealy mouthed rhetoric.

I wondered about "secondary gain"—the possible reward that can come from real or hypochondriacal symptoms, such as sympathy and attention or being excused from work. Did being a victim of incest have a payoff? Yes, it did. It freed me from guilt feelings about weird sexual fantasies and desires. But it had great costs too. It was so painfully shameful that I would only talk to Nan or Linda about what was going on inside me. I felt cut off from people I'd met pursuing my MA. After two years of going to seminars and workshops almost every weekend, I was no longer willing to participate in them.

I was still trading hypnosis sessions with Dan, a friend I had met in a hypnotherapy class. I could not bring myself to tell him what was happening, but we continued to work with guided visualization in the imaginal room behind the arched doorway. One of the characters, Honey, the sexy black woman, died. The preacher went off somewhere with Red, the tough, humorous, red dwarf. They probably had sex. The bear continued to protect the little girl.

SPLITS, EGO STATES, AND MULTIPLE PERSONALITIES

One thing I was beginning to understand psychologically about myself was that I exhibited a great deal of "splitting." My painful conflict over homosexuality and kinky sex was one example. Often in hypnotic guided visualizations I wouldn't see one figure but two or more in conflict with each other. The division between the child within me, Robert, and my current personality seemed more and more real. We seemed to have different emotions, perceptions, and knowledge. Many times during these early sessions I would cry, but the tears only came out of one eye and without any accompanying feelings of sadness. This was another aspect of severe splitting. I took it as evidence of healing six months later when I began to have tears in both eyes at the same time and to consistently feel sadness as I cried.

Another long-term pattern that seemed to be an effect of splitting was that I would almost never react to something right away. Typically, I'd have to sleep on it before a coherent feeling would form. This may have made me appear blasé, even numb, but in fact I didn't know what I felt. Feelings didn't enter my awareness directly. I subsequently learned there's a technical word for this—alexithymia. I've actually had to train myself to know what I feel.

This splitting and numbing out are also responsible for my lifelong search for intensity. I've always done things intensely. I had taken huge doses of psychedelics; I work and play very hard; I become obsessed with whatever I'm involved in. The thirst for intensity seems to be an attempt to compensate for the numbness.

I've always prided myself on my ability to see through bullshit. I'm hardheaded and cynical. I would have dismissed all this as imaginary foolishness, but in working on my MA I'd read a great deal about ego-state therapy and the relationship between posttraumatic stress and multiple personality. Often when children are traumatized, they dissociate, splitting off and compartmentalizing the part of themselves that experienced the trauma. In milder forms, this splitting produces the "child within" or "ego state" phenomenon. Robert, the personality who appeared in my trances, seemed to be an example of this. In severe cases it leads to full-blown multiple personality disorder (MPD), in which the various ego states or "alters" take control of the body.

Everyone dissociates to some degree. When we concentrate on a task, we're dissociating from distractions. When we take on a specific social role, such as Good Employee, for a specific social situation, we're dissociating from such other roles as Lover, Tennis Player, or Parent. It's the same basic mechanism that underlies the mind's response to trauma—the same mechanism that's at work in hypnotic trance. Some theorists explain trance in terms of cerebral-hemispheric dominance, as a process of the imagistic and holistic right brain rather than the verbal and analytical left brain. I prefer the view first advanced by Pierre Janet and others over a century ago: that hypnosis is based on dissociation.

I was beginning to feel that the real reason I'd gone back to school was to prepare myself to do therapy. Having studied this stuff objectively from the point of view of a (potential) therapist made a great difference in how much, and how quickly, I could accept and understand.

I had just about completed rewriting my thesis on trance and dreams. I had planned to go straight on to a PhD, but now I decided not to. My business was producing enough income for me to live on and only required a couple of days' work each week. I think one reason therapy didn't drive me completely nuts was that the rest of my life was not demanding energy or attention.

It was now late October. At my request Nan agreed to expand our sessions to two hours. One-hour sessions felt too short to me; we often had to stop just when they were getting interesting.

I began to bring a journal to each session and read or summarize the week's entries at the start. I had told Nan that as a child I loved to feel the ribbon on the edge of a blanket between my fingers. She began keeping a length of smooth, yellow ribbon with her notes. Every time I went into trance she'd give it to me, and I'd intertwine it in my fingers. Subjectively, the ribbon felt comforting. I knew from my academic training that this kind of repeated physical stimulus is called an anchor. It facilitates the reinduction and deepening of trance. Because of my bad back, it was painful for me to sit very long in Nan's canvas director's chairs. We would talk sitting up, but when it came time for trance I would lie on the floor on my back with pillows propping up my knees. When I am in a long trance, my circulation often changes, and my extremities get cold. Nan would cover me with a small, soft blanket. It provided warmth, as well as privacy and safety; when we were dealing with the highly sexual memories, I would often get a partial erection.

I can't recall just when the ego states I met in my imaginal room began appearing in trances during therapy. I think they may have been lurking in the background from the start. Trance logic is a lot like dream logic; it doesn't correspond to conscious reality. I had formed the tentative hypothesis that Honey represented the pattern of relations I had developed to handle sexual energy. Her death represented the dissolution of these patterns; I wondered what would emerge to replace them. Red was afraid he would die too, but despite this fear he seemed to want to change. He resented being small; he wanted to grow. I believed that he was the resistant, rebellious part of me. Robert seemed flat without his energy.

I had a lot of theories about Red but no answers. In searching to understand this image in Jungian terms, I noted archetypal parallels. Asclepios, the Greek god of healing, for example, had a small, red assistant who carried his erect phallus before him. Red also reminded me of a weird beatnik I used to see standing in a park in Greenwich Village shouting, "Imgrat, imgrat!" He meant immediate gratification. Was Red the part of me that loves to get high? The fusion of anger and sex? A valuable survival asset? A source of caustic insight? The outsider?

Around this time my mother found some boxes of family photos, and we went through them together. In this way I learned a lot about the family and my childhood without broaching the subject of incest. My father's mother had been in and out of mental hospitals, probably due to bipolar disorder. Dad had refused to discuss this with Mom. He and his father hadn't spoken for years; Mom didn't know the reason for this either. I learned that Dad's gay lover, Hugh, had lived with us on and off from before I started kindergarten. Going through the pictures, which we did in several sessions over a period of weeks, let my unconscious know that I was making a real effort to establish a chronological framework for reconstructing my childhood. The visual images communicated in a way that words could not.

Part of me wanted to scream my memories in my mother's face. I was really split about confronting Mom. Sometimes I saw her as Dad's accomplice, but more often I saw her as just another victim. In any case, I was far too emotional and confused to handle a confrontation well.

I was drinking wine and smoking pot more and more. I was also eating too much. I've always had a tendency to eat and drink too much, especially between Thanksgiving and Christmas, but this year was worse than usual. I realized that I was overdoing it and couldn't continue. I told myself that after New Year's I'd get straight. It was strange that during this period of anger and sadness, I often dreamed of parties. In waking life I don't much like parties; I especially don't like large parties, but my dreams were full of them.

One dream from this time stands out. All my life I've loved dogs; I often joke that I get on better with dogs than with people. In the dream there was a dog that had been very bad. At one point it had been a poisonous snake that a girl had let loose in my apartment. It moved very fast, too fast to catch. The girl mixed up some poison and put it down for the snake. The snake turned into a dog that looked like my dog, Lola. The dog ate the poison after I/we encouraged it to come and eat. I felt *horrible*. I knew the animal was doomed. I got up to go to my room. I punched the door because I was so sad and upset that I'd poisoned the dog.

Poisoning the snake-dog seemed analogous to dealing with my childhood memories; in attempting to deal with a snake (the incest), I poisoned something that I love (the childlike part of me).

The last weekend in October was miserable for me. I was in a lot of pain, both physical and mental. My back was the worst it had been since I first injured it, and I was unhappy with Linda. The strain of the discoveries of therapy was pushing us apart.

Linda was a college professor, classically attractive, six feet tall with blue eyes and flowing light-brown hair. I'd met her through an ad I placed in a singles newsletter. I have herpes, and it was difficult for me to meet a woman, become attracted to her, and tell her about the condition before having sex with her. The ad I wrote began, "HERPES: Damn, I've got it. . . ." It went on to describe the woman I was looking for: an intelligent person with a life and career of her own. That was Linda. Now her career was keeping her busy and pre-occupied, and, despite my neediness, I felt I couldn't make demands on her. She came over on Friday night, but she was so exhausted that she had no energy for me, sexually or emotionally. I felt abandoned and resentful.

She called Sunday morning. I'd been too hurt and angry to call her. She asked if I was okay. I said, "Yes, I'm fine." She said, "Baloney." I broke down and cried. She came right over; thank God she could see through my bullshit. She was wonderful. She held me for a long time, and we made love. I wouldn't admit it, but I needed the physical contact and the emotional support. I needed the love-sex.

For the first time the link between my emotional state and my back pain was clear to me. I was beginning to feel that the force of the molestation had so warped my sexual energies that they were literally twisting and deforming my lower spine; the muscles were pulling each other apart and were red, puffy, raw, and hamburger-like.

One day early in November, I got stoned and lay down after lunch. As usual my thoughts drifted toward wondering about what Dad had done to me. I started to get the feeling of being rubbed by a big, blunt, lubricated penis. This was a memory I often had in trance. It felt like I was being prodded all over my ass, under my balls, and between my legs.

Suddenly I imagined (remembered?) a sharp, shallow penetration of my asshole. When that happened my hips and legs twitched and jerked convulsively. This occurred several times: repeated images and memories of penetration accompanied by involuntary twitches and jerks.

A little later I said to myself, "Your daddy really did fuck you." My body twitched sharply again.

Chapter 2

Young One, Honey, Dream Woman, and Bear: Memories Are Made of This

November 1987-February 1988

I didn't go nuts, attack anyone, try suicide, or mutilate myself. I maintained a relatively normal life, though the emotional impact of the realization was tremendous. I retreated to my bed and spent three days crying and thinking.

Daddy really did fuck me, didn't he? He got me to suck his dick. What else did he do? There were memories of being greased and prodded, memories of being held in that bent-over position. I reviewed the memories over and over and wondered where they stopped.

I was astonished by the intensity of my emotions. I'd always been primarily phlegmatic in temperament. Now for days at a time, I would be depressed and weepy or angry and irritable. The anger was harder to deal with than the depression. When I was sad I could be with people, but when I was angry my bristling hostility isolated me from all human contact.

At the same time I was growing increasingly aware of a disturbance in my sexuality—a knot, a cramp, scar tissue. Every kinky, homosexual fantasy I'd ever had was being stirred up, in Technicolor, vivid and full of energy. An inner voice said, "You're just a greasy faggot like your dad, except you don't have the balls to do anything." It sounded like Dad's voice. It also sounded like the preacher in the imaginal room, who was seeming more and more like Dad.

A strange image started bothering me about this time. It may have come from a dream. A penis is sticking out of a mouth as though it were a tongue. This shifts into a close-up of a turd emerging from an asshole.

Was this a memory? I was starting to think that the only way to deal with the confusion and pain was to stay with the physical sensation and the strange mixture of terror, excitement, and shame that accompanied it. It felt as though the memories I didn't have access to were tied up in my body. The back pain and the strange twitches were clear examples.

I looked for physical ways to release the memories and the pain. I considered Rolfing, acupuncture, a new exercise plan. For ten years I'd been doing yoga almost daily. It had kept my back pain under control and may have helped me build inner strength. Athletics—wrestling, soccer, tennis, running—had preserved my health and saved me from going totally nuts. My athletic history seems to be a progressive refinement of the urge to kick and fight. This experience parallels Arnold Mindell's (1982, 1985, 1987) concept of the "dreambody." In essence, his idea is that the same message, the same information, is trying to come through your dreams, your body symptoms, and your patterns of relationship. Much later I would learn that "body memory" is a well-known concept among therapists. People who have been traumatized often recall a particular sensation, position, or movement without any associated emotion or narrative. Sometimes it's so vivid it feels like it's happening in the present. The concept does not seem so bizarre when you consider that the procedural memories we all experience are a kind of body memory. Procedural memory, as distinct from narrative, story-like memory, is what we use when we ride a bike or drive a car. It is so reliable that we trust our lives to it.

The worst aspect of my memories was that I wanted it. I wanted the contact with Dad. I wanted to suck his dick. The bald fact was that it turned me on. To have him reach out to me made me feel honored, chosen, and valued. I wanted to please him. I wanted to be told I'd done well.

Nan and I worked a lot with the intense shame and self-contempt this feeling produced. I knew I was starved for attention and approval as a child. I don't think Mom ever hugged me. Until I was about six I was largely raised by Gloria, a black woman who was not unlike Honey. She cared for me while Mom pursued her career. As an infant, I lived at her house in Harlem for a time while the rest of my family were away on a long trip. Dad's incest was probably the only physical contact I got from my parents. I remembered him saying frequently,

"You don't have to love me just because I happen to be your father." I was now realizing that he meant, "I don't regret anything and I don't love you."

Around this time the trust fund I'd inherited when Dad died was finally terminated, and I received the money. Just as I was struggling to free myself from him psychologically, the last vestige of his control in the real world ended. His will and the administration of his estate had pissed me off for years. He gave Mom part of his estate, and I was to receive the income from part of it until I turned fifty. The greatest share went to his long-term lover, Hugh. It was just about the maximum Dad could give him without having the will contested. The executor of the estate was another of Dad's gay friends and Hugh's one-time lover. The lawyer for the estate was also part of their circle. Often they took as much money from the estate in fees and commissions as I received. Still, they were careful to stay just within the bounds of the law, and I couldn't challenge them. The only reason I got the money was that the trustee died and his replacement terminated the trust. Maybe my strange shame and secrecy about money is because a lot of it came to me through Dad's hands, though the source of most of it was his own mother.

Nan took a two-week vacation early in December. I reviewed where I was. I had met one dream monster, and it had shaken me profoundly. It had two main components: My father had coerced me to suck his dick, and to some degree I had liked it. There were also partial memories of other sex acts with related shame, self-hatred, and anger. Since then I had tried to integrate this information. I was still getting memory images, but they were coming less and less frequently.

Sometimes the memories appeared as dissociated visual images. I saw myself as though looking at an old photograph or a short bit of film. Even though they upset me greatly, these dissociated memories usually had a numb quality. They were cut off from direct body sensation and feeling memory.

Sometimes the memories would be associated visual images. I saw what the young me would have seen from the point of view of the child's eyes. These memories often stopped or turned black at crucial points.

Then there were memories of physical sensation—the bent-over position, the feel of grease on my ass. They were directly tied to feelings, usually sexual excitement and fear. Typically, these body memories were at first restricted in scope and then expanded slowly. They often were accompanied by an odor. They too often stopped short of crucial points, and they seemed hard to catch and fix in my mind.

All these memories were autonomous. They didn't come when I wanted them, and they often remained fragmentary no matter how I tried to get them to complete themselves. They were largely silent; there were almost never any comprehensible words. I guessed about what happened, but when I examined these guesses in trance, they seemed very different than the memories. They were only ideas without substance or energy.

STRUGGLING TO BELIEVE THE MEMORIES

I struggled toward agreement and congruence between parts of myself. How could I have "forgotten" this stuff? Part of me still didn't want to believe any of it. Every once in a while an inner voice would say to me, "This isn't real. It's just a bad dream; don't believe it." I wanted to deny the whole thing; I had no hard, external evidence. But the intensity of the emotions, the pain, and the memories themselves seemed to make the reality of incest undeniable. I had cried more in the past four months than in the previous twenty-five years. Yet I still wavered and questioned and agonized over what was the truth. What remained beyond my comprehension was:

How did the abuse stop?

How did the amnesia begin?

How old was I when this happened?

What about my brother Eddie, who was Dad's favorite?

I wondered whether my unconscious hadn't revealed the abuse when I was younger because I wouldn't have been able to handle it. Perhaps I would have been sucked into a downward spiral of more intensely bizarre sex acts as I acted out the fantasies and memories. The breaking of the amnesia seemed well timed. I was financially secure, and the management of my business affairs was not too demanding. I had a solid relationship with a strong woman who had been through difficult therapy herself. She was supportive and understanding and didn't freak out when I'd start weeping or retreat into myself. I thought I knew a great deal about active imagination, amnesia, and post-traumatic stress syndrome from an objective, intellectual viewpoint. This knowledge made it much easier for me to deal with what was happening to me, but my real education was only beginning.

I was trying to get a profile of the diagnostic signs that clinicians would look for if they suspected a male client was an incest "survivor." I now believe that there is no single coherent pattern. There are many ways a boy can respond to incest: problems with trust, a peculiar style of guarded posture and speech, passive-aggressive tendencies, drug and alcohol abuse, alexithymia, numbing out with a compensatory desire for intensity, dissociation, depression, self-contempt, shame, difficulty with authority figures, overly responsible or irresponsible behavior, a calm, well-modulated speaking voice, and a history of being a sexual abuser one's self. While I was studying psychology, one behavior I could not understand was self-mutilation. I had no empathy with people who were (in therapists' jargon) "cutters." Now I understood. Several times I had a strong urge to cut myself. It somehow seemed that it would make the pain understandable, external, and easy to heal.

Drinking and smoking pot provided my only relief, my way of medicating the pain. I've never liked my stomach, even when I was in great shape. Now I weighed 210 pounds; it was perhaps the fattest I'd ever been. The idea of abstinence through the holidays seemed gray and grim.

I had hoped that meeting the monster would be like lancing a boil: messy and painful, but something I could get through by gritting my teeth and anesthetizing myself. I'd assumed that all I had to do was recover the memories and everything would be okay. Had I been trying to turn a process into an event?

I felt isolated. The only people I trusted enough to tell about what was happening were Nan and Linda. I was still trading hypnosis sessions with Dan, but I was unwilling to discuss incest with him, and Robert clearly preferred Nan. Eventually the sessions with Dan petered out.

Hypnosis can be like mental massage, relaxing and content-free, but what I saw in the imaginal room disturbed me. The splits between ego states seemed to be becoming larger and more hostile. There had been a fight between the bear and Red. The bear was gone; the little girl stood beside his cave entrance and said not to bother him now. Red's stomach had been punctured by the bear's claw. He appeared small and shriveled, like a punctured balloon. The preacher was gone; I worried about him being on the loose.

My attitude toward the inner figures had been partly in error. I'd been assuming that Red was the holder of the memories, but now I was beginning to think it was Robert. He seemed to be feeling better, somewhat less angry and raw. It was as if he had experienced a reduction of pressure, as though the pain I felt in my conscious life was relieving him of some of his burden.

Nan returned from vacation, and our first session was unproductive. As I drove home I felt defeated. My stomach hurt all day—I "couldn't stomach it." I thought of Red being deflated by a puncture in the midsection.

The feeling in my stomach grew worse. It turned out to be a bad infection. I had to quit drinking wine and smoking pot. The infection cleared up after about a week, but I stayed abstinent. Was this a positive instance of somatization? A beneficial psychogenic illness? I thought so, but I couldn't prove it.

In any case, I quit getting high. A few days later my emotions came back. I was either irritable or tearful, all the time. The Saturday before Christmas I was almost uncontrollably angry. I was looking for someone to hurt. Badly. I was obsessed with fantasies of fights, revenge, hate, and mortal insults. On the street I would see nothing but stupid, ugly, fat people who deserved contempt and physical beatings. I knew this was irrational, but that didn't lessen its impact or make it go away. Fortunately, I had the self-control to avoid people. That night I had persistent, arousing homosexual dreams. Sunday morning I could not stop crying. There were no particular thoughts or memories in my mind, just intense sadness. After it subsided somewhat, I was exhausted. It was a struggle to function even minimally.

YOUNG ONE: A SECOND CHILD WITHIN AND A SECOND MONSTER

During the fall, as Nan and I went over my childhood memories consciously and in trance, I had become aware of a lot of images of myself as a child. One of them had grown into an ego state, or subpersonality, with autonomous qualities comparable to Robert's. This boy was about six. He didn't choose a name for himself, so we just called him "Young One." At first he was only an image, but during the holiday season we made contact with him.

It happened at the end of a particularly harrowing and upsetting session of probing my memories. There was a clear image of myself at about age six, in bed in the house at Lake George, curled up in fetal position and facing the wall. When we met Robert he had responded with defiance and sexualized anger. Young One didn't respond at all. He didn't seem to be crying. He would not turn over and face us. He didn't want to move.

Another split-off child within had emerged. We took the same attitude toward him as we had toward Robert, offering respect, support, and patient observation. There would be no physical contact unless the child okayed it, and firm boundaries were set against sexualized touch. As Young One began tentatively to develop trust, he let us see a little more of himself. It was apparent that he was badly hurt. The entire left side of his face and neck was an open, oozing wound, and he did not want it to be seen.

As we worked steadily to establish relations with the boys, we continued to watch for memories. We went back to that dream of the three monsters. The first monster now appeared to be lying motionless in front of the shop. We prodded the second monster imaginally and tried to drag it out into the street. We did this a couple of times without results. Finally we were able to get the monster into the street, but no memory came immediately.

We moved on to exploring other memories. There were various unresolved fragments of sex and terror in my bedroom in the house at Lake George, the room where we'd met Young One. We worked at them one at a time, trying to let the complete memory emerge.

On January 11, in trance, I remembered.

I'm lying on my back on the bed. Dad is here. I'm terrified. Turning my head from side to side. I can smell him. He's naked, crouching over me, kneeling on my arms. His ass is right in front of my face. It's coming down on me. He lowers himself, wiggling his ass around. . . .

At first when I realized what he was doing, I wouldn't tell Nan. It was too painful, too humiliating. I wanted to curl up and face the wall like Young One and bury this disgusting secret. But Nan could tell something was happening. She kept asking me, gently and firmly. I was crying and shaking as I told her:

"He made me lick his asshole!"

Nan started calling me back from the trance and the memories. I didn't respond right away. I felt shattered. I wanted to hide. I didn't want to look Nan in the eye. Again she called me, more firmly this time. As I started to pull away from the memory, Dad slapped my face, hard. I was momentarily unsure what was real. That stinging slap was absolutely tangible.

Nan postponed her next appointment to give me time to get myself together. I had to concentrate very hard to drive home safely. I slept most of the next day.

I didn't feel angry. I just wanted to hide. I felt isolated. I was unwilling to tell Linda or even to write down the memory in my journal. Linda sensed that I was keeping a secret. She said she felt cut off and somewhat rejected. For days I just hung on and tried to numb my surging emotions. I built my life around therapy sessions, hoping they would provide some relief.

It was almost three weeks later that I finally told Linda. I cried and choked as I told her. She responded with love for me and anger at my father. When I told Nan how much better I felt for having told Linda, she said, "Of course you do! What you were trying to do is like walking around with a dog turd in your pocket and pretending it's not there."

The memory of being forced to lick Dad's asshole seemed to be the second monster. As with the first, fragmentary memories came with the most cogent one. In subsequent trances, there was another man involved besides Dad. I had been aware of a shadowy adult figure in the background while Dad was using me for his pleasure. Now I became aware of a different touch, much gentler and kinder than my father's. This man oiled, massaged, and stretched my asshole before fucking me, and he penetrated me slowly. Holding his dick with its head wedged in my asshole, he pulled the cheeks of my ass apart, working it into me. It was Hugh, my father's long-time lover. At one point when they both were there and my dad was being especially cruel to me, Hugh cried out, "Oh, Harland, don't!" (Harland was Dad's middle name; it's what everyone called him.) I almost never heard words in these trance memories, but it was clearly Hugh's voice.

The animation of the second monster took me on another spiral of belief and disbelief. I wanted to deny the whole thing and forget it. No father could do that to his child. It's too gross to be true. Yet there did not seem to be any possible secondary gain in this kind of memory, and its emotional impact was overwhelming. I had no hard evidence and no possibility of getting any, but I believed the memory.

BLOCK THAT FANTASY!—OR NOT?

The second monster also brought a new surge of intense, homosexual desire and fantasy. This was not loving or kind sex I was fantasizing about. It was sadomasochistic and raunchy: active and passive rape, dominance and submission, bondage, degradation, whipping, ass-licking. It reeked of abuse—there actually was a smell to it, funky and repulsive. The fact that I never acted on these fantasies didn't make me feel any better about myself. My internal critic, the Dad-voice, berated me for having them and berated me for being too cowardly to act them out. I felt tremendous self-contempt. I was glad I didn't have a son of my own. I felt sure I'd compulsively abuse him.

The desire to repeat the trauma seems bizarre, but repetition compulsion is a familiar concept in therapy. John Bradshaw explains its dynamics simply: By recreating the trauma, you allow yourself to reexperience some of the cut-off and denied emotions surrounding the original trauma. Virginia Satir compares denied emotions to hungry dogs locked in the basement. They get hungrier and hungrier, and you have to put increasingly more energy into keeping them locked up. The compulsion lets out some of the emotional energy; but because it doesn't really change anything, it tends to happen over and over. Susan Forward mentions that incest "survivors" often feel intense desire for degradation and self-punishment. My fantasies had a flavor of humiliating dirtiness. Sometimes I thought I needed to reexperience it all. Perhaps only when I felt the full force of the forgotten emotions would I be able to end these desires. The cut-off memories held the pain and degradation I was both drawn to and struggling against. I was beginning to understand my fantasies; but understanding had little impact on my shame, guilt, and self-hatred.

Two things helped me through this storm of kinky sexual energy. One was the reassurance that whenever I was in a room full of people, it was the women who attracted most of my sexual attention. The other was my adolescent memories of a girl named Ruth. I liked Ruth and respected her, and at the time when I knew her I would have told you I loved her. She never let me fuck her, but we did just about everything else. I remember her naked body, her beautiful slim stomach and dark pubic hair, her gentleness and kindness. I remember her smells and the curves of her legs and butt. I remember her beautiful cunt and what it felt like when she let me caress her and put my finger inside her. I clung to these memories whenever I was besieged by stormy and degrading sexual energies—the memory of her feel, moist and fresh and gentle on my finger, made me feel saner, cleaner, and more loving.

Linda and I were making love only about once a week, but when we did it was pleasant and satisfying. I had almost always given her oral sex as part of foreplay, but now I stopped that. It seemed tainted with abuse. For a long time I had held the cynical and arrogant view that if you ate a woman's cunt patiently, artfully, and caressingly enough, you could fully satisfy her, and this would make her dependent upon you. I believed that often a woman would delude herself into experiencing this sexual dependence as "romantic love." This crude theory sometimes worked, but I was beginning to see that its manipulative cynicism owed a lot to what I had experienced as a child.

Nan and I talked a lot about the weird fantasies. She told me about a "survivor" she had known who could only achieve orgasm when she allowed abuse to enter her fantasies. This woman made a decision not to allow these fantasies, even if it meant no orgasms. Nan suggested that I similarly refuse the stimulation of the kinky images. I was not ready to do this. They were too strong and contained too much energy. Refusing them seemed like repression and denial. For me, gay sex was profoundly tainted by incest and abuse, but intellectually I believed that bisexuality is the healthiest, most complete sexual orientation. I hoped that the work we were doing in breaking the amnesia and reexperiencing the feelings would cleanse my sexuality.

I would have liked to take credit for not having acted out these desires, but that would have been dishonest. My conscious mind—my ego—had always been ready, willing, and eager, but it was always blocked. By what? In the imagery that developed, two figures seemed to symbolize this force. One was the bear that appeared in my hypnotic room. "Bear" was large, shaggy, hulking, and almost always silent. He protected the little girl and liked it when she rubbed his ears. He usually sat motionless. When I was hurt or sick, the wounds would often show up on his body. But this time the stomach problems that helped me quit getting high were preceded by his puncturing Red's stomach with a claw.

Bear appeared in trance, daydreams, and active imagination, never in sleeping dreams. "Dream Woman" was a figure that appeared first in sleeping dreams and later in trance. I had met her before therapy began. I'd been about to be hypnotized by another student, and I asked him to give me a posthypnotic suggestion that I have a dream which would answer the question, "How can I relate better to my unconscious?" In that dream I was a police detective. I had broken into an apartment to search it. There was a sexy woman there, naked. I made her get down on the floor and tried to hog-tie her, but my thick rope kept stretching into elastic string. The woman laughed good-naturedly at my futile efforts. I ended up literally having to kiss her ass. At the time I took the dream as a warning that my attempts to control the unconscious weren't working; but now, kissing someone's ass to gain access to unconscious material had taken on a new realm of meaning.

THE INSIDERS

Dream Woman continued to appear in my dreams from time to time. At first I conceptualized her as a Jungian anima figure—a female archetype who could be the gateway to deeper realms—and I was eager for more contact with her. After the "ass-licking" session, she began to appear frequently in my trances too.

All this may seem pretty farfetched. Animals and naked women! A child within, yes, but this guy's got a whole family! How could someone like me—a cynical penetrator of hypocrisy, an intellectual, a businessman, a hard-headed realist—come to value and cultivate these images? How could a distrustful and suspicious outsider come to rely so much on the testimony of "insiders"?

There were three reasons. First, my study of psychology had convinced me of the importance of imagery. Jung, Erickson and many other theorists rely on the power of images. Gregory Bateson has explained perhaps more clearly than anyone else that the language of the unconscious consists not of words, but of images. Like the communication systems of animals, unconscious communication is "iconic" and operates under different laws than our conscious, "aniconic" verbal systems. In trance, for example, as in dreams, there is no past or future tense. Everything happens in the present. There are no negatives either—it's like someone saying "Don't think of a rhinoceros"; you can't not think of something. It was important for me to have this objective understanding of the role of imagery in psychotherapy before my own therapy began.

Second, these images were autonomous. Like dreams, they were not under my conscious control and seemed to have a life of their own. They often did things I didn't like or want and left me feeling confused and frustrated.

Last, these images had, and have, power for me. My emotions were, and continue to be, deeply affected by them, often in ways I don't consciously understand.

It became standard in therapy sessions to check in with both Robert and Young One at the beginning and end of trance. We'd look for them and ask if they needed or wanted anything. Robert was usually standing, often with his arms crossed over his chest with an air of protective anger. Young One was lying on a couch, recovering from being ill. When he felt bad he would curl up in fetal position and face the wall. I gave them food, hot compresses, clean coverings, anything I imagined might help.

Somehow the little girl from my imaginal room started to be associated with the two boys. She was even younger than Young One, about four. She usually appeared happy and childlike. I realized that I had first met her in a posthypnotically suggested dream, just as I had met Dream Woman. In that dream the girl and I were at a lake beside a dock. She went to play in the water and came back covered with sticky mud. I washed her in the lake, dried her, and covered her with my shirt. As I washed her forearm, a cabin cruiser pulled up and anchored. The people onboard stared at us with binoculars, and I worried they might think I was molesting her.

When the girl started taking her place with the two boys, she was accompanied by Dream Woman, who protected her like Bear did. The little girl eventually chose to be called "Honey," the same name as the black woman from my trances who had died. I liked Honey. Seeing her gave me good feelings at a time when they were few and far between. I formed the tentative hypothesis that Robert represented the pattern of adaptations I made in order to deal with my emerging sexual energies in early adolescence; Young One was the one who underwent the bulk of the abuse and wounding; and Honey was the child in me before the wounding who had somehow dissociated.

The question of when the abuse happened continued to bother me. The trance memories had a quality of being out of time and out of sequence. If it had happened when I was an adolescent, I felt I would have remembered it all along. Yet it was hard to believe Dad was vicious enough to have sex with a really young child. I reviewed my childhood memories, asking myself, "When was my daily behavior most disturbed?" The answer was from about age six to age nine, a time of almost constant tantrums, bed wetting, fighting, and stealing. By age eleven I was learning rapidly, making up for the time I'd wasted at school, even though I was an unhappy, surly bully.

Could the abuse have started when I was six? Even earlier? Those accidents when I was in kindergarten—impalement on a wrought iron fence seems an accurate physical metaphor. Something big was forced into my mouth. I was stuck there. It left scars.

Another question that still bothered me was, "If all this really happened, how the hell could I have forgotten it? How could the amnesia have formed?"

I tried to get an answer from my dreams. This was not like consulting the oracle at the temple or New Age mumbo jumbo. There are about eighty articles on the subject in scholarly journals, and researchers agree almost unanimously that posthypnotic suggestions can influence dreams. Within two weeks I had no fewer than six dreams about escaping from something terrifying (often the police—a "legitimate" authority figure, like a father) by going up to a roof or attic or up a chimney (up "into my head").

Two other dreams also cast light on the psychodynamics of amnesia formation. In one there was a rattlesnake loose in my bedroom. Somehow I was responsible for it being there. Very scary. It was hiding under something. At the end of the dream I had the idea of using a vacuum cleaner to get it out. The snake is a good expression of what my father was to me, and I did put those memories in a vacuum for over thirty years. In the other dream, I'd been taken under false pretenses (kidnapped?) to a raft on Lake George. Several people were there. I felt woozy, perhaps drunk. I staggered off the raft fully clothed and swam to shore. I wanted to accuse the kidnappers. A crowd arrived, disembarking from a plane. I pointed out some of the kidnappers. The leader of the kidnappers appeared at the top of the stairs from the plane and received a warm welcome, recognition, and applause. As the dream ended, I was totally confused and disheartened. It was an intensely poignant feeling, similar to what I must have felt as a young boy considering accusing Dad—the well-liked church deacon, the smooth talker, the dominating force in our home.

MORE SPLITTING

Nan and I began to attempt to wake up the third monster. When I went back to the three-monster dream in trance, it appeared as though the rugs that had been covering the shop window were down in the street. Two monsters were sitting or lying on them. In my imagination I went into the shop to get the third monster out.

I prod the monster with a stick, taunting it. The monster moves, but it doesn't proceed dully out into the street like the first two. It moves quickly, trying to hide in corners of the shop. Finally, I chase it outside. Somehow I get it secured by one foot. It's sitting on the ground, next to the other two monsters. It's tied fast by the foot and can't get free, but it won't tell me anything. No memories emerge. I keep taunting and interrogating the monster, but it won't answer. At one point it says, "Suck my dick and I'll tell you!" I'd do it, but Nan thinks it's a horrible idea, reiterative of the abuse. I have to agree with her.

We kept working at the third monster. When we got no movement we focused on other things. In one memory I was face down on a bare, wooden floor. My face was being pushed at an odd angle against the baseboard. There was a thin, round wooden leg of a table near my face and a strong smell of old shoes. At first this memory was limited and largely free of emotion. I was only aware of things in the immediate vicinity of my face, and there were no sensations or sound. But as this memory recurred in trance, the emotion came back. It was terror—sexualized terror. The memory was more like a still picture than a film. Some psychologists have developed a theory of "flashbulb memories." The concept is that certain traumatic events are burned into the brain with such intensity that they are stored by a different physiological process than ordinary memories. This memory, and others, returned to me like moments in time that had been frozen by a flash.

I had several weird dreams about feet. Some of them involved breaking glass and worrying about cutting my feet or my dog's feet. I didn't know what to make of these feet dreams or of the third monster being caught by his foot. I didn't have any special associations with feet, but that was where these images were pointing. I wanted to do something to honor that. I bought myself new walking shoes, the best I could find. I went to a deep-tissue bodyworker and had her work on my feet and lower legs.

I had been getting regular massage ever since my back injury became serious. I like traditional, strong massage. If some part of my body was cramped up, I'd get some deep-tissue massage like Rolfing or Hellerwork. I got into massage just because it felt good, but it became emotionally important once therapy grew intense. It was wonderful and reassuring to be get naked, lie down on a table, and let someone work me over knowing I was sexually safe, that I could trust her hands on my body. It was especially good when I could schedule a massage right after therapy. Later I developed a routine I followed almost religiously: After therapy I'd write up the session while eating lunch, then have a massage.

The insiders, the characters in my imaginal room, seemed to be becoming ever more separated and hostile. It appeared that a fight was imminent between the preacher and Red on one side, and Bear and Honey on the other. Red now looked less like a dwarf than like a healthy, erect penis. I didn't know what to do about the split; all I could do was observe the imagery as it emerged.

Another painful, persistent split was caused by that aspect of me that didn't believe the memories. Whenever I was at my weakest, the voice that sounded like my dad's would attack: "You're just a greasy faggot like your dad; you wanted to suck his cock and you want to suck one now. You're a coward, a clown, a closet case! Hypnosis, dreams, make-believe—you don't really believe that shit, do you? Blaming it on Dad frees you from responsibility for your disgusting fantasies. Isn't that convenient?" In the language of psychology, this voice was an introject, an absorption into my unconscious of someone else's aspect and attitude. I made some attempts to initiate a dialogue with it, but they were fruitless.

Nan and I were getting no further with the third monster. It was frustrating and painful. Almost all my energy was going into therapy. Other areas of my life were on hold. I couldn't make any long-term plans.

One day in late February Nan left a message on my answering machine. She was very tired and wanted to postpone an appointment. I became irate. "Well, to hell with that jerk!" I thought, "She doesn't give a damn. Who needs her anyway?"

I didn't return her call right away. I wanted to find some other helper and not ask Nan for anything. I spent about an hour stewing over it; then I entered trance to see how the insiders felt. Young One was curled up in fetal position and facing the wall.

I realized that getting rid of Nan would be cutting off my nose to spite my face. I wanted to berate and humiliate her and walk away; but instead, even though it was difficult for me, I called and asked her not to postpone my appointment.

Nan agreed. Years later she told me that she considered that phone call a turning point in my therapy. I had looked inside, seen what Young One's needs were and taken steps to meet them. I'd expressed my anger at her clearly and negotiated for what I wanted. At the time, however, I could only feel stunned by the realization of how much emotional energy I'd invested in Nan and how much I'd come to depend on her. I wanted to get the memories out. I wanted to get this damn therapy over and get on with my life.

Chapter 3

Child Abuse and Its Discontents

March-May 1988

As I continued to work at establishing trusting relations with Nan, she and I continued to work at establishing trusting relations with the insiders.

We'd always check Young One's wound. Instead of a wet, open sore covering half of his face and neck, there was now a smaller, dry scab. It itched around the edges, and I tried to get him not to pick at it. In one session he was so frustrated with his wound that he ripped the scab off. When I looked in the wound I saw a little, white worm. Then there were three worms, looking like a tiny cock and balls. After this the wound continued to heal; the scab seemed to get smaller as time went by. Once there appeared to be some unraveled, black-brown wire in it.

Bear seemed ill. He moved slowly and with difficulty, and this worried me. Dream Woman had become the predominant caregiver for Honey. They usually stood side by side, Dream Woman with her arm around Honey's shoulders.

As the standoff with the third monster continued, we were still getting random details of the memories of sexual abuse. One session had a lot of stuff about leather belts. An unbuckled belt hanging down in front of a man's pants turned into a penis. The image flashed back and forth between belt and penis. There were vague memories of being whipped with the belt.

Several times I recovered memories and images in trance only to have them sink back into amnesia. It seemed analogous to the difficulty of recalling dreams unless they're promptly recorded. I have no idea how many memories I regained and then lost again in this way.

I had many dreams and nightmares. Many of them were about building or remodeling houses, of houses half-built or half-demolished. I was doing electrical work, repairing leaks, building fire walls. In one dream I was admiring a complex installation of circuit breaker boxes and subpanels. I took these images primarily as metaphors for the state of my ego, my personality.

One dream seemed especially important. It took place in Australia, on a dock that serviced offshore oil-drilling platforms. (Before I entered therapy I'd had several dreams about oil fields, oil creatures, and "the grease area," a dangerous and terrifying place which was often walled or blocked off.) Barges were bringing in oil. One of them brought in an injured man in a medical emergency carrier shaped like a coffin. The injured man's name was Fricatee Jones. He was hurt badly. A bunch of his relatives were there. A friend of his happened to come by looking for him, and they told him, "Yeah, he's here." A guy from the oil company opened the container and pointed out how Fricatee's spine was sticking through his chest and that he'd probably die: "Ain't much chance he'll live, and he *has* to be made aware of this." *Sad.* Very sad. There was some feeling among the relatives that Fricatee was so tough he'd make it. The oilman explained that Fricatee had been standing over a "dome" when it exploded from built-up pressure. At one point the oilman bantered with a supplier of parts. The supplier said, "Where can you find somebody to pick up these pants?" The oilman said, "That's easy—just pay money." They also discussed where to eat.

I was not in the dream. I observed it as if watching a film, but I identified with Fricatee Jones. He seemed like the wounded Young One I was striving to rescue. The dream contained great sadness, which I continued to feel after I woke. I thought about the dream for months afterward. Its symbolism seemed so exact and revealing. I think the oil fields, as well as the earlier dreams of oil creatures, were references to the lubricants Dad would rub on me. Fricatee's injury connected my back problems to my dream symbols and to the emotions from the abuse—Fricatee's spine shoved through his chest was like being fucked up the ass till it breaks your heart. The coffin was a perfect metaphor for amnesia. The name "Fricatee" is like mortgagor/mortgagee, lessor/lessee—fucker/fuckee? The casual, cynical callousness of the oilmen reminded me of my father. The dream carried a lot of complex emotions, and this account only begins to point toward its meanings.

THE REWARDS AND FRUSTRATIONS OF AMNESIA

In March, body memories began to return. The awareness that had been limited to my face now expanded to my head and then to my feet and knees. I was pulling away, arching and struggling; then I collapsed. I thought this was the memory of Dad's cock actually penetrating my asshole, but it was vague and tended to sink back into amnesia.

Was this amnesia merciful? I didn't know. It frustrated me. I worked against it as hard as I knew how. I felt I needed to have my memories back, no matter how ugly they were. If I was going to heal, I needed to feel what I felt, no matter how painful it was. But the process did not go according to my conscious wishes. I couldn't get all the memories at once. I only seemed to get new material when I had emotionally digested the last batch. Arnold Mindell says of psychotherapy that you can heal as fast as you can integrate the material into your life. Did "integrating the material" mean healing the splits in my personality? Grieving for the wounded child and the lost years? Letting out the unexpressed anger and pain? Silencing or satisfying the internal critic? What did I need to do?

April 4 was my fortieth birthday. Linda and I went away for a few days. We saw old friends, visited a hot spring, went wine tasting in the Napa Valley, and ate too much gourmet food. My unconscious cooperated. I actually was able to stop obsessing about incest, weird sex, shame, anger, pain, and sadness. I enjoyed this vacation, this respite.

One month later I had found another hole in my memory. Between the ages of about five and eight, I had a bedroom on the third floor of our home, quite near my parents' bedroom. I could not remember the bed at all. While revisiting the bedroom in trance with Nan, the memory came back.

There are several dissociated images—asses, erect penises. A growing feeling of excitement and fear. I remember the bed now; it's the bottom half of a bunk bed. I'm lying face down in it. Can't move

my feet. They're tied to the corners of the footboard. There's some-
thing flat and wide around my ankles—belts or straps, maybe sheets.
Dad is kneeling between my legs. I try to pull away. He pushes my
legs apart at the knees. I struggle to get away. I distinctly feel intense
stretching on the inside of my legs. He pushes my knees apart with my
feet tied down, my legs bent. My ass can't help but open and move up
and back toward him. Toward his goddamn erect cock. Disgust. De-
feat.

The sequence started as associated memory. I was in the child's body, seeing through his eyes and feeling what he (I?) felt. Then it flipped into dissociated mode, like watching a movie. I could see his cock touching my ass, but at penetration the memory faded out. The fucking was still in amnesia, but the sexual energy that accompanied the recall was tremendous.

. . . Dad takes my ass in his hands. He pulls it apart, hard. The heels
of his hands are together over my asshole. His fingernails dig into my
ass. Hugh is here too. I see his face with eerie, photographic clarity. I
look down his naked body. His huge erection. I am forced to suck his
dick. Or am I forced? . . .

During the trance my body twitched. I had gooseflesh all over, and I cried and cried.

That night I told Linda what had happened. She held me and tried to comfort me, but I felt awkward and irritable. I was glad when she left me alone. I found no comfort or refuge in her arms, and this scared me. I didn't want to touch anyone or to be touched. Like Young One, I wanted to curl up in a ball and not see anyone. My crying felt like a choked, silent scream.

These memories started me on yet another spiral of disbelief and denial. That critical inner voice, the Dad introject, was giving me a hard time. It expressed vast, bitter contempt for me, my "memories," my sexuality, and my attempts at therapy. It was clever and persuasive. It knew exactly how to shame me, exactly where I was weak. Its contempt burned like acid, but those body memories were clear, vivid, strong, exact. They were real. Where the voice was most successful was in attacking my sexuality and making me feel like a perverted, foul worm.

I enjoyed giving them blow jobs. That bold fact shamed me painfully. I covered it, justifying it by thinking it was so much better than other things they made me do, no wonder I would prefer to suck them. There were images of being fucked, of sucking dick, of a man's naked ass; all permeated with dark, masochistic sexual energy. Should I willfully refuse these fantasies? What should I do with the stressful energies, the weird, powerful, stimulating, guilty excitement? Was this my sexuality, or only the emotion-laden memories of abuse? Would these energies fade or transmute? Was I gay? Would I ever be able to have sex with a man that was not a reiteration of abuse? Would I end up hating faggots?

In reading the literature on childhood sexual abuse, I found that the more graphic descriptions turned me on. This horrified and disgusted me. How could the rape and torment of children stimulate me? I was feeling untempered hatred and disgust for my sexuality and myself. One of my deepest fears was that I was really like Dad and Hugh, "one of them," an abuser. With all the reiterative abuse arousal, I was afraid that at some point I'd find myself aroused by a child—or worse, that I might actually have abused a child at some point. This terrible thought haunted me. With all the amnesia I had, why couldn't it be true?

There was so much amnesia that wouldn't move. That fragmentary memory of being on the floor, face twisted sideways, in the corner where the wall meets the floor. The smell of old shoes, the table leg. This much was burned into my memory by overloads of pain, terror, and excitement, but I couldn't get anything more. What was happening? Where were my hands and arms; why wasn't I protecting my face?

My relationship with Linda was strained. She complained that I didn't seem to care whether she was there or not. It was true I was self-involved and sometimes would not tell her what was obsessing me. Once I tried to let some of the intense, kinky energy of the memories into our lovemaking. I was a little drunk. We were engaging in mutual oral sex. I started playing with her ass and asshole. I could feel the flavor, the odor of abuse begin to surface, and I let it come. Then Linda said, "No, not my butt." I stopped at once and went to the missionary position.

I was hurt by this seemingly trivial incident. We had engaged in anal stimulation before, and it was okay. I didn't understand her reaction. We didn't talk about it for a week. When I mentioned it to her, she said, "Boy, were you weird!" Her tone was one of disgust mixed with fear. She went on to say that she didn't like the intercourse afterward; she was scared and it hurt.

COPING WITH WINE AND WEED

I was crushed and deeply shamed. I felt perverted. I was civil to her, but I was thinking, "How could I ever have been such a jerk as to rely on her love? I don't need her. I'll get her for this." I knew my feelings were overreactive, but I felt betrayed. I wanted to hurt her back; I wanted to cut her out of my life.

Fortunately I didn't strike out at Linda or try to hurt her. My love and trust slowly returned. We realized that she needed support. I was almost impossible to be with, no matter how hard I tried to act normally. This small attempt to find an outlet for the weird sexual energy nearly destroyed my relationship with Linda. I had no idea what to do with it. Would it clear itself? Should I deny it and suppress it? Should I get a male lover and fully explore it?

I was back to consuming a bottle of wine and one big joint a day. I'd typically smoke pot during the day and play the piano for hours—blues mostly, but also jazz and pop. Then I'd drink wine in the evening to relax. I wasn't doing it for fun; usually I'd get high alone to dull my feelings. It was excessive and abusive use of drugs. I knew it and I felt bad about it. I was afraid that the drugs would put Robert, Young One, and Honey back to sleep and I would lose contact with them. I made plans to quit, eat better and exercise more, but I kept putting them off.

I didn't want to admit this problem to Nan. I wanted to handle it on my own. Nan had displayed an A.A. attitude which I didn't like. I knew that A.A. and the other twelve-step programs were the most successful way of dealing with addictions. I also knew that the understanding of compulsiveness and codependence that has grown out of A.A. was very significant. I just did not accept a lot of their ideas. This may be partly because I've always been a loner, and A.A. is based on groups. Nan said several times that she thought my dad was an alcoholic. I wouldn't accept this. I felt that it let him off too easy (ie, "The poor man was sick; he had a disease"). Fuck that. He was an adult. He should be held responsible and accountable. His actions shouldn't be blamed on a bottle. Where does sickness end and evil begin?

I quit drinking and getting high and went on a diet. I promised myself I'd stay straight and eat right for forty days. It seemed an appropriate, biblical duration, long enough to have a real impact on my health, but not so long that I would feel seriously deprived.

During the fast I tried to focus on determining when the abuse happened. Based on my size in the memories, the places where the abuse occurred, and the number of incidents, I guessed that it probably went on approximately between ages five and nine. Nan and I asked about this in trance. We got no answer regarding the beginning of abuse, but when we asked about the end I saw an image of a hand drawing a figure eight.

It was a visual image, not a spoken word. The trance images were still almost completely silent. The inner figures communicated through images or body sensations. The major source of words was that glib, critical voice. Its contempt and bitterness were almost exclusively communicated through words. I don't know whether these patterns of intrapsychic communication are peculiar to me or if they are typical. Wilson Van Dusen, PhD, longtime chief psychologist at Mendocino State Hospital, observed that the hallucinations which really harmed his psychotic patients were typically glib and convincing talkers. The more benign hallucinations generally used few words or were silent.

I knew that if I were going to heal, I would have to unravel and change some of the effects of incest on my life. In an attempt to assess how my personality compared with descriptions of other "survivors" I worked up quite a list:

- Weird S&M homosexual fantasies and attraction/repulsion
- Multiple psychological splitting and dissociation
- Distrust, cynicism, social isolation
- Numb, out-of-contact feeling countered by drugs and a desire for intensity
- Shame and shyness
- Compulsiveness
- Trouble with facial recognition; unwillingness to ask names
- Blasé demeanor; unwillingness to express surprise
- Overuse of booze and drugs
- Not liking my body, even when in top shape

- Periods of "workaholism"
- Disgust about sexual desire; tremendous relief and release after making a sexual connection with a new lover
- Extreme bookishness and intellectuality, especially in childhood and adolescence
- Family role as bad boy-scapegoat, later as caretaker-therapist for Mom
- Very early physical maturation
- Hatred for bosses, government, and other authority figures
- A career without status or recognition; doing work that's dirty, hard, and "beneath an educated man"
- Little or no intimacy or peer-group contact
- No trust of intuition, inner voices, or perceptions
- Inability to feel; disconnection from feelings; delayed emotional reactions to events
- Anhedonia; no pleasure even in major successes
- Discomfort about dressing up and looking good
- Extreme hatred of hypocrisy and phonies
- Somaticizing: chronic back problems, herpes, childhood accidents, rashes
- Not having a family of my own
- Nightmares and sleep disorders

I also made a list of positive effects:

- Contempt for phonies sharpens perceptions of dishonesty.
- Self-reliance and independence lead to self-discipline, tenacity, lack of pretense, and a certain strength of character.
- Bookishness produces a well-read, scholarly mind.
- Being an outsider provides perspective and originality.

"THE COURAGE TO HEAL," THE COWARDICE OF DENIAL

I tried to analyze my life in terms of my coping strategies. Denial, forgetting, repression, and splitting were important. Anger and hate were covers for pain. Drugs, wine, and food provided a sense of fullness. Intellectualism was an elitist and snobbish escape. Compulsive and intense involvement in work, athletics, or other projects absorbed my energies. My interest in non-Western history and culture now seemed like a desire to occupy my mind with matters far from home. My interest in yoga and meditation also seemed partly escapist. (There may be a distinct personality type that becomes involved in meditation to armor itself against its emotions. Meditation and yoga can calm your fires and strengthen your ego structure. Meditation appears noble, exotic, beautiful, and respectable, while dealing with personal wounds often isn't.)

I coped with fear of betrayal by not trusting. I coped with shame by having no peers to shame me and no status or persona that could be shamed. I coped with painful emotions by splitting myself off from all emotions.

I don't want to make my life sound all bad; there was much I was proud of and happy with. My financial success pleased me. Even though I had inherited money from Dad (and this still galls me), it was a long way from a modest monthly income to owning eight homes. It had taken hard work and determination. There had been several good, nonabusive love relationships in my life. I had a few long-term friendships I felt good about. I was pleased with my intellect and my cultivation of knowledge in such diverse areas as history, architecture and drafting, religious studies, psychology, and anthropology.

In fact, the cultivation of knowledge was one defense mechanism that was serving me well. I was investigating the literature on incest and on adult "survivors" of childhood sexual abuse. At first it was hard to buy these books. I'd feel overcome with shame and have to force myself to take them to the cashier. Sometimes I bought books on other subjects to camouflage the incest books. I'd occasionally wait until there was no one else at the counter, but I'd be unable to look the cashier in the eye, and I'd feel myself flushing with embarrassment.

Although I disagreed with much that was in these books, reading them was good for me. They gave me different viewpoints and filled in pieces of the puzzle. I learned that most authorities agree that at least one in four girls and one in seven boys are molested before the age of thirteen. It made me feel less like an isolated freak. Most of the books moved me, even the poorly written ones. Many ideas they expressed seemed to apply to me. One woman spoke of memories stored in her body, of physically feeling the screams that she could not scream as a child. A woman breaking through amnesia spoke of how sexual arousal for her was linked to feelings arising from her childhood abuse: shame, disgust, pain, and humiliation. Another victim attested to isolation, addictions, and intense emotions shielded by outward aloofness.

Probably the best, most helpful book I read was *The Courage to Heal: A Guide for Women Survivors of Child Sexual Abuse*, by Ellen Bass and Laura Davis. It is a well-balanced combination of exposition and case histories that conveys both factual information and emotional impact. The authors don't shy away from even the most painful, intimate problems. Even though I disagree with much of it (especially when the authors confuse feminist theory with the healing process), this is the first book I would put into the hands of anyone trying to deal with having been abused.

The best book specifically for men is Mike Lew's *Victims No Longer.* It too presents a balanced blend of didactic material and personal stories. Lew has a gentle and reassuring tone, and he never speaks from the one-up position where so many therapists seem to live.

An important subject discussed in many books is Sigmund Freud's original theory of neurosis. In his 1896 paper, "The Aetiology of Hysteria," Freud stated that neurosis resulted from childhood sexual abuse, often incestuous (Freud, 1959). The paper was not well received. Then, as now, people didn't want to hear about child abuse. Jeffrey Masson's book, *The Assault on Truth,* documents how Freud collapsed under the pressure of criticism and ostracism. In an act of great cowardice, he changed his theory, claiming that his patients' memories were fantasies. The origin of neurosis, he asserted, was in children's fantasies of sex with their parents, not in real acts of violation. This idea, the celebrated Oedipus complex, was much more popular and became the foundation of psychoanalytic theory. When one of Freud's students and closest friends, Sandor Ferenczi, began to assert the reality of child abuse, Freud worked to suppress publication of his papers. Freud blamed the victim and, in the process, made himself rich and famous. His cult-like, pseudoscientific following came to dominate European and American psychotherapy and probably set back the understanding of how to help abuse victims a hundred years. In my angrier moments it seemed appropriate that a man who made a career out of lying should have died of cancer of the mouth. Freudian analysis, like bloodletting, will go down as one of the truly stupid errors in the history of medicine.

100 WAYS TO KILL MY FATHER, GIVE OR TAKE 85

Extreme anger continued to be my most difficult emotional problem. When this mood was upon me, it completely cut me off from the support of other people. I could not stand to be with anyone. The anger seemed to be free-floating. I would get angry at whatever was in my immediate environment. I always had enough control not to do something stupid, but there were times I felt strained to the breaking point. It bothered me that the anger was directed to all sorts of trivial people and events in my daily life instead of where it belonged—right in my father's face.

Nan suggested I get a tennis racket and pound on my bed. I refused; it seemed inane. Moreover, because I had been a bully and a fighter as a child, I didn't want to start hitting again. Instead, when I took my daily two-mile walk to the beach, I imagined that with each step I was stepping on Dad. I stepped on his face, his stomach, his cock, and his balls. I got the most satisfaction from walking on his hands and fingers over and over. I'd think, "You'll never be able to grab a child again."

Doing this provided some satisfaction, but it did not solve the problem. Nan suggested that I might make a list titled "100 ways to kill my father." I started this task with glee. I added to the list slowly over a period of a weeks, and at first it felt good. It felt as though my anger was going where it belonged. After a while, however, I began to feel that my enjoyment of these fantasies made me an abuser like Dad, and I quit adding to the list. My problems with anger were far from solved.

100 WAYS TO KILL MY FATHER

1. Hold up a straightedge razor and as he comes at me let it split his cock down the middle.
2. Cram him, hog-tied, in the bottom of a frequently used outhouse, and leave him there until he drowns.

3. Surround his limp dick with razors, and show him films of boys being sexually abused and tortured. As his dick gets hard he'll slice himself up and bleed to death.

4. Nail him down spread-eagled and naked in the Arctic during spring season, where the mosquitoes are the worst in the world. Allow the bugs and slow starvation to kill him.

5. Drill holes in his flesh where it won't kill him quickly. Pour fluids from the genitals of a bitch in heat into these wounds. Tie him down and release male dogs, one after another.

6. Put dynamite up his ass and light it.

7. Immobilize his head, prop his mouth open with sharp sticks, and use his eyes, mouth, nose, and face for an ashtray at a smokers' gathering.

8. Shove two one-half-inch round pieces of metal pipe up his ass. Slowly force them apart until he is ripped in two.

9. Starting with his feet, burn him over a fire until he passes out. Give him enough medical attention and time to heal between sessions, so that he lives at least until his genitals are burnt away.

10. Chop off his fingers and allow his hands to heal. Then put fishhooks into every square inch of his body, including his eyeballs, and lock him in a padded cell. Give him enough water and food to live.

11. Make a large, splintery wooden dildo and line the urethra with metal. Fill it with a viscous acid solution instead of semen. Fuck him in the ass and mouth a couple of times a day. Be sure to spill acid on his face.

12. Plug his ass with a huge dildo with fishhooks or spines on it, and sew it in place. Force-feed him slowly until he bursts.

13. Make a wire mesh cage which encloses his body from the waist down in a squatting position. Put a sharpened stick between his knees to hold them far apart. Introduce large, starving rats to the cage. When his genitals have been completely eaten away, remove the rats. Being sure the rats are fully fed and sleepy, place them in a similar cage around his face. This will give him plenty of time to think about what is coming.

14. Ram a glass tube up his penis and shatter it. Give him lots of beer so he pees himself to a bloody, slow death.

15. Pluck out one of his eyeballs and fuck the socket.

TRYING TO SHOW KINDNESS TO THE INNER CHILDREN

During one session Nan and I focused on Honey. Her left arm appeared to be injured. There seemed to be sticky dirt all over it from near her shoulder to her hand. This reminded me of that dream when I had first met her and rescued her from the lake. Nan and I tried in trance to clean and help heal her arm. It looked something like an X ray. I could see the bones meeting in the elbow. The bones looked like an erection and ass almost converging.

Later during this session a fairly coherent memory of a specific incident returned:

I seem to be about five. There is the sensation of having my penis grabbed hard. Someone sucks and licks it. Now there is a huge dick in my face. I can feel its heat against my cheek. I can feel it pressed against my lips. Someone is turning me over, laying me down on my stomach. The dick rubs against my wet or oiled ass. Between my legs. Does he come? I guess so; I don't feel it. I feel terry cloth wiping me off, and this seems reassuring.

I bought a stuffed animal for Honey, a small white bear with very soft fur and a ribbon around her neck. Some months earlier Linda had given me a large, vaguely human-like stuffed doll which I came to associate with Robert. It was comforting to have it around when I was alone and crying. I developed the theory that having a physical object at a particular location provided a sensory anchor for the memories and emotions that formed Robert. I placed it in a spare bedroom of my house. When I wanted communication with Robert, I'd sit down on the couch in that room and let myself drift into trance while holding or touching the doll. Later that winter I'd bought a second stuffed animal for Young One, a furry light-brown bear with a gentle expression. I'd felt a little silly—a tough, grown man playing with stuffed animals—but I was not going to let embarrassment stop me from doing something that seemed to help. Now I had one for Honey too. At first I worried about leaving the little girl on the couch in the spare bedroom with the two bigger boys. I (she?) feared she'd be molested. The boys agreed to protect her, and Dream Woman stayed with her also. The couch became a place of refuge for me, and the three animals were a source of comfort.

More and more, I was finding myself able to check with the insiders on my own. It didn't occur to me at the time, but in hindsight this was an important healing step. One evening I lay down on the couch and went into trance. I greeted the children and asked if they had anything they wanted me to know. I quickly got the image of a hand grabbing a penis and pulling it hard. It seemed to come from Young One. Fearfully, I rejected the image because I was concerned about sexual contact with the children. However, I soon came to feel that this was a valuable communication, and I apologized for my reaction. Did Dad yank on my cock? As punishment? Sadistically?

There were still big blanks in my memories. I didn't feel the feelings I'd had as a child. I remembered none of Dad's or Hugh's orgasms. I remembered no intense, physical pain. How much would I have to reexperience before I could heal? When would my emotional state settle down? When would I be able to undertake a big project and get on with my life?

Thinking about these questions that weekend, I lay down and relaxed. I went into trance and greeted the children. It required a great deal of clarity about boundaries to deal with intensely sexual memories without having the kids feel seduced or reabused. I reaffirmed these boundaries and asked if the children needed anything or had anything they wanted to say. I saw an image of a pile of shit in the corner of the room. I took this to mean that there was more stuff that had to be cleared out.

Nan and I went looking for the feelings in our next session. We checked with the boys, and then let them go to the park and have ice cream. Honey was upset, and Dream Woman held and comforted her. In trance I followed my heartbeat.

Robert has his arms crossed over his chest. Now he opens them. . . . There is a turd on the floor. My face is pushed toward it. Now a huge penis is in front of my face. I suck it. No emotions. I ask Dream Woman for help. Image of myself as a boy, alone and curled up in fetal position facing the wall. Numb. Confusion in the numbness, the confusion of an unjustly punished child. I want to hide under the bed or between the bed and the wall. I remember pain but do not feel it. I remember being fucked, trying to get away from each thrust. Images of a boy's ass—sexy. (I had an erection.) Moving diagonally across the bed with Dad on top of me. Trying to get away from the thrusts. He grabs my hair pulls my head back keeps thrusting. (My body jerked; my buttocks contracted.) I think I'm screaming. My body collapses; I guess I pass out. Tears. Emotional pain that feels like it could go on forever.

I very much wanted to curl into a ball myself, but I didn't. We had to end the session. In the process of reorienting from trance, we greeted the children, and they hugged and supported me. I continued to cry, less bitterly now. I thanked the children for their strength and help.

I'd had a memory of remembering the physical pain, but the memory of the pain itself was still blocked out. It was not a direct reexperience; it was filtered through that confused and hurt boy lying curled up, facing the wall. I wondered if this was the trauma that split off the Young One.

Two days later I tranced and checked with the children again.

Robert's arms are uncrossed. I see his broken heart: a clear image of a stylized, red Valentine heart split vertically down the middle. Jagged edges that look almost like the profiles of faces. An erect dick appears between them. Robert is tired of keeping his arms tightly crossed. He does it so that his heart won't fall apart. I tell him that at the next session with Nan, we'll see what we can do. Young One's wound is much smaller. A slit. A big cock comes out of it. Violent, sadistic images of being slapped in the face, raped, having his ass pulled apart. Now someone on his hands and knees, waiting to be fucked. Someone sucking dick.

Honey is happy with her stuffed bear. Her arm is still covered with sticky stuff—mud? dirt? pus? We wrap it in bandages so that the bear will stay clean when she holds it. Dream Woman is with her. Dream Woman warns me not to get high if I want to learn more in the next session.

This was the first direct comment about drugs I'd had from the inner figures, and I honored it. The fast was going well. Some irritability occurred the first week and some loss of joy in playing the piano, but that was all.

In my next session with Nan, the memories were different. I remembered being abused gently. At first I was sucked, and then my ass was fingered.

I can feel the finger massage inside of me. Now I'm being rolled over on my stomach. Greased. Penetrated. It's Hugh; different smell and much gentler than Dad. He rolls over on his back and pulls me on top of him, keeping his cock in my ass all the time. I am so small. The top of my head does not reach his chin. I feel his hands on my lower stomach and groin as he fucks me from underneath. Now he's finished. He rolls me off him. I catch a glimpse of his dick, covered with shit and come. Waves of fear. Internal voice: "This ain't real! It couldn't be!"

Sucking their dicks now. Clearly two men. Conversation between them. Indecipherable. Hugh puts only the head of his dick in my mouth; doesn't smell much. Dad's crotch smells acrid and sharp. Not gentle when he fucks my mouth. Really cramming his cock deep down my throat. Hugh's relative kindness seems to inspire Dad to be more brutal.

As often happened during trance, I experienced a lot of spasms and cramps in my upper stomach. They were strong enough that my whole body twitched. Toward the end as I was slowly reorienting, Nan expressed sympathy for my pain. The Dad introject said, "What pain? You enjoyed it, you little creep. You little whore. Sometime you'll be longing for a big, stiff dick up your ass or in your mouth."

Again the memories of pain were dissociated. I didn't feel pain. I felt fear and a desire for numbness, a desire to space out. Afterwards the muscles of my upper stomach and lower chest were tired and sore. I felt like I was near the edge of a vast reservoir of sadness.

I took time the next day to trance on my own. I asked Dream Woman what I needed to do. She pointed to the pile of shit in the corner of the room. What did I need to do with it? Let my face be pushed into it? Find gold in it? Eat it? Clean it up? Use it for fertilizer?

The next day I was browsing in a bookstore, and a painting on a book cover riveted my attention. A Middle-Eastern potentate was sitting on the floor against a wall in a spacious, shadowy room with his henchmen on either side of him. Standing in front of him, facing him, was a naked boy. He held a large serpent which was partially wrapped around his body. The artist's use of color and light was richly sensuous. The boy's naked ass was in the exact center of the picture. It was beautiful. It appeared that the boy had just finished a performance of some kind. The potentate was staring at him with a mixture of desire and cruelty. I felt a little turned on and intensely ashamed.

That afternoon I was filled with fantasies of confrontation and hate. My neck and shoulder muscles were tied up in tense knots. I wanted to hit someone. I wanted to cut myself. I wanted to smash and destroy Nan's office. Everything and everyone I saw provoked fantasies of confrontation and striking out to cause pain.

Inside, Dream Woman was still pointing to the pile of shit. Was it my sexual energy, tied to passive, sadomasochistic, homosexual fantasies? That jeering inner voice—"You liked it, you little faggot!"—the horrible fact was that, at least in part, it was right. There were times when I longed for a good, stiff dick up my ass or in my mouth. The shame burned like acid. I felt disgusted by it; I hated myself for it, but it was true. These were not clean desires. They were painful. They reeked of abuse. Repetition compulsion, the twisting of immature sexuality, the punitive father introject—none of these theories could mitigate my massive self-contempt and shame. That book cover picture had evoked something in me. If that boy had been performing in front of me with his snake, I would surely have fucked him.

Chapter 4

Anger, Despair, Self-Hate, Binges

June-November 1988

Dream Woman points to the shit in the corner. It looks like a coiled snake. Or a penis. An eyeball appears in the palm of Dream Woman's hand. Means what? . . .

Her pointing finger looks like a gun. Now like a cigarette. A sinking, sickening feeling in my stomach: it's the glowing coal at the end of a stick from the fireplace. Panic: He couldn't have burned me. He couldn't have burned me. Calm down, calm down. Quiet and receptive. The coal is pressed into an ass—mine?—on the bottom of the tailbone. No feeling or memory of physical pain. A clear moving image, like a film, but totally dissociated. . . .

My face and head are twisted at an odd angle against the wall. My face is shoved into someone's ass. I'm lying naked on the floor. Dad is kicking at my asshole as though trying to fuck me with the toe of his shoe. I'm being held, stepped on. There's something that looks like a golden asparagus tip: a strong image.

Is it important to recover the sensations that go with the memories? Dream Woman nods, but I get the feeling that what is really important now are the memories themselves.

The children appear as their stuffed animals. Young One: Dad threatened to put my eye out with the glowing stick. That's what the asparagus is, the glowing coal seen from very close up. . . .

I kept wheeling through the same cycle. In trance I would recover memories of abuse, and the insiders would symbolically confirm them. My emotions would swing back and forth from intense anger to deep despair. One day it would take all my self-control not to hit people when I went out to buy groceries; the next day I would be sinking in an ocean of sadness. The emotions brought on my back pain and other physical distress. To deaden the pain, emotional and physical, I would binge on pot and wine. Tensions with Linda would mount until I couldn't stand having her around. After a while I would get the urge to do more work in therapy, recover more memories, and continue healing. I'd stop bingeing and go on a diet. Then the dreams would return, along with the memories, and the cycle would begin again, each time revealing a little more.

I had no clear goals, but I felt that I couldn't stop. Without the hope of healing that therapy provided, I would drown in an emotional cesspool or kill myself.

Robert: sad and distraught. Clenching and unclenching his hands by his sides. His head hanging down: shame and helplessness. Nan: "The shame is his father's, not his. Imagine something for his hands to do, give him a towel to wring. . . ." Young One is lying on the couch. A penis and balls are sticking out of the wound on his face. He wants to rip them out. Honey is glad to see me. It is good to hold her. Dream Woman is with her. Pointing. More images of a glowing stick coming very close to my eyes. . . .

I went in and out of believing the memory of the glowing stick. It seemed impossible a father would threaten his son that way. Yet the feeling in my body when that stick approached my eye was strong and convincing: tingling, shivering, gooseflesh and a sensation in my gut like when you go down in a fast elevator. The blatant sadism weakened that contemptuous, "you-wanted-it" inner voice. Nobody wants their eyes burned out.

All my life I've strongly disliked having anything near my eyes. I have a hard time when I get my eyes examined. I don't even like it when a lover's caressing fingers come near my eyes. Was this why an eyeball appeared in Dream Woman's palm? The time I saw the racehorse with its head held still and its eyes wide and rolling in terror—did that also touch this buried memory?

I was sleeping ten or more hours a night. At first I thought I needed all this sleep because I was processing stuff in my dreams. I came to realize it was just exhaustion. The strain of holding all the anger and irritation and not striking out cost me all my energy.

Robert needed (I needed) a way to express the anger that was free
of abusive or sexual overtones. I felt like I was the one suffering from
the anger. In some ways, it felt as though I was being abused again.
Would simply feeling the anger free me from it? Or would I have to
act on it, or perhaps experience its connection to the abuse?

*Robert clenches and unclenches his hands, recrosses his arms on
his chest. (Is this the symbolic equivalent of my withdrawal from
Linda and hiding my feelings?) We work with Young One to pull the
cock and balls from his wound. ("When you've got 'em by the balls,
their hearts and minds will follow.") A knee comes out and we pull on
it; then a foot, the other leg, then all of him. His hands are last; they
are trying to grab and hold. It's Dad. Fuck you, Dad! Get out, you
piece of shit! You bastard creep! Nan: "Can you separate the good
Dad from the bad, and keep the good?" There is nothing I want to
keep. The "good" is nothing but bullshit, blandishments and seduction.*

*No pain or strong emotion. I feel mildly anesthetized. Young One
quickly goes to sleep. We roll him on his side with the wound facing
down so that it can drain. We put a loose bandage over it. Dream
Woman cares for him, stroking his forehead and guarding him. We
put Dad in a garbage can, but that doesn't seem secure enough. We
put him in a dumpster and make sure he can't get out. . . .*

I checked with the children often while processing these memories. Almost every day I'd spend time in the bedroom with the stuffed
animals. I put Honey with Robert. I sat and held Young One's bear
and cried. Several times I hypnotized myself and imagined that my
breath, like warm, slow ocean waves, was washing out Young One's
wound.

*Young One looks better. He wants food. I give him chicken soup.
He wants to sit up. Robert holds Honey, guarding her. He's tired and
irritable. Pissed off that he's not getting much attention. He feels that
the strength of his self-control hides how deeply he hurts and needs.
Dream Woman helps with Young One. The eye-in-hand image has
changed. It's a field of black with a transparent "X" in it, like the
crosshairs of a rifle sight, in which I see a close-up view of an eye.
Sometimes the eye appears normal and sometimes opaque.*

Nan and I tried to understand the X-eye image. It was hard to enter, but when I did I saw a naked woman's body, including a close-up of her genitals. Was this Mom? I was dismayed by the thought that there might be whole new realms of abuse, but we didn't get any more images or information.

Young One's wound is healing well. Image of male genitals in the wound. Not Dad's; too small. Maybe they're Young One's genitals. I tell him yes, you're a sexual being, and Robert has done a great deal to integrate these energies. I tell him that in his life he will have many beautiful women as lovers. . . .

Young One is afraid that Dad will return. The image of his wound looks a little like an orifice. I think that when his ass heals from one assault, he knows it's time for another. Dad is dead, I assure him; he will never attack you again. Look at all your protectors: Dream Woman, Robert, Bear, Nan, and me. Young One looks much healthier. He sits up and eats a big breakfast. . . .

We kill Dad's image with a pistol shot to the temple. I take the corpse to a crematorium and watch as it enters the flames. Then I sift through the ashes. The X-eye is there in the ashes, and so is Honey's bandaged arm. Young One feels quite sad, and so do I. Like having to shoot a beloved, but rabid, dog. . . .

I TRY TO HIDE, BUT THEY STILL FIND ME

I slacked off on the inner work. At the time I felt that something had come to a conclusion, but with hindsight I realize I was avoiding what lay ahead. There were too many loose ends.

What about the inner children? Would we be unified into one person, remain separate ego states, or function as a team?

What about my sexuality? In *The Courage to Heal* I'd found several quotes that seemed to apply to me. One of the quotes spoke of "a kind of imprinting. . . twisting together pain, humiliation, violations, and arousal" (p. 263). Another victim said that because of her abuse, "Shame, secrecy, danger, and the forbidden feel thrilling" (p. 255). A third said, "I was so horrified that those were the things that turned me on. I just wonder if that isn't really the hard core, the pivot of this whole thing—the shame and horror and utter self-despair about being turned on by terribly abusive, sadistic situations" (p. 262). It reassured me to know that other people had experienced the wounding, pain, and self-hate that I was struggling against; but my sexuality still seemed tainted.

What about Mom? Knowing her patterns of denial, I still couldn't imagine anything positive coming out of talking with her. At one session with Nan I had remembered having seen Mom naked and then lying down beside her. It felt sexual. This was about all we found. It was easy for me to believe that as a child, I could misinterpret other adults' behavior as sexual because of what Dad and Hugh were doing to me. Nan felt that the memories of contact with Mom were very different in quality and tone from the memories of abuse. Nevertheless, I still felt a lot of anger toward her. Even if she didn't actively participate in abusing me, at some level she must have known. She'd abandoned me.

Did I need to retrieve more memories? I still had no recollection of physical pain or the abusers' orgasms. I didn't understand the third monster, the X-eye, or Honey's arm. And what had happened on those wrestling mats in the basement?

Part of me still hoped it was all just a bad dream. I tried to go on vacation. I quit reading about incest and child abuse. I put more energy into my business and thought about what to do with the rest of my life. I was forty, I had no dependents, and I was financially secure. I could go in any direction. I considered writing, teaching, starting a family, getting a PhD, doing more real estate projects, starting a Far Eastern art-import business, becoming a therapist. Joseph Campbell's (1988) clear and convincing answer to this kind of life-direction question is, "Follow your bliss." My trouble was that I didn't know what my bliss was.

When I was high on pot, the memories stopped cold, and I paid no attention to dreams. I rarely checked inside, but when I did I saw a spoon in Young One's wound. The spoon held a dark-brown viscous liquid in it. With an "Aha!" I realized there was still a spoonful of bitter medicine I had to take, and that I would continue angry and frustrated until I did. At Nan's, waiting to see her, my feelings of "I don't want to do this" were countered by an inner voice that said, "This is the most important thing in your life—don't blow it!" I was irritated at Nan, even though I understood that the feeling of irritation was really due to my avoidance. It was a relief not to feel, struggle or remember, but I knew that path led to boredom and to more and stronger drugs.

I was bored with myself and therefore bored with Linda. She didn't like me when I got high, and most of the time I felt annoyed by her presence. Our sex life was almost nonexistent. I've always had a quick escape hatch in relationships, and I was close to using it with her. The least insult or sign of untrustworthiness, real or imagined, causes me to cut the connection and transmute the emotional bonds into hate and anger.

When my pot ran out, I decided not to get any for a while. I started reading and thinking about sexual abuse again. I listened to tapes of Pia Mellody's seminars on abused children. Mellody, an addictions and codependency counselor, says that the child picks up and carries the unexpressed or denied emotions of the primary caregiver, even if this transfer is accompanied by abuse. If the abuser represses shame, the victim feels shame. If the abuser is consumed by hidden self-hate, the child will hate itself. Maybe this was why Robert experienced his father's shame as his own, and why the contemptuous father-like inner voice was so strong and withering. To a young child, its parents are godlike in their powers. If something is wrong between parent and child, the child necessarily feels at fault. The gods could not be wrong. If they were, the whole universe would be bad and crazy.

Mellody speaks of three levels of dissociation: side-by-side, up-on-the-ceiling, and the black hole. In the first you experience yourself beside your body as the abuse occurs. In the second you witness the abuse from as far above as possible. In the third you completely disappear into a black hole. I knew all three dissociations. For me, the black hole is like the eye of a tornado.

Nan once said to me, "You go so far inside yourself to hide." This seemed wrong. I went outside myself, far, far away to outer space. For years I'd had repetitive nightmares about invading aliens. I recognized them now as a symbol of the dissociated parts of my personality and the dissociated memories, which have, in a sense, returned to conquer me.

Nan and I started exploring what went on in the room with the wrestling mats. There was a clear, frozen image of Dad sitting naked with his knees apart and my brother Eddie standing in front of him, holding Dad's erection in his hand. Eddie had a pleased look on his face, almost smug or proud, as if he were enjoying the attention and preference. If there was anything that came before or after that image, it was quickly lost to amnesia.

Consciously, I had always known that Eddie was Dad's favorite. Was he Dad's sexual favorite too? Were we trained and seduced into competing for Dad's sexual attention? Was I a rejected second best, even as an incest victim?

I dreamed repeatedly about Dad approaching me sexually. At first this was gratifying: the dreams confirmed what I had learned in therapy. Still, three such dreams in one night did not seem positive. In some dreams I fought back, attacking Dad's face and threatening to tear his eyes out. In other dreams I was curious and turned on, and this flooded me with shame.

I stayed depressed for days, except for the times I was so angry my hands and body shook. In either state I'd get drunk. I'd get pissed off at Linda and send her away, then wake up with a hangover and hate myself for being such a jerk. Meanwhile, I kept working with Nan on memories from the basement.

Eddie stands between Dad's legs. He's shorter standing than Dad is sitting. He holds Dad's erect cock, looks proud. I'm there too. I feel rejected, jealous. . . . Now we're both standing between Dad's knees, playing and giggling. The heat of his hard cock. His hands running down our bodies. His big fingers playing with my ass. Sucking me and Eddie, this memory hazier. . . . Me playing with Eddie's genitals. . . a kid's ass seen from behind. We are so small.

Now I'm lying face down on the mat with Dad on top of me. I feel his weight; smell him. He rubs his cock around my ass, between my legs. No penetration, no pain. Wiping me off now. I see him cinching up his belt and going up the basement stairs. Confusion, total overwhelming confusion. What happened? I'm abandoned, alone. . . .

As I reoriented from trance, I felt tremendous sadness. For the next two days I cried so much it was difficult to function. Was Dad's weight pressing down on me the first time I knew this wasn't giggles and play? Was I passing back beyond Young One's era and into Honey's? Those accidents I'd had in kindergarten—were they my (Honey's) only means of expression? My mute scream?

I remembered another accident I'd had in that room, years later, after the wrestling mats had been replaced by a Ping-Pong table. One day, while playing Ping-Pong with Mom, I fell against a corner of the table and hit my balls very hard. I waited hours in a hospital emergency room for a specialist to show up and decide if I needed surgery. He finally arrived, direct from the operating room, with blood splattered on him. He said I just had a bad bruise and could go home. When we got home Dad was drunk and angry that his dinner was late.

This accident now seemed to have double significance. It was my mute cry to Mom, telling her that my sex had been damaged in this basement. It was also a nearly perfect screen memory, both for the sexual abuse that had occurred there and for my anger at Dad. (A screen memory is a memory of a real event that is somewhat acceptable to the conscious mind and is not subject to amnesia. It has an eerie, distinctive emotional tone to it because it carries the meaning or energy of a repressed, "forgotten" memory.)

At our next session Nan told me about a group starting locally for men who had been sexually abused. She suggested that it might help me, especially with working on shame.

My reaction shocked me: shame-filled fear, almost panic. I tried to defend myself against these emotions by turning them into anger, but that didn't work. All my life I've been a loner. I've never identified myself as part of a group. Support groups were something mushheads went to when they didn't have enough strength of mind to form and hold their own opinions. And now I was scared shitless at the mere idea of going to one.

I had thought I was well on my way to being done with therapy. My panic made me realize that I was only at the beginning of integrating the material, of real healing. Nan didn't try to push me. She just gave me the group leader's name and phone number, telling me that groups are not for everyone, but reminding me again that it might help.

Then I went into trance.

We work on Honey's left arm. It still appears wounded and covered with sticky mud. I seem to see lips on her elbow. Between the lips a cigarette . . . a little penis. Dad's face looms above me in an off-white room. I'm lying on sheets on my back. I'm a baby. A ring—a circle of wire. It's the circle of wire in a safety pin. I'm being poked with the pin—an accident? It can be made to look like an accident. He's poking my penis with the pin repeatedly. A wave of feeling: sadness, overwhelmingly intense; my hairs standing on end; gooseflesh all

over my body: The critical voice says, "You couldn't remember any-
thing that young!. . . "

It seemed significant that the voice didn't say, "Dad wouldn't do
that to you."

I left Nan's in a daze. Much of the session was lost to amnesia,
even minutes later. I didn't believe I could remember something that
happened at such an early age, but that wave of feeling was not something I could have made up.

Thankfully, I had a lot of work to do that week: a few small remodeling projects, road work, and maintenance. It felt great to put in long,
productive days, to be tired and sore at night and not to be thinking
about abuse all day.

That weekend I took a friend and his three-year old son to one of
my rural houses. We swam nude in the pool there. Seeing that child's
naked body had a strange and powerful effect on me. He crawled and
walked and played by the pool, exposing his genitals and ass without
a care. I was not turned on at all. I felt queasy and scared. I wanted to
shout a warning to him. I wanted to cry. He was so small.

EDDIE AND HOW HE DIED

In trance Nan and I continued to focus on Honey. The memories
seemed to be coming from ever earlier times; we were clearly passing
out of Young One's realm and into hers. Her left arm still had sticky
stuff all over it. We tried to wash and then bandage it so it wouldn't
make a mess. We tried everything we could think of to see what was
wrong with her arm and figure out how to heal it. Honey liked being
held, but she didn't want to sit on my lap. Dream Woman nearly always stood beside her, protecting her.

Who was Dream Woman? I had identified her and Bear as images
of the amnesia, the force that protected me from my memories. Did
she represent some benevolent power within my mind? Or was amnesia a product of survival mechanisms? One of the cliches of therapy
is, "Trust the process." What was the nature of this process, so clearly
stronger than the conscious mind? Dad had been dead nearly twenty
years, and yet the impact of the returning memories was nearly destroying me.

Wherever the amnesia came from, it had probably saved my life. Literally. I hadn't died in a teenage "accident" like Eddie.

I often thought about the weekend of Eddie's death. Dad and I had planned to drive up to Lake George to celebrate Eddie's eighteenth birthday with him and his friend, Chuck. Eddie and I had been getting on very well since he'd been away from home. He had invited me up to Cornell a couple of times for wild parties at his fraternity.

Dad was teaching me to drive. He let me drive up to Lake George on back roads. While I drove, he drank. After a few hours I didn't want to drive anymore. Dad piloted the car a few hundred yards, but he was obviously too drunk. I got him to stop, and I drove the rest of the way. When we got to Lake George, I gave him a hard time about getting so loaded that he couldn't drive.

We weren't expecting Eddie and Chuck until late that night or early the next day, so we went to bed. In the middle of the night I got up to pee. Just as I was getting back into bed, Dad appeared in my room, naked. I was afraid. He came over to the bed and started telling me that Eddie had had an accident and was dead. Then Dad said he was cold and told me to move over and let him into the bed with me. I did. I froze up and didn't move. I didn't cry for my brother. I felt confused and ashamed that I didn't cry. I held my body rigid and as far as possible from Dad. He told me all the details he knew, and then just lay there naked and silent in my bed. Finally, even though it was about three in the morning, I said with as much force as I could muster, "I want to get up now." He got up and went to his room. I got dressed quickly and went downstairs to start a long and painful day.

Eddie had been driving. No other cars were involved. He just drove off the thruway and crashed. He was killed instantly, and Chuck was only slightly bruised.

At the time I didn't understand why I was so frozen with fear when Dad got in my bed. (I knew Dad was bisexual, but the incest memories were already in amnesia.) Later that weekend Dad told me how he had learned of Eddie's death. The police had called Mom in the city. She called our Lake George neighbors, the Churchills, who were good friends of ours. Harold Churchill came over in the middle of the night, sat down on Dad's bed, put his hand on his shoulder and told him the news. Dad made some crack about thinking at first that Harold was a homosexual trying to make a pass at him.

My understanding of that weekend had been changed by what I had learned in therapy. I think this story was Dad's way of simultaneously discounting and exploring my feelings about the sexual abuse. From the time of Eddie's death, Dad was cold and hostile toward me. There was not even a pretense of affection. I thought at first it was because I'd given him a hard time about driving drunk on the same day Eddie died in an accident that was his own fault. I also thought that Dad wished I had died instead of Eddie. Now I think the real reason for his animosity was that I would not have sex with him that night.

I still feel bad that I didn't cry for my brother, but I no longer blame myself. It's one more thing my father took from me.

THIS IS NOT WHAT'S MEANT BY A RICH INNER LIFE

Nan took off on a five-week vacation beginning in late September. The week before she left, we discussed the course of my therapy to date. She said that many people breaking the kind of amnesia I had need to be temporarily institutionalized. She guessed that it would be another year before I felt settled and whole. Hearing her say these things made me sad. I didn't want to keep my life on hold another year, but I knew I was still too distraught and unstable to make long-term decisions. She also commented, "It doesn't get much worse." I had a sharply split reaction to this pronouncement. One part of me appreciated the sympathy and her respect for the enormity of what I had endured. Another part of me thought it was complete bullshit and questioned Nan's judgment.

On the whole, though, I thought she was doing a very good job, and I told her so. I admired her strength. I doubted I could have tolerated the emotional pain if I were in her position. There was much we disagreed about, issues of politics and worldview, but this was no impediment to our working together. She kept her ideology to herself. There were firm boundaries, and we related as client and therapist.

I wasn't expecting much from the last session before Nan's vacation. I wanted a rest too. While she was gone I planned to get high, make music, eat and drink, and not think about incest. I thought the last session might tie up some loose ends and smooth things over, but the insiders had a different agenda.

Young One is still ill, still an invalid. He is not ready to get up and be an active child. The bandage on Honey's bad arm is smaller and slit up the side. It looks like an Ace bandage. As I examine her arm, I notice it looks like an oar held in an oarlock by a pin. I don't understand. Pin . . . pinned to the mat . . . safety pin. . . unsafe?

Honey is/I am lying on her/my back. Her/my left arm is out to the side, the elbow bent at a right angle so that the forearm is sticking up into the air. My arm is greased. . . . Dad comes and sits on it. My hand and most of my forearm go into his asshole. Heat and the pressure on my arm as it is gripped by his ass muscles. . . . Now Dad is on his hands and knees, his ass in the air, my arm stuck in his asshole almost to the elbow. . . . My hand and forearm are covered with grease. Intense disgust and fear. . . .

Even after a year of processing such memories, my immediate reaction was denial: Dad *couldn't* have done *that*. But the images wouldn't go away, and the physical sensations were very real.

I didn't tell Nan at once. I had told her many painful, intimate, and humiliating things, but somehow this was the hardest. My body was twitching and jerking. I was unaware of it, but Nan knew something was wrong. She asked me about it, gently but firmly. I mumbled something about "arm up asshole." It was easier to keep talking once the gross fact was out. After telling her I sank back into trance. Honey was nodding her head, and the bandage was off her arm.

I tried to go back on vacation. I got high and drank and tried to have a good time, but my emotions wouldn't cooperate. I felt a lot of anger, toward Mom in particular. She abandoned me and Eddie. She let that psychopathic, sadistic, drunken pedophile have us. Just closed her eyes and let him have us so that her life would be easier. Fuck the bitch.

I put off calling about the survivors' group. My resistance challenged me. Was it shame? A lifetime of being a loner? If I did join a group, it would externalize and validate my memories. Maybe this was why I didn't call: It would make incest a part of my social reality.

I wouldn't tell Linda what was going on inside. She was so busy that it was easy to keep secrets from her. She had a new and demanding job. On short notice she had taken over as the head of a badly disorganized department at her college. We didn't spend much time together, and when we did she was often exhausted and preoccupied. I had no emotional reserves, and it was hard for me to be supportive.

One Friday night I went over to her house, eager for some R&R. I brought good wines, ingredients for a fancy dinner, and a treat from her favorite bakery for breakfast the next day. She was an hour and a half late. When she got there all she did was talk about her work and ask for input. When I made suggestions she started crying and gave me the impression that my ideas were stupid. Shit. I felt useless. She had helped me so much that I was glad to have the chance to help her, but my efforts had backfired. It was a strain to be with her. I went home alone.

In October we gave a big dinner party, a housewarming. Linda had just moved into one of my homes, a World War I-era vintage farmhouse I had remodeled. For me, this party marked a major effort toward normal sociability. I worked with a hired man to prepare the house for the party. I ordered catered food and bought a couple dozen bottles of good wines.

The guests seemed to have a good time. *I* had a good time. After the guests were gone and we'd cleaned up, Linda and I sat on the couch and talked. I told Linda I thought everyone had enjoyed themselves. She said she was exhausted; the party hadn't been fun for her. All she'd done was heat stuff up and serve people; we should have hired someone to do the serving.

I was crushed. I'd been feeling such pleasure in knowing I could still act like a normal human being. Now these feelings quickly drained away and were replaced by confusion and anger. I'd tried hard to make a good time for us, and I'd fucked up.

Selfishly, I thought, Fuck her; she can go to hell.

That night I was sick. Linda had a very soft bed, and it hurt my back. I had allergic reactions to her cats. My nose and eyes were running, and it was hard to breathe. My stomach hurt from all the rich food and wine.

I was sick the next week. Sleep was difficult. I was full of fantasies of getting Linda out of my life, even though by now I could see that this was a long-term and not-very-functional pattern. I was afraid of losing her, even though it felt as though I'd already lost ninety percent of her.

FEELING ABANDONED

Once again my attempts to take a vacation through partying were not working. Once again I quit drinking and getting high, went on a diet and increased my exercise. Once again the nightmares returned and the anger came back. I felt contempt for everything and everyone, particularly Linda. I fantasized telling her what a shitty lover she was; what a jerk she was. I got mean and guilty pleasure from savoring the most hurtful insults I could create. Part of me was rational enough to know that this emotion had little to do with Linda, and I stayed away from her and expressed none of this. Part of me recognized, too, that some of the distance between us arose from my unwillingness to tell her about the memories from the last session with Nan.

Nevertheless, I felt abandoned. I was deeply hurt and ready to hurt Linda in return. Being with her had become a duty, not a pleasure.

The negative emotions took a toll on my body. It felt as though someone had laced my shoulder blades together and was continually tightening the laces. I spent a lot of time on the heating pad; I did stretching exercises and got regular massage. But my back was still sore, and I had a constant headache from the tension.

Nan returned in November. I must have looked as bad as I felt, because she asked me if I had been considering suicide. I told her no. I said that if I did go completely nuts, I didn't think I'd kill myself. I'd kill other people first. We spent that first session talking and reestablishing connection with the insiders, but it wasn't long before we were back at the work of letting the memories emerge.

Robert is satisfied. He indicates that we need to work with the younger kids. Young One is sitting up. He seems more chipper and alert. The wound on his neck looks well healed. A coin is sticking halfway out of it. I start pulling it out. . . . I'm lying on my back, and Dad is crouching over me, his ass in front of my face. He's flicking my cock with the nail of his index finger, saying, "Lick it. Lick it." He masturbates me for a while. He grabs my cock and yanks on it, hard: "Lick faster." He reaches under my balls and grabs my crotch with his fingers in my ass, squeezing and pulling, shaking me. I lick his asshole, but I don't do it just like he wants—did I bite him? He says, "Boy, you're going to get it now!" He rolls me over. He's either whipping me or shoving something painful up my ass. . . . My face feels wet and slimy: a clear sensation. Now his cock is in my face. I'm being rolled over. My body is jerking, twitching involuntarily: strong cramps like being repeatedly punched in the stomach. The memories black out. ". . . unbelievable, silly . . . and you're paying money for this! . . . what a jerk . . . sucker . . . "

Young One giggles a little. Not a pleasurable giggle, one of shame and fear—fear of not being believed, of expressing bad emotion, of being punished again. Honey reaches out for hugs. Her need and desperation scare me. Nan: "It's great that Honey could reach out and express emotional need at all." Reassuring. We must be doing something right. Maybe her desperation will fade as Honey grows used to getting love . . . as I grow used to it.

Dream Woman is still pointing to the pile of shit. I go toward it. The turd becomes a snake with a huge open mouth. I go into the mouth. Memory fragment of being fucked; blocked as usual. . . . I'm being held down by the back of the neck with my face on a sheet. A thumb is being repeatedly shoved up an asshole. Dissociated. Now the thumb is a penis. The imagery blanks out. . . .

More coherent now: on my hands and knees under Dad. Being raped. I try to lie on my stomach. He shoves his knee between my legs from behind, into my balls, forcing me back onto my knees. His elbows by my head prevent me from moving away. No sensation from the rest of my body. Some sense of movement. He gets off and wipes me dry. Blocked again. . . .

I try to explain to the children that this is an effort to heal. Young One is doubtful; it seems abusive to him; maybe I get off on it. The Dad voice, not so convincing this time: "Yeah, this is your cowardly pornography. You like it. Your dick gets hard, doesn't it? You want what I wanted, but you're too chicken. . . ."

Trying again to let the memories complete themselves. We take the kids aside and get Dream Woman, Bear, and Robert to guard Honey and Young One. We focus on oral-sex memories because memories around my face are much less strongly dissociated. . . . I'm standing in front of Dad. He is naked. A very early memory; my head is at the level of his crotch. I look up his body to his face, and he nods encouragement. I take the tip of his cock in my mouth, holding the shaft in both hands. Very clear memory: I put my hands in his pubic hair. More fragmentary: my face being held in his crotch next to his dick. Now back to holding the head of his cock in my mouth. He's telling me to lick it. I rub my tongue back and forth on the underside of it. He doesn't push it deeper. No orgasm. . . . Convulsions in my stomach, tremors that progress from my stomach toward my chest.

Coming back now. A dissociated memory of me with Dad's cock in my mouth; a wall behind my head and back, I can't get away. Ominous, strong, and clear. Looking up at Dad nodding encouragement for me to suck him. . . . Dream Woman points to the pile of shit. . . .

Chapter 5

My Man-of-Anger Takes Charge

November 1988-April 1989

I had a stone, a piece of obsidian the size of a large olive, that I had begun taking with me to therapy. I got it from a very interesting man, Terry Tafoya. He is a PhD, a psychologist, a college teacher, an Ericksonian hypnotherapist, and a Hopi Indian. When I met him he was an apprentice Hopi healer. (In his midforties, he was not old enough to be a full-fledged medicine man.) I attended a workshop of his at which we performed several Hopi healing rituals. In one of them he gave us each a piece of obsidian and told us how to put our pain in the stone. He then instructed us to bury or hide it someplace where it was unlikely that anyone would find it. He warned us not to keep the stone, but I did. I didn't know whether it was because I didn't believe in the ritual or because at some level I knew I wasn't ready to throw away my pain.

In any case I started taking this stone to Nan's. I'd hold it during trance as a way of trying to experience the feelings I'd had to stuff away as a child. I took it only when I felt ready for such feelings. I rationalized that doing this could be a physical way of communicating my wishes to my unconscious, but I soon found that it also gave my unconscious a channel for communicating with me. Not infrequently I would "forget" to bring the obsidian, a message I interpreted as a warning to be gentle with myself.

I had the stone with me the session after Thanksgiving. I was trying to prepare myself to "feel the feelings." Over the holiday weekend I'd been thinking about therapy, about how so many of my returning memories were dissociated or numb. I wanted to let the pain out. I had fantasy images of puking, screaming, shitting in my pants, bleeding from my nose and asshole. I brought a change of clothes to Nan's in anticipation of something like this happening.

Nevertheless, I didn't want to push too hard. I tried talking with the insiders about what I was trying to do, assuring them that it would be for healing, not sexual stimulation. I guessed that there had to be some benevolent entity (Dream Woman? Bear? the "process"?) that knew better than I did and that I could trust. I no longer wanted to bulldoze this entity; I wanted to work as hard as I could to help it.

It had been a lousy holiday. I'd been dieting again, forty days with restricted food and no pot; I wanted to indulge myself. Mom had announced that she was having stomach problems. They were hypochondriacal, but they gave me an excuse not to invite her. I anticipated a weekend alone with Linda. I hadn't seen her for a while; I wanted sex and a good time. Instead she was so overtired and stressed from work that she was weeping and haggard. The distance between us hurt and angered me. We each felt abandoned by the other. I'd hoped the holiday would give us a chance to reconnect, but instead it was a grim failure.

I'd had several dreams that week about graduation ceremonies. They seemed to symbolize healing: a confirmation of accomplishment, but also the sense that more work lay ahead. "Commencement." Maybe I was completing developmental tasks, that in a more normal life, I would have finished decades ago. One dream involved a graduation at a prep school where I'd been a teacher at the time Dad was killed. It was full of images of healing, dependence on Nan, and hatred and confused fear of Dad. He had died exactly eighteen years earlier, a few days before Thanksgiving. The unconscious has a strange, cyclical sense of time, and I was just beginning to realize how emotionally important anniversaries can be. I thought about Dad's unsolved murder, how the police had thought it was over a woman. Now I suspected it more likely had involved a boy.

There was one positive aspect of Thanksgiving. I took the time to think about what I was thankful for. I thanked each of the inner children for being who they were, for surviving, and for letting me know them.

I told Nan about all this before going into trance. We greeted the insiders, and then Dream Woman, Bear, and Robert guarded the younger children while I looked for memories.

I'm on my back. Looking up at the underside of Dad's erect penis and balls as he kneels over me facing my feet. He rubs my dick enough to excite me. Now he starts to sit on my face. It's like an alarm is going off, a loud bell or a siren, but I can't move. Panic. I try to turn my head. Feel his leg against my cheek. I try to bring my knees up, curl up, and roll over. He pushes me down. He grabs my balls and cock in one hand and squeezes, twists, fingernails digging in. Fear. I lick his balls. Then I give in and lick his asshole. I don't feel afraid anymore, just numb, with a desire to hide and cling and forget, to disappear into oblivion. The memory becomes foggy, dissociated. He gets off me. I can see his hard-on. He's not finished. . . .

We start reorienting, but it feels like we're abandoning the child. We reassure him that we'll come back and give him as much time as he needs to be complete. Tears. A wave of intense sadness from Young One. He's worried that no one will ever want to kiss his lips; a kiss from him would be foul aggression, not love. . . .

During the session I felt a lot of cramplike twitches. I'd experienced pains before during trance, sharp, single cramps like punches in the solar plexus, but these were different. They were almost like tremors that moved around the front of my body.

MASSAGING THE FEELINGS LOOSE

I'd been getting deep-tissue bodywork from a woman named Peg. She was trained as a Hellerworker, a forceful style quite unlike the relaxing Swedish massage I usually got after therapy. Peg's work often seemed to free those old emotions and memories that had been bound up and carried in my body. As they say, "the issues are in the tissues." Peg was one of the very few people in whom I confided anything about the abuse or my therapy.

That week she worked very hard on the area under my ribs. She also worked between my shoulder blades, a chronically sore area when I get tense. Peg put her elbows there and pushed hard. This brought up fragmentary memories of abuse. It was sexually stimulating in the weird, shameful way of the abuse itself. As she worked, my body jerked and twitched. I found myself breathing hard and making quiet noises. Peg encouraged me to let go, not to inhibit the sounds.

She told me to make noise. For some reason this angered and scared me. At the end of the session my jaw hurt, and I felt depressed and alone. Peg seemed to sense this; she stood by my head awhile and stroked my brow.

Later, thinking over the session, I realized that the intensity of the pressure of her elbows was fine. It was the demanding way she told me to make noise that was the problem. It caused me to shut down and feel shame. I realized that as a child, if I yelled or made too much noise when Dad was abusing me, I'd get hit, usually in the face.

The release of these feelings led me to anticipate a tense session when I returned to Nan's. I held the obsidian throughout the trance. We checked with the children, then took them aside and protected them like the last time. Robert stayed with us to help.

I see a closed, locked door. Robert tries to smash it down. Now a key appears. We unlock the door and open it. At first nothing; then . . . I am back where the last session left off: Dad sitting on my face, making me lick him. His asshole is blurred, fogged over. Now he gets off, rolls me over and fucks me. My breathing is jagged. I'm panting. My body is bouncing, arching away from him. I feel it all the way down to my diaphragm, but nothing from my anus. Sometimes I can feel him pull my head back toward him. He's saying something now. He's angry. Ramming his cock into me, hard. He seems to enjoy my twitching and panting and jerking. Hits me if I yell too loud. . . .

Coming out now, pulling away from the memories. Not smooth. We shut the door, but goo oozes from under it. I'm still twitching; random sex images keep coming. The area between my shoulders is tense, contracting painfully. . . .

Calmer now. We greet the children. Robert first. Honey: scared. Wanting hugs. She has pillows to sit on. Now Young One. I greet him, and suddenly I am overwhelmed with grief. . . .

I spent a restless, unhappy night. In trance my body had convulsed a great deal, at least partly in response to being raped. A couple of times I had let out a big breath and blanked out. Did he make me suck his dick clean after raping me? Did I pass out, dissociate totally in an attempt to avoid this?

Surprisingly, these memories did not leave a lot of bad emotion in their wake. I simply felt exhausted. I'd had an uncomfortable reaction to Nan's expressions of sympathy and her labeling of what I experience as "pain." It made me want to deny everything, to say (with a nervous grin), "Who? Me? No, not me."

We didn't talk much at our next session. We worked again at receiving the feelings and the memories. I lay down and drifted into trance. We checked with the kids, and Bear and Dream Woman took them aside and protected them. I opened the door and waited. I was learning not to try to force the memories, not to guess or imagine what might have happened. I'd been *trying* to recover memories, and the attempt clearly got in the way. Therapy rarely went according to my agenda or expectation. A less directive attitude was definitely better for me. I had to keep my mind open, to pay attention to whatever sensation, image, or feeling might come, no matter how seemingly irrelevant it might be.

The memory that came was a repetition of the very first incest memory I'd had, the first dream monster.

I see Dad clearly pull his belt out of his pants and unzip his zipper. Now I'm sucking his dick. He has the belt wrapped around one hand, hitting me occasionally with it. . . .

Now the rape begins. I can feel a hand pushing on my upper back, holding me down while he fingers my asshole. He gets on me and starts fucking me. (No sensation from my ass, but in trance my body was jerking around, and there were spasms centered in my lower abdomen.) *Dad reaches around, rubs my lower stomach and my cock. It starts feeling good. He grabs my cock and pulls it hard down toward my feet. I can't get away when he shoves himself in deeper. He swears at me, the tone angry but the words unclear. Grabs my balls and pulls on them to keep me from moving away. My head is pushed down toward my ass: a clear sensation. My neck hurts; it's like it's being jammed down between my shoulders. . . .*

We try to withdraw, to close the door, but it won't stay closed. The memories keep coming. Dad forces me to lick his dick clean after he's fucked me. There's some shit caught behind the head of his dick, and he makes sure I get it clean. Now he leaves. Finally I hear the door latch.

We check with the insiders. Bear returns first. Dream Woman won't let the others back just yet. There are quiet tears and a wave of sadness, but no overwhelming explosion of grief and pain. Young One looks agitated, feverish. He's sitting funny; I think his butt hurts. It takes him a while to calm down. . . .

Similar memories kept emerging throughout December: Dad yanking my head down as he raped me, forcing my legs apart, arching my back, pushing my ass so hard it felt like it would touch the back of my head. Dad making me suck his cock clean after he fucked me. This memory brought gagging sensations, a hot, flushed feeling, dissociation, and loss of consciousness. My body seemed to be responding with little conscious control or understanding.

My emotional reaction to this singularly nasty bit of abuse was numbness and a powerful urge to deny, which led to confusion. Anger, shame, and grief connected with the memory emerged slowly over a period of months. I remembered how as a child I would compulsively brush my teeth for a half an hour or more. This behavior was now perfectly understandable.

In trance, after checking with the insiders, I would open the inner door and ask Dream Woman to take me back. There seemed to be a built-in delay between opening the door and the onset of memories. There was a similar delay between closing the door and stopping the flow. Was this lag a necessary structural part of trance communication with the unconscious, like radio communication in space?

The children were needy. Honey was scared and wanted hugs. She still sat on pillows. Young One's butt still hurt. He wanted a long, hot bath, and I honored that. There was a memory of trying to look around at my ass to see how much damage was done. I could remember reaching around and gingerly touching it. At the edge of tears I tried to comfort Young One: "I love you. He is dead. It won't happen again. You are safe now. It was horrible and it must have hurt so much."

I told Peg that the bodywork was releasing abusive memories and feelings; that if I let myself go into them, I'd likely start crying, and I'd get an erection. Peg told me that deep-tissue work frequently released old patterns and tensions which often had a sexual component. In all the years she'd done Swedish-style massage, no one ever got an erection, but since she'd been doing deep-tissue work it had happened several times.

After we'd talked about it openly, I no longer worried when Peg worked on me. When I lay down on her table I'd tell myself, "You can let it go, you can let it out." Peg had an excellent sense of boundaries. She could work intensely and intimately without my ever feeling she was being sexual with me. I had gained a second healing helper.

A CHILD MOLESTER IN A SURVIVORS' GROUP

Meanwhile the group for male survivors of sexual abuse had begun to meet. It was led by a woman, a marriage, family, and child counselor (MFCC) whom I'll call Roseanne. I'd had an intake interview with her and decided to give the group a try. She promised that it would be a safe place. No sex offenders would be allowed in the group. As it turned out, the hardest thing about it was my nervousness while sitting around, waiting to start.

I'd thought a lot about the word "survivor." As a name for people who had been abused as children, it seemed dishonest, like calling a jail a correctional institution or a garbage collector a sanitation engineer. There's denial in these names. Confucius said that one of the first tasks of a leader in reforming a corrupt state is the "rectification of names." It is almost impossible to think clearly when the very names you are using represent lies. I felt that a more accurate way to refer to myself was as "someone who had been a victim," with emphasis on the past tense. This, however, was awkward. I didn't have a one-word replacement for "survivor," so I decided to use it until I heard something more acceptable.

There were three other men in the group. Rick was a well-dressed, soft-spoken man of about forty. Michael was thirtyish and gay, an attractive man with an easy smile. Phil was a long-term client of Roseanne's. He was in his mid-forties and described himself as a "natural healer." He seemed sad and at loose ends. All three of them seemed to be just starting to deal with abuse issues.

Roseanne handled herself all right. There were some introductory questions about who we were. I said something about my back problems, and at the end of the session Phil asked for my phone number and offered to work for free on my back. I didn't want him to work on me, and I didn't ask for his number. Later I hoped I hadn't hurt his feelings.

The following week we talked together for a while; then Roseanne divided up the remaining time, and we each took a turn talking. She used a kitchen timer. Rick described how he was molested by his father's best friend. I felt sympathy and respect for him. Michael had had sex with his older brother for a year and a half as a preteen and remembered one incident with his father at about age four. I thought Phil was something of a jerk. With Roseanne's encouragement, he got up and pushed against her hands yelling, "No, leave me alone." Then as he sat down, he said in a self-satisfied way, "I'm used to doing deep work."

I talked about meeting the first dream monster, remembering sucking Dad's dick. I asked about amnesia. I didn't know then how common amnesia was among victims of trauma, and it bothered me that I could have buried all this for so long. As it turned out, everyone in the group had had at least some amnesia.

It bothered me, too, that none of them seemed to have had abuse similar to mine. It made me feel freakish. I wondered whether they'd resent hearing about the severe, sadistic abuse. Maybe they wouldn't believe me. Maybe they'd think I was bragging.

In thinking about what to say, I realized I could describe what happened without much emotion if I stuck with generalities. It was the specific incidents that held intense shame and pain. In trance Robert reluctantly agreed that it would be okay to talk about his memories a little. It was not okay to talk about Young One's or Honey's.

According to Roseanne's plan, the third meeting was when we would agree either to continue for twelve sessions or to drop out of the group. We all agreed to stay, myself with some reluctance. I was having second thoughts about Roseanne. I was trying not be hypercritical, but I thought that as a therapist she rated a C-minus at best. At the start of every session she'd go around and have us each say something we did that week that was positive in our recovery. This seemed Mickey Mouse and phony to me, but a couple of the guys had responded seriously, and I didn't want to make them feel bad. She had also been giving little lectures on recovery, which I thought were inane. Before I could express this opinion, one of the other guys diplomatically got her to agree to stop. I resented paying her when I felt she was not earning the money. I'd wondered whether it would be grossly inappropriate to ask the other men if they wanted to meet without her.

The next meeting was the week after Christmas. I'd been depressed all week. I'd asked Linda to read an early draft of the manuscript that became this book, and after a hundred pages she'd refused to go on or even to talk about it. Her lack of response was like the silence and denial I experienced in my family as a child. Perhaps her reservoir was empty. What would I have done without her love? Murder? Suicide? Hard drugs? The nut house?

At Nan's suggestion, I told Linda what I was feeling: "It seems to me that you don't want to hear this stuff any more. . . ." She denied this point-blank. She said she didn't want to read more because it was too painful, and it made her feel weird about me, sexually. Linda wouldn't talk about the sexual stuff, and I didn't push her, but her seeming lack of interest was very painful to me.

Our sex life had continued to deteriorate. She had stopped having orgasms. From the little she said, I guessed that she felt repelled by the abusive sexuality I wrote about; disgusted to be a sex object for me. She did not seem warm or lovingly attracted. Sometimes she acted horny and made sexual jokes in a semihostile way that left me feeling repelled. Although I later came to understand the role my own sexual fear and self-contempt played in our difficulties, at the time I blamed her entirely.

Partly because of Linda's response it was still hard for me to talk about my stuff in group. The strength of this feeling was a major factor in convincing me that the group was valuable. Anything that stirred my emotions that much was obviously having an effect.

The group followed its usual pattern. After some general talk, Roseanne got out her timer and divided the remaining time among us. Phil was the last to speak. He started talking about his daughter. He described how, when she was three years old, he would let her grab his cock and play with it. He said she did this "several times."

I couldn't believe what I was hearing. That whimpering piece of shit was a child molester! My body became rigid with tension. The creep was whining and asking for our sympathy because his daughter had seduced him! He was not only an incestuous father, he was trying to blame his three-year-old daughter for initiating it!

What happened next deepened my shock. Roseanne, the alleged therapist, congratulated Phil on his honesty! She asked the rest of us to express our support. Rick, codependent and placating, said something about how children will grab anything. He then looked at me and asked if I was okay. He said I looked like Thor about to throw thunderbolts. I kept my mouth shut. Roseanne quickly changed the subject, closed the meeting, and left the room. Phil left almost as quickly. I was stunned. I tried to talk to Michael, but I don't remember what was said.

As I drove home my sense of reality resolidified and my anger grew. Roseanne had emphasized that trust was a paramount issue for "survivors" and that group would be a safe place, an intimate meeting where it was okay to be vulnerable. *A safe place.* And what was absolutely the worst sort of person to have in such a place? An unrepentant child molester, a simpering creep like Phil, who was still trying to blame his victim. I'd been encouraged to open up and tell my most shameful and intimate secrets, and a goddamn child molester had been listening to them.

Phil was Roseanne's long-term client. He had boasted that she recruited the group around him. A stack of his business cards sat prominently displayed on the windowsill of her therapy room. I hadn't liked the way they "worked" together or the way Phil kissed Roseanne's ass. Phil claimed not to remember being abused, but Roseanne kept insisting that "something horrible" had happened to him.

I also remembered Phil mentioning that his divorced daughter was coming to live with him again.

THE INSIDERS AND I DEAL WITH BETRAYAL

At home I phoned Roseanne and demanded an explanation. Had she known Phil was a child molester, a perpetrator? She had. Why hadn't she told us? She forgot. She rambled on, saying she didn't know what she'd been thinking. She repeatedly said, "I don't know where my head was." I told her, "It was wedged up your ass." (I was sort of proud of this remark. Usually I don't think of things this obnoxious to say until at least a day later.)

I demanded her MFCC license number and, after some resistance, she gave it to me. I swore at her. I called her a jerk, a fool, an incompetent. I told her that people lose their licenses for stuff like this and she hadn't heard the last of it. I told her she was lucky I hadn't destroyed that child molester right there in her office.

I was still pissed off when I got off the phone. She had been apologetic and conciliatory, but as I thought about our conversation several things bothered me. She'd repeatedly expressed sympathy for how upset I was, as though the problem were my reaction and not her stupid and unethical actions. She'd asked me what she should tell the others the next time the group met, implying that the group would continue, that it was okay for her to conceal a child molester.

My anger at that duplicitous bitch was hardening. Underneath it was a great deal of pain, betrayal, isolation, and despair, but the anger kept these other emotions at bay for a while.

I called Nan and told her what had happened. I wanted her to find out whether Phil had been reported to Child Protective Services (CPS) as California law requires in cases of child sexual abuse. I asked her for the name of the most feared, most obnoxious malpractice attorney in the field. I asked her how I might register a formal complaint and try to get Roseanne's license revoked. I told her it was okay for her to contact Roseanne. I almost never phoned Nan or asked for anything outside of our sessions, but I phoned her several times that week. The calls were businesslike, but my real reason for them was a need for contact and emotional support.

It turned out that Phil was a registered sex offender who had been reported to CPS. Roseanne knew this, but she was not the person who reported him. She had failed to comply with the letter of the law. She took Phil's word that he was registered and never checked herself. It seemed impossible that she just "forgot" he was a child molester. He was her long-term client; she had formed the group around him. It wasn't like she was running a lot of groups; she'd been trying to get this one started for months. Maybe it was her "experiment" for a special client. Or else she was so eager to lead a group that she'd take anybody. Or so neurotic that this was her sick revenge against men or some other such acting out.

I was not really angry at Phil. He made my skin crawl, but in a distant, intellectual way I felt sorry for him. I had no fantasies of destroying him. I did have fantasies of destroying Roseanne. I thought about burning her house down, sabotaging her car, beating her to death, hiring street people to gang-rape her. I took sick pleasure in the idea that if caught, I could claim temporary insanity caused by her own malpractice. One thing that really pissed me off was that I had told Roseanne about my problem with anger. She said that group would be a secure place to express and explore such feelings, and she'd gone and snuck in the kind of person most likely to set them off. She snuck him in with no warning, no safeguards, and no choice. What a betrayal!

In the real world I was doing a good job of handling the matter. I confronted Roseanne forcefully but rationally. I was checking with the appropriate authorities. I had the numbers of the other guys in the group and planned to talk with them. I was evaluating my legal and other options. But whenever I thought about it, my body would start twitching, and I'd feel cold and shaky. Just as I had learned as a child, you can't trust anyone. Even the kindest, best-intentioned people were likely to let you down hard when you really needed them.

It was the week between Christmas and New Year's, traditionally a time for relaxation and evaluation. I was no closer to being able to make long-range plans than I'd been the previous year. I was hurt and angry about Linda. I couldn't help but feel that the real me was too frightening and disgusting for her to deal with. On the rare occasions that Nan canceled a session, I felt abandoned by her; I wanted to strike out at her and hurt her badly. Yet if she called and expressed concern about how I was doing, I'd feel afraid that she was checking up on me and planning to have me institutionalized against my will. I felt like I was barely hanging on. I was a bomb ready to go off.

Roseanne had really hurt me. The foul, sagging, middle-aged twat, the leaking sack of shit, the phony, ambitious self-seeking creep. She shit on my soul.

Young One seems to be revealing a new side to his personality. He's always been a compliant invalid. Now, suddenly, he's a wise-ass, making mischievous remarks. I like it; I'm proud of his spunkiness. It's the ancient, raw, skinned-alive anger that Roseanne's betrayal touched: helpless, desperate, and vicious. . . .

There is a new wound inside me. It bleeds, slowly cleansing itself. We spend time washing it out and placing hot compresses on it. After washing, it looks like an asshole or a mouth. The wound is not on any of the insiders. I can't see who or what is wounded.

Nan and I reported Roseanne to CPS. They agreed to appoint a worker to investigate and to ensure the safety of Phil's daughter, but for reasons of confidentiality they refused to give us any more information. I called Roseanne and demanded that she refund the money I'd paid her and write me a formal letter of apology.

Young One clearly has a new aspect. I wonder if that invalid role was a mask? . . . Random, dissociated images: a big cock poised at small boy's ass . . . a huge, distended asshole in a small ass . . . a memory of being fucked, but no sensation . . . a close-up of Dad's naked ass. . . . Now a memory sequence that seems to be Red's: not of Dad's abuse, but of masturbating as a young boy, full of anger and hate. "Beating the meat": angrily beating at my own genitals. . . . The wound that was free-floating in the last session is on Bear. He is slashed open. Something is in the wound. . . .

I received a letter of apology and a refund from Roseanne. The letter had obviously been written or edited by a lawyer. It said nothing, and it said it in a mealymouthed way. At first this irritated me, but Nan pointed out that it meant Roseanne was seriously worried about losing her license. She also got the amount of the refund wrong. The error was in her favor, but I never contacted her again.

I had lunch with Michael, the gay man from group. He was polite but distant, and he showed no interest in continuing to see me. Part of me wanted sex with him, but I didn't communicate this feeling. Therapy hadn't changed this painful old dilemma. I tried asking the insiders about homosexuality. They were split on the issue. Red seemed to be the one most interested. I felt sad after the lunch with Michael. It was my last attempt to get what I'd gone to group for: a peer, a confidant, someone I could talk to.

There seemed to be immensely more distance between Nan and me. I felt that a bond had been broken. I had no rational reason to feel that way. Nan had told me she had no direct knowledge of Roseanne's work as a therapist. She'd also said that groups were not for everyone. But my defenses were up, and my independence reasserted itself by mocking her ideas and her stodginess.

THE RETURN OF RED:
THAT'S WHAT YOU GET FOR THEORIZING

Robert is exhausted. He feels despair; he has lost hope of healing. We try to comfort him; he curls up and goes to sleep. Bear's wound appears clean; we sew it up. Red is horny. He wants homosex. Threatens to cause a lot of pain if he doesn't get it. He is angry at Nan's insistence that any sex that's reiterative of the abuse is bad. He is angry at me. Says he can destroy any and all joy I find in sex unless I do what he wants. He threatens to lash out with a whip. He wants to go to San Francisco and buy a boy. Red will not be calmed. All we can do is try to contain him.

The reemergence of Red confused me. He hadn't appeared in over a year, and now he was back and somehow associated with Young One. I was beginning to accept that my theories were usually wrong and often interfered with my perceiving what really was there, so I didn't speculate much about Red. I tried to listen to him without prejudice and to see him clearly, to treat him with care and respect and boundaries, even when he angered me.

I realized that Red was the major source of my desires to drink, get high, and eat excessively. "Imgrat." I had gone off pot and wine again and was filled with hate for Nan, Linda, and the world. Part of me wanted to stay in bed and ignore everything. Part of me wanted to kill someone with my hands. Everything was ugly and repulsive. I had nightmares and would wake with gooseflesh and intense fear. I would get into a frightening twilight state, half-awake and half-asleep. Sometimes I would rouse myself to full wakefulness just to escape the fear.

Meanwhile, in my conscious life I was trying to complete a complex tax-deferred, three-way, real estate exchange. It kept me busy enough to avoid feelings. I had already found a buyer for the parcel I wanted to sell and had been looking for the property I wanted to buy. I found a promising prospect, an old fixer-upper ranch with three rental units. That weekend I had a pleasant time with Linda. I was happy for the first time in months. On Monday my offer was accepted. I was manic. It was natural to be excited, but the intensity of the feeling probably had nothing to do with business. It was so wonderful to be thinking of something other than incest, child abuse, and sadism. I had been so down just a week before, and now I was so up that I couldn't sit still.

Bear is moving around, clowning. Robert seems jittery and shaky. Bear gets him to get up and dance, stomping around in a circle. Now he's calm enough to sit and hold Bear. . . . Young One is an invalid, but Red is hiding behind him as if Young One is a mask he is wearing. Red is too sore to touch. He is encrusted with filth and scabs. I prepare a white sterile pad for him to lie on. He gently soaks off the crud that covers him before he lies down. Vivid image: erect penis with shit and blood and come on it. Red is too sore to rinse with a stream of water and too sore to scrub or pick at himself. He lies down on his pad and rests.

Now the sex memories come: a huge dick and a small ass with a distended asshole. I'm lying on my back with my legs up and pulled apart to form a "V." I remember this clearly both as a dissociated image and as physical sensation. I think my legs are tied in this position, but they might be held. Dad licks and sucks my genitals. He greases up my ass. Image of his erection from below . . . the tip of his dick pushing at my asshole . . . dissociated, sensation-free image of penetration. Fear of being punished for getting shit and blood on the sheets. . . .

The memories stop. We check again with the insiders. Maybe as Red grows new skin it will become possible to put soothing salve on him, but for now he just needs to be clean. Honey wants and gets her hugs. Dream Woman seems happy. Bear is clowning. He wears a headband with an upside-down feather and pretends to do Native American dances. . . .

I'd been reading more books. Several of them maintained that adults who were abused as children suffer from a form of post-traumatic stress disorder. One of the hallmarks of PTSD is what's called "biphasic response": on the one hand, the sufferer experiences repression, amnesia, numbing and/or denial; on the other, the sufferer experiences invasive return of repressed material. I clearly had the first half, but I'd been unsure about the other. Now I realized that my frequent nightmares and the weird sexual fantasies were an invasive return of the repressed.

The abusive memories, the body positions, the sadomasochistic dominance and submission still held sexual energy for me. A lot of books mention that "survivors" adult sexuality is often imprinted with the flavor and circumstances of their abuse. (This may well be how many child molesters are created; most studies report that a very high percentage of abusers were themselves abused as children.) I felt that this reiterative arousal was an unconscious attempt by the repressed memories and split-off parts to return. I hoped that this energy would fade away once I had remembered everything and had reconnected with all parts. When would that be?

Another symptom of PTSD is an exaggerated startle response, as in the case of Vietnam vets who jump when they hear a car backfire. I had my own exaggerated startle response. All my life, whenever I caught my toe or stumbled slightly, I would feel an unpleasant flush throughout my body, and my heart would pound. I had accepted this as normal. I only began to see it as an exaggerated startle response because it was fading. This change in a long-standing somatic pattern beyond my conscious control felt like confirmation of the value of therapy. When PTSD goes untreated, its sufferers classically go into "post-traumatic decline," progressively restricting their actions, human contacts, and gratifications. They grow hard and bitter. They often become addicts of some kind. This could easily have happened to me.

Bear is cheerful and active. Robert looks a little worried. Young One seems more substantial and real, less like a mask for Red to hide behind. Red lies on a cushion, looking like a burn victim with cracks and fissures in his skin. He wants hot soaks and tears to wash his wounds. Perhaps he'll be ready for salve soon. We try to keep him with us when we turn to the memories, but this hurts him. He goes off with Dream Woman and the others. . . .

I am lying on my back. Dad is kneeling on my arms facing my feet with his ass right over my face. He's holding me down so that Hugh can fuck me. He holds my ankles and pulls my legs up and apart. Clear, detailed, associated somatic memory. It becomes dissociated and the sensation is lost when Hugh starts fucking me. Intense emotion. . . .

A problem developed with my real estate deal. The rental units on the property I was buying turned out to have been built without permits. I had been told repeatedly, and in writing, that they were legal. The deal was turning into an emotional roller coaster. I handled the business aspects all right, but I was drinking nightly because of the stress, and I didn't like it. I wondered if I was ready for a big, demanding project after all.

Robert wears a fierce, toothy monster mask. He leads me to a room. . . . Dad sits on my face, making me lick his ass. Difficulty breathing. Fear. Did I bite him while struggling for air? . . . Something is interposed between my face and his ass. It's a piece of shit. He shit in my face and made me eat it. Punishment for biting him? I try to ignore this memory, to deny it, but it persists. The texture and size of the piece of shit are vivid. Slimy, but no smell. Smell would make me retch. Distinct sensation of wetness. Waves of sadness. . . .

I bring the children back and tell them I love them. I'm crying. It was so hard for that child to let others see his face.

The anger I expected after that session never did arise. I had some flashback experiences, intrusive memory fragments of the texture of shit in my mouth, intense night sweats, and moments of denial, but none of the killing rage. Only sadness for the child who had lived through it.

I thought about all the insults involving shit—crock of shit, shithead, shitfaced, shit-for-brains. When I was younger I used the word "cock-sucker" as an insult, but since I had gay friends I'd substituted the word "turdsucker." This choice was now painfully ironic. Early in adolescence I'd had several dreams and fantasies of being drowned in a septic tank. The imagery had felt sexual and very shameful.

My real estate deal collapsed. The sellers backed out of guaranteeing the legality of the rental units, and I canceled my offer to purchase. I felt bad about this, but I realized that what I needed was cleansing and recovery, not a demanding, high-risk economic opportunity.

Robert takes off his toothy mask. There is shit all over his face and neck. He wants to tear and scratch it off, but knows this will hurt. The others help him wash his face. Young One appears sleepy, out-of-it. Red is perched on the back of the couch, angry and alert. His anger covers black despair. Honey whispers in my ear: Stuff like this happened to her too; memory of being hit in the face with dirty diapers. Diaper changing was scary; I didn't know what to expect: sometimes tormented with a pin, sometimes sexually played with, sometimes hit with dirty diapers. Robert: This happened more than once. A memory of being held by the back of the neck, my face pushed into a pile of shit. . . .

TRAUMA, EGO STATES, AND WHY I'M NOT A MULTIPLE

I was in bad shape. I felt resentful toward Nan, Linda, everyone; and my condition went downhill from there. Every time I saw dog shit on the street, I wanted to gag and puke. I couldn't keep my eyes off it. I saw shit everywhere.

My body was mirroring my emotional state, my persona, and my sexuality. By Friday that week I had two large, red, infected cysts on the left side of my face. My left ear was infected, and so were my sinuses. My left eye was twitching sporadically, and I had a constant headache. Chronic skin problems in my crotch and ass were acting up. They were itchy and sore.

I read Dr. Eliana Gil's excellent books on abused children. She comments that excessive scratching is the most basic and ordinary form of self-mutilation and that skin problems are a major form of somatization. Both those observations apply to me. The bottom of my balls and, to a lesser extent, my ass, itch chronically and sometimes very intensely. I'd seen several doctors about it, and they found nothing. Sometimes, asleep and awake, I scratch this area till it bleeds. It's as though I'm trying to dig or rip something out with my fingernails.

Robert holds the toothy mask. He seems calm and tired, but there is a lot of unexpressed sadness. The inside of the mask is caked with shit; Robert wants to find a way to clean it. . . . Red is perched on the back of the couch. He enjoys stretching his healing skin. I turn to Young One lying on the couch. . . . Kaleidoscopic images: big erect penis, young boy's ass, a shit-smeared neck, an ass coming down toward my face. My body twitches sharply. I feel dizzy, upset, nauseous. . . . Honey climbs up on my shoulder, clinging desperately like a cat seeking safety on high ground. A memory of wrapping my arms around a knee—Mom's, I'm pretty sure—and trying to hang on, screaming while Dad pulls me away. Confused, ambivalent memory: lying on my stomach while huge hands fondle and spread my ass. A penis in my face: distinct, unpleasant. . . .

Bear does a slow dance, standing in a semisquatting position with his hands on his bent knees, rocking from side to side, deliberately and powerfully stamping one foot after the other. . . . I catch a glimpse of Dream Woman; she nods that she's okay. . . .

I felt somewhat rested after that session and slept well that night. I enjoyed recalling Bear's dance. It was like the movements sumo wrestlers make before they fight. What a wonderful expression of placing your feet in firm contact with the ground!

I was reading a textbook on multiple-personality disorder. The authors saw most instances of MPD as the result of childhood abuse or trauma. Psychological splitting, the formation of subpersonalities, of "the child (or children) within" seems crucial to how I survived the abuse, and to how I might heal from its aftereffects. There seems to be a continuum of psychological splitting from normal dissociation to the "child within" to ego states to amnesia and fugue states to full-blown MPD, on to chaotic, polyfragmented systems where sub-personalities cannot form.

Each subpersonality within a multiple is typically very sure of itself. It has no doubts; its judgments are black and white. This is a result of splitting, of the walling off of any parts where there's disagreement. Since multiples are usually aware of only one subpersonality at a time, they appear very sure of themselves and are often self-righteous and contemptuous.

I'm not a multiple. I never "become" Robert or Honey or Red. They influence my behavior, but they never take over. They have their own emotions, memories, consciousness, and attitudes, but I need to be quiet and listen to communicate with them.

This splitting is important not only as a pathology or symptom, but also as a therapeutic technique. Many forms of therapy treat sub-personalities explicitly: the "parts work" of Virginia Satir and others, the "ego-state therapy" of John Watkins. Gestalt therapy encourages the separation and interaction of parts; transactional analysis divides the client into parent, adult, and child parts. Jungian analysis, with its archetypes, autonomous psychic complexes, and concept of the shadow, can be viewed as a form of parts work. Even such "occult phenomena" as channeling, spirit possession, and past-life regression can be rationalistically interpreted as expressions of autonomous, split-off parts of the psyche.

It was only much later that I came to understand that healing is a movement down the continuum, from the rigidities of MPD to adaptive, normal dissociation. Yet in working with the insiders, I was clearly addressing dissociated parts of myself. A paradoxical problem faced by therapists is how to interact with dissociated ego states in order to gain their trust and cooperation without increasing their separateness and the degree of dissociation. Nan's approach was always to address the insiders through me. She'd always ask me to interact with them and report what happened; she never asked me to step aside and let them speak directly.

I enjoyed the intellectual exploration of psychology. It made me feel that I was working at my problems, while allowing me some temporary refuge from the feelings.

Robert seems angry at me for getting high and not being effective. He's exhausted. Young One doesn't want to feel anymore. He wants to "go away," to die. Red wants to get high and stay high. Honey wants to be held and hugged.

There were many sessions when all I could do was check in and see how the insiders were feeling. I didn't realize how depressed I was until the depression started to lift a little. Physically I felt low. Fragments of abuse memories would surface while I was in the bathtub or being worked on by Peg. A voice kept saying, "I want to die. I want to die. I want to curl up and go away and stop trying." Arguing with the voice seemed ineffectual. Functioning in the world was unbelievably difficult. It took all my self-control and discipline to accomplish even the simple tasks of daily life.

Walking on the beach, seeing all the happy, sunny, frolicking people enjoying themselves, made me feel self-conscious and out of place. One morning, as I walked out along the jetty to the water's edge, I "saw" the dead body of a very young boy, floating face down in the water. The waves seemed to be repeatedly banging the body headfirst into the rocks. This was not a true hallucination. Even as I saw it, I knew it wasn't real, but it was vivid, moving. I cried. I was that child. The forces that ruled my childhood were as overwhelming and inescapable as the sea, and I was trapped like flotsam banging against the rocks.

Nan was glowing with good feeling when I saw her the next day. I think her daughter was coming to visit. Her cheeriness irritated me. She noted how tired I looked. She suggested that I get away for a few days, that I was "not having enough fun."

Robert is exhausted. He wants to nap, but he's afraid he'll die if he lets go. Image of a drowning man's hand letting go of a rope. Bear is angry at Nan's suggestion. He pretends to be happy, drunk, but he has painful wounds and feels immensely lonely. He is as faithful as a dog in the best sense. Young One seems sleepy, dreamy. Almost as though I'm looking at him through water. Red is up on the back of the couch with his arms crossed over his chest. Honey wants her hugs. She re-

members why she needs a pillow to sit on. Dad was fucking her butt while he was changing her diapers. Somehow she had the idea that this was some kind of medical procedure, something being done for her own good. . . .

I was angry at Nan. I'm seeing visions of dead children in the surf, and she thinks I'm not having enough fun. Jesus, what a jerk. I wrote a couple of pages in my journal about how inappropriate she was and how she hurt my feelings. I ripped these pages out and sent them to her.

My birthday was the following Tuesday. Linda brought me a cake. I wanted to smash it. It felt like a rebuke, a reminder of what a lonely, friendless, joyless man I was. The phrase "Happy Birthday" on the cake seemed like an ironic insult. I felt like a weird, isolated freak. I wanted to throw the fucking cake out, but that made me feel ashamed. I pretended to enjoy it. I hated pretending. I didn't want to celebrate anything. I didn't want to see Linda. I didn't want to feel or be aware.

I've never really enjoyed my birthday. I wonder if it's the anniversary of some particularly bad abuse. I have the same kind of bad feelings about Thanksgiving and Christmas. In general I don't like holidays or weekends. This makes sense. Dad would have been home, and I would have had no place to hide.

Chapter 6

Sex Rears Several of Its Heads

April-August 1989

Robert's arms are crossed on his chest. Bear is with Robert. He has big wounds all over. It looks as though the flesh is rotting off the bone. Bear is not panicked; he feels he will endure. I see one wound close up. It's like a hole blown open so that something can be expelled. Bear and I have paid a big price to open this hole. I want to be sure all the shit gets out.

Young One seems more alert. The coin is sticking out of his neck again, moving in and out. Red is confused and uncertain, unusual for him. His skin is crusty and cracked, but he doesn't seem to care much. Honey appears in two forms. She's the cute, cuddly little girl I first met in a dream, cradling her bad arm, but she's also an intent little animal, with the tenacity of a weasel. She jumps on my neck with strength and determination. Her skin is a little reddish; she seems to have some of Red's strength.

The I-want-to-die voice is here, like someone's ass moving behind a curtain. I invite it in to talk, but it hides from me. . . .

My birthday proved to be both the low point and the turning point. The preceding three weeks were emotionally the worst period I had endured. I couldn't remember ever experiencing such bleak despair, such desire to give up. I couldn't remember ever thinking about killing myself so much. Before this episode, anger had been the most difficult emotion for me to deal with. This time the return of anger was a relief. I felt a return of my spirit and will to live.

I spent most of the weekend with Linda. I actually enjoyed being with her. Saturday we made love for the first time in weeks. That night I slept soundly for over eleven hours. We made love again on Sunday. I'd been so low I hadn't even noticed my lack of a sex drive.

I wanted to meet the part of me that wanted to die. I wondered if it was the same part that wanted reiterative sex. I'd been "forgetting" to bring the obsidian to Nan's more often than not, but this time I remembered it.

> ... Whirling, kaleidoscopic images of abusive sex, almost a review or summary of what we've uncovered.... Bear's wound appears. The flap of flesh on it looks like a penis and balls. Images of Dad's ass coming down toward my face and my neck. I arch back, trying to free my nose so that I can breathe....
>
> Young One looks dreamy and sensual.... A memory of having my ass rubbed with oil and someone sucking my dick. I enjoyed this; it was pleasurable.... Honey is still split in two. As a little white animal on my shoulder, she is no longer tense and clinging. As a girl she appears larger, but she still cradles her left arm....
>
> We ask to meet the figure behind the curtain who wants to die. There is a clear image of me as a child, naked, on my hands and knees with my ass sticking up in the air. Waiting to be fucked. Is this an image of blocked desires for reiterative sex: passive, masochistic, anal?

I was flooded with sexual energy again. My mind was filled with images and fantasies of men and women, being fucked in the ass and mouth, eating pussy, licking assholes, group sex, sexual massage fantasies, and slave fantasies. I would masturbate repeatedly and still find myself with half a hard-on while walking down the street. At night I would wake up with an erection and jack off to get back to sleep. Sometimes I massaged my asshole while I masturbated. I felt great shame about getting pleasure from my ass. It was the old, painful pattern: self-hate for having passive, submissive, "feminine" sexual fantasies; self-contempt for not acting them out.

It was a week before Linda and I had sex again. It wasn't much fun. That night I masturbated to strange fantasies. Their imagery had an intensity that made normal sex seem pale.

What sex was okay for me? Was this compelling intensity wrong or evil? I had thought that any sex acts between consenting adults were fine, but I was no longer sure. Nan felt that any sexual stimulation, even fantasy, that was reiterative of the abuse was unhealthy and should be refused. I was not willing to refuse anything. I felt furtive and unclean and driven, but I didn't want to reject that part of me that was an ass sticking up in the air, wanting attention. I wanted to integrate it. How could I overcome the splitting so that my actions and fantasies coincided better?

"Is sex dirty?" Woody Allen once asked. "Only if you do it right."

The next time at Nan's the image of that boy on his hands and knees came up before we had a chance to check with the insiders.

The boy, like Red and Young One, has a rough "gallows" sense of humor. I'm at a forty-five-degree angle to him. The message seems to be that I have to get right behind him and look into his asshole. There's a rip or tear on one side of it. How painful it must have been to be fucked in an open wound! Before we check with the kids, I tried to assure that boy that I/we will be back.

Robert is okay. Bear: The rough edges of his wounds look like the boy's ripped anus. Bear likes having Robert with him. Young One seems better. He pulls the coin from his neck. . . . Memories of being fucked in the mouth. Red: alert, vigilant. Honey: less tense when she grabs my neck. Dream Woman points to the boy's asshole. . . . Drawing back now, ending the trance. I really want to welcome back that young-boy-on-hands-and-knees part of me. . . .

This image of myself combined two things I've long been anxious about: submissive sex and sexual rejection. Together they stimulate a bitter voice: "You're a fat, old, pathetic queen, a repulsive pervert! Nobody would want you at all if they really knew you." I used to have sex with almost anybody who indicated an interest, yet I wouldn't ask for sex unless I was sure the answer would be yes. I've always feared sexual rejection and felt euphoric whenever I was accepted. I've never been able to flirt or take sexual attraction with any lightness or humor.

The boy is lying on his side, looking at me over his hip. Now he gets up on his hands and knees. We both knew he's about to be fucked. A clear associated memory of waiting with my ass in the air for Dad to start. "Assume the position": the phrase resonates in my head. Like waiting for a spanking—sex as punishment. Fear: I want to run, to scream; but I am restrained by a greater fear and the beginnings of dissociation and numbness. No pain. Like I'm drugged: dizzy, spinning, out of control of my body. I have an idiot grin, like I'm going under anesthesia. . . . The rape memory is dissociated, like watching a movie. I feel it only around my head. Dad digs his fingers into my throat and chokes me when I scream. Sticks his fingers in behind my ears to hold me still. I feel my face moving back and forth on the bed and the rocking movement of Dad fucking me. No sensation from my ass at all. Fear that he'll shove his cock in deeper. He seems angry, slapping and punching the back of my head. He rams it in hard and hurts me when he comes. He keeps hitting the back of my head even after he's finished. He leaves the room, and I curl up alone.

As the flow of memories came to an end, there was an overwhelming rush of emotion. I lay there on Nan's floor, crying and choking and twitching. My neck was twisted to one side, as it was when Dad had dug his fingers into my throat.

Nan asks me whether we can leave this now and check with the insiders. The idea of leaving brings up tremendous pain. As a child, I wanted to leave so badly. . . . Can't talk. Tears. Overwhelming pain, sadness, and loneliness.

This went on for about a half hour before it subsided. Nan said something about finding a safe place for the child within. This started the grief again.

There is no safe place. The best I can do is to pass out, become unconscious. . . . The insiders are trying to sing or chant a lullaby. More tears and grief, body twitches, jerks. . . . Hair standing on end all over my body. Waves of this sensation.

Finally the boy goes to sleep. Bear posts himself as guard. He is so angry that he is implacable. . . .

At home that night I wrote in my journal, "Dear child, I (we) will be back, you're not alone anymore. You and I survived. You deserve all the time in the world to cry and grieve. I will do what I can to help you. You are safe now. Dad is dead. I'm glad you trust me enough to let me know this stuff. I love you."

WORKING IT OUT WITH LINDA

I felt so alone. There was no one I could talk to. Friends in whom I'd confided seemed to be avoiding me. The man I'd considered my closest friend betrayed my confidence to a mutual acquaintance. The group had been a disaster, and my attempt to make friends with the men in it hadn't worked out. I hadn't told Linda the really bad parts since she refused to finish reading my manuscript.

The gulf between Linda and me and the withering failure of our sex life were taking a toll on us both. Did I want to save the relationship? Yes, definitely. Linda had come a long way with me in recovery. Most women would have left long ago. What connection there still was between us was very important to me. I was glad my resentment hadn't destroyed it.

Still, part of me wanted to strike out at her. I was deeply hurt over what had happened after she read my manuscript. We hardly ever made love, and when we did I felt that she was being vigilant, expecting me to do something weird. Probably because of some unconscious attempt at self-defense, I no longer felt strongly attracted to her. Nan had encouraged me to talk with Linda; she suggested couples therapy. The idea felt totally unacceptable. I had reached out to her once. It would be very difficult to do it again after having been rejected.

I didn't want to see anyone. I unplugged my phone. I stayed home alone as the waves of despair, sexual energy, and anger washed over and through me. The I-want-to-die voice came up again. I tried to invite it in to talk.

I recognized that my attitude of just-hang-on-and-numb-yourself-and-get-through-recovery was exactly the same attitude I'd had as a child, while Dad was fucking me.

I read *Reclaiming Our Lives,* by Carol Poston and Karen Lison. One item in it helped me. The authors cited an abuse victim who could only remember the beginnings of incidents of abuse. She never remembered the conclusions or her abuser's orgasms. This paralleled and validated my experience. I believed that the last session with Nan was the first time I had remembered a complete incident.

Far more helpful were Eliana Gil's books, *Treatment of Adult Survivors of Childhood Abuse* and *Outgrowing the Pain.* They include lists of questions for therapists to ask clients, some of which really started me thinking. One question is, "Do people ever greet you whom you don't recognize?" Sometimes people greet me and I'm unsure whether I recognize them. I have a strange fear about admitting my uncertainty and asking their names. This is an indication of dissociation and possible current amnesia.

Gil also writes, ". . . a few members [of a survivors' group] mentioned that they endured great shame because they could only become aroused when they had sexual fantasies of the abuse. (This issue comes up frequently and is a source of great pain to survivors.)" Unfortunately Gil doesn't discuss how to deal with the problem.

That weekend, the last one of April, I was experiencing sudden mood swings as well as much tension and pain in my neck. At home I tranced out in the room where the insiders' stuffed animals were arrayed on the couch.

Robert and Bear are together and okay. Bear's wound looks like a ripped anus. Young One is okay. He pulls the coin out of the wound on his neck, pulling and pulling until he turns inside out and looks like a flower. Red is badly hurt, bending over as though cut in the stomach. He is crying. Tough, angry Red. I try to tell him it's a sign of strength to cry. I try to comfort him. His skin is too raw to touch. He wants to soak in a hot bath. Honey is a little animal again, biting my neck and hanging on fiercely. Dad is standing in front of me, reaching out to grab my shoulder and pulling me down to suck his dick. He puts his thumb inside the collarbone and rotates his wrist so that his thumb digs into the soft flesh between the collarbone and throat. This is how he controlled me. This is how he'd force me to open my mouth and suck him just the way he wanted. As I remember this, Honey stops biting my neck. I offer comfort to her and the other children. Dream Woman is here with them. . . .

I honored Red by taking a hot bath as soon as I was out of trance. This was the first time I'd recovered a big chunk of memory on my own. The stiff and sore neck I'd had all week took on new meaning.

The memories were confirmed in the next session with Nan. The image of Dad forcing me to suck his dick by shoving his thumb down inside my collarbone came up as soon as I drifted into trance.

Bear's wound comes into focus. There is still stuff coming out, some liquid, some bigger pieces that hurt as they come out. Robert is

*hard to find. He is back on the porch swing in Lake George where I
first met him. Swinging and singing softly to himself; resting. He
seems deeply bothered by the shame I've been feeling. He wants to go
back to grooming and caring for Bear.*

*Red is in trouble. He's been slashed across the stomach. He holds
his arms over the wound so that his guts won't spill out. Tears in his
eyes. We get him down off the back of the couch and lay him on his
back. Dream Woman bandages his stomach. Young One is sitting at
the other end of the couch. Honey is happy to see me. I enjoy hugging
her and being hugged. The new boy is there in both his poses: on
hands and knees, and lying on his side. . . . A swirling array of sex images and memories, shattered, fragmentary, dissociated. . . .*

I went to a toy store to buy Red a stuffed animal. I spent quite a bit
of time choosing one. Finally I settled on a skunk. It seemed to cap-
ture Red's feisty, combative character. I was concerned that Red
might not like it; he might feel it made fun of him. I tried to give him
the message that if this were so, he could let me know and I'd get another
animal. Since Red often appeared perched on the back of a couch, I
placed his skunk on the back of the couch that held the other animals.

It was a week of nightmares: dreams about disasters, earthquakes,
giant waves, and volcanic eruptions; dreams about secrets and loneliness and betrayal of trust, containing layer after layer of meaning.

One morning I felt intense anger and sadness all at once. I did everything I knew of to take care of myself. I went for a walk, did back
exercises and yoga, tranced out. Nothing helped. I was so angry and
unhappy I couldn't sit down. I had to get out, but I had no place to go.
I went to a bookstore, but I wasn't able to focus enough to read the ti-
tles. I came home. My dog, Lola, started shaking. Finally I just sat in
a chair holding my stomach. Anger . . . pain . . . lost . . . useless . . . no
rewards . . . tears . . . hate . . . contempt. I totally dissociated for ten to
twenty minutes at a time. I'd look at the clock and realize the time had
passed and have no memory or awareness of what had happened. I remained in this state for hours. I couldn't stand it. I wanted to become
unconscious, to die. As the intensity of the emotions abated, I tried to
understand what had happened. The feelings were so strong and jumbled that I couldn't even clearly name them.

Saturday afternoon Linda came over. She complained that I didn't
seem to want her around anymore, that I'd cut her out of my life. I told

her what I'd been feeling—that I'd stopped telling her what was happening inside when she had refused to finish reading the manuscript, and that I felt she had come to find me sexually disgusting and watched me closely any time we had sex. She immediately denied this.

We lay on my bed together, fully clothed. Haltingly and with tears, I told her about the memories: the beatings, the rapes, the choking, dad's shit in my mouth. I told her how horrible I'd been feeling but not that I'd wanted to die. She'd had a brother who committed suicide, and I never mentioned such thoughts to her.

We lay in each other's arms for a long time. I felt better but drained and tired. We made love the next day. It felt so good that we did it again. As difficult and painful as it had been to talk with her, I was very glad we had done it.

REMEMBERING ABUSE, READING ABOUT RECOVERY

Robert keeps seeing Dad sitting in his own place of refuge, the old porch swing. We try all sorts of images to deal with Dad. We pour Drano on him, shrink him down to the size of a tick and hammer him on an anvil, but he keeps laughing at us. He claims my getting pleasure from anal stimulation as his victory. Finally we get him tied by his feet in a cage, and Robert turns his attention to Bear. He still has a large wound with chunks of material in it. Young One seems okay. Red is improved, somewhat angry, lying down with his stomach wounded and bandaged. He likes the skunk! . . . Strong cramplike sensations in my jaw: were these sensations the release of chronic patterns of muscular tension that had kept all sensation below the neck, out of consciousness?

I started going to another group for male survivors. It was led by an MFCC whom I'll call Wendy. The group had completed one twelve-session cycle and was being opened to new members. Michael and Rick from the group with Roseanne were ongoing members. I met with Wendy and told her how hurt I'd been by Roseanne's horseshit, and how I needed a group with no abusers in it. She was sympathetic and promised that abusers would be screened out.

It was hard to go to the first meeting. Nervously, I arrived early and sat in my truck until it was time. I was sweaty and uncomfortable walking up the stairs and into the room. Half-a-dozen men were there. I was burning with shame at the thought that they all knew I was an incest victim. When Wendy arrived and the group actually started talking, my discomfort level came down into bearable range. Wendy seemed a big step up from Roseanne. She was emotionally present, she seemed kind and warm, and she didn't lecture. By the second meeting I was starting to have high hopes that the group would actually help me heal.

I'm lying face down on my bed, naked. Dad is whipping me with a long, thin piece of leather. He shoves his knee hard into my balls, forcing my ass into the air. He greases my ass and starts fucking me. My head bangs rhythmically into the wall. I'm screaming. Dad yells at me to shut up. The strip of leather is the dog's leash. He puts a choke collar around my throat. He wraps part of the leash around my head and in my mouth and pulls it tight to silence me. I struggle to breathe. After he finishes he makes me suck him clean, holding me by the shoulder and pushing his thumb down between my collarbone and throat. He leaves. I feel physically numb, but I'm scared that my balls or ass are badly hurt. I want to go to sleep and pretend it was all a bad dream. . . .

On my way out: The insiders seem okay. Bear is impassive. There appear to be two Reds, one angry and one wounded. Young One is clowning nervously. Honey gives me hugs; I really enjoy them.

For a few days after that session, I had difficulty concentrating on anything. I imagined taking a hammer and smashing Dad's teeth down his throat one by one. Just as when I was a child, I had a strong urge to go to sleep and pretend it was a dream. I was remembering complete incidents now, but, ironically, being in a group made the recall more difficult because I couldn't imagine telling them about this.

A flood of memories: I'm tied up; Dad and Hugh are choking me. I clearly feel my arms tied too tightly behind my back while they fuck me. . . . A wide belt is pulled deep into my mouth and tied in place. . . . Dad pinches my nose closed and plays with my terror of suffocation. . . . My arms are tied above my head while I blow them. They gag and hog-tie me in a painfully contorted position, then leave the room. Painful confusion: I'm torn between longing for them to come back and free me and wishing that they'd die.

A whole string of stuff has been pulled from Bear's wound. Chunks, some of them still hanging out. We change the imaginal door into a double door and close it with a massive bar. . . .

I read Steven Farmer's book, *Adult Children of Abusive Parents.* He presents the idea that there are often not one, but many internal children. Seeing this in print was good for me; it made me feel less like a freak. Farmer places inner children in three categories: hurting child, natural child, and controlling child. The hurting child is the part that was traumatized (Red and Young One); the natural child is the innocent, authentic and creative core (Honey); and the controlling child is the part that took over, tried to protect itself and managed life (Robert and, perhaps, Bear). Farmer's categories didn't fit me perfectly, but they gave me new tools to think with.

There is a huge, roundish chunk of stuff behind the double doors. It has split in two, but even the halves will barely fit through. I try to get ready. I imagine ropes to pull it out and lumber to repair the doorway if it breaks. I grease the door frame and the floor. I ask the insiders if they'll help. They all agree, some fearfully and some gleefully.

We open the doors, and the kids start pulling. The big glob comes out. . . . Dad rubs my dick with oil until it gets hard. Flicks his fingernail at the tip of my dick. Rolls me onto my stomach. Greases and rubs the bottom of my balls and my ass. He sticks a finger up my ass, pulls me up on hands and knees, and lays his dick on my ass. After a while he starts trying to fuck me. The force of it pushes me down. He pulls me back up on my knees, this time with my head against the wall so I can't squirm away, and pounds his dick into my ass again. My ass is pushed up over my head; he pulls me back down. Finally he penetrates me. A voice in my head puns, "Pop . . . he's in." Vivid images of a cock in a small boy's ass. . . .

Later: I'm lying there with a blank, unseeing stare. Maybe I passed out or went into shock. Lots of tremors, sensations in my lower body. We tried to close and bar the double doors, but there is a lot of slime and debris and a big penis that won't go away. We put it in a cage and hose down the area. . . .

I took this long, coherent memory to be the first time Dad anally raped me. My initial response was numbness, but the next day my body seemed to be expressing the emotions I refused to feel. Besides the usual back pain, there were stabbing pains in my groin and down my left leg. I had trouble walking. The next day I had a double massage, but even that didn't feel good.

Then the anger and sadness crept in. I begged off seeing Linda that weekend, afraid I'd take my anger out on her. I was sad about my dog, Lola. She was old and aging quickly; her rear end was weak, and she had to struggle to stand. I felt so helpless; I feared her decline and death. I thought of Mom, next door. There was so much unresolved shit, but confronting her seemed hard and unlikely to do any good. I wished she'd hurry up and die.

I ate and drank and smoked pot until I felt nothing.

I pull the second chunk from behind the double doors. . . . A clear memory of my face being pushed downward. Two memories: my face pushed into the toilet bowl and my face pushed into a pile of puke. Dad is yelling. Some of the words are clear enough to understand: "You little shit, I'll kill you." Panic, suffocation. I'm let up for a moment, gasping for air; then my face is pushed down again. And again. And again. Overwhelming panic. Dad ranting. I'm desperate to please him, to suck and lick him just the way he likes. Intense shame. I try not to gag or resist; I want to appear willing and eager. . . . Fragmentary images: being whipped with a belt and fucked, sucking Dad's dick clean after, adult hands pulling the cheeks of a young boy's ass apart. . . . Dad making me lick something disgusting up off the floor. Deep, abyssal sadness and shame about trying to please him. I just let the edge of it touch me, and I'm crying so. . . .

I felt little emotion the week after that session. I occupied my brain with my continuing study of abuse and recovery. I had discovered Pia Mellody's fascinating idea of the emotional triangle. She says the three basic emotions in recovery are sadness, fear, and anger; and whenever any of them is "up," in consciousness, like the tip of an iceberg, the other two are waiting below, in the unconscious. Mellody is an important and original thinker. Like Ellen Bass, Virginia Satir, and other creative figures in the field of recovery, survivors and co-dependency, she's not a licensed therapist. She's an RN.

I also found a reassuring quote attributed to Viktor Frankl in *Man's Search for Meaning:* "Abnormal reactions to abnormal situations are normal."

The session with Nan on June 20 was the last one before she left on vacation. We sought no new memories and spent the trance time with the insiders.

Bear still has a string in his wound. He carries a rope over his shoulder to pull out more stuff, but he's willing to put it down when we ask. Robert is in the porch swing. The memory of licking something off the floor (mucus? semen?) feels especially shameful to him because Dad didn't hold me down to do it. Dad laughed and gloated over his successful intimidation.

There are clearly two versions of Red: an angry Red marching around with a sword, and a hurt Red who has something protruding from under his bandages. Young One is angry, resentful, and isolated. He gives Nan the finger. Honey seems larger and more mature, but sad and worried.

I went about eating, drinking, and getting high and basically not feeling. I experienced back pain, extreme itchiness in my crotch and ass, running sores, and repeated fantasies of fights and angry confrontations. Later it seemed obvious that the emotions freed by the two big chunks of memory were beginning to leak through my walls of numbness; but at the time I didn't have a clue.

Dad's holding my face down in the toilet bowl and in puke had totally defeated me. After that I had done anything I could to please him. Licking something off the floor without coercion represented murder of the soul. Dad had me broken to his will. I was a trained animal performing his degrading tricks on demand. I might have stayed that way, but he made a mistake. His abuse was so violent that it suffocated me as surely as being held face down in puke. The panic induced by his "training" collided with the life-threatening panic of suffocation. The crushing impact drove me crazy, and this craziness reanimated my spirit. The unbearable pressure made me continue to fight after total defeat.

The early part of July was horrible. I was tormented by every negative emotion and sensation the memories had called up. I wanted to hide in my room with the drapes closed, but I spent time with Linda as

I'd promised. It took all my self-control not to be angry with her. She wanted to plan a vacation, but the idea filled me with hate and irritation. Everything filled me with hate and irritation. Each morning I'd wake to discover I'd scratched my balls and ass bloody. I keenly felt the need for a purpose, a task, something to fill the emptiness inside, but I still felt way too unstable to make major decisions or commitments. In group I carefully chose the memories I discussed, avoiding the recent ones. I was so repressed in the way I expressed myself that I don't think the others had any idea how hard it was for me.

Sometimes I would cry, and that was a relief.

In a daydream Honey appeared as a sexy adolescent. I drew a firm line against any fantasy of sexual contact between us, but I did notice her beautiful, athletic body. She seemed determined, fearful, and somewhat angry.

I looked forward to Nan coming back. We went right to work.

BIG HONEY, THE CHAMPION

Honey puts on work boots to start dealing with memories. She becomes a large and determined young woman, but she's there as a small child too. Bear still has a string hanging out of his wound. Robert is crying, but he doesn't want attention. He lets a tear drop into Bear's wound. The angry Red is a guard marching back and forth. The ill Red now has a hugely distended stomach. Honey and I massage him gently. Strange images arise: His stomach looks like a tit, its nipple like a penis. Memory of turning my head side-to-side, like a baby refusing food. But it's Dad's cock I'm avoiding. I'm being put down in his naked lap to play with his erection. I was a baby. . . .

Ill Red's stomach bursts open like a ripe fruit. A tiny living creature is in the material that comes out. It has a big head with closed eyes and tiny curled-up legs and arms. Is it human?. . . Big Honey has a hammer and is anxious to get to work on Dad. She and Young One agree to care for the being. Robert washes it with a tear, and Young One puts it into his marsupial pouch.

Big Honey rushes with her hammer to attack Dad. She smashes his face and eyes and dick. She rolls him over and uses the claw of her hammer to gouge out his asshole. She smashes his balls like grapes. She rolls him over again and smashes at his face. She puts the claws up his nose and rips it off his face. She takes a spike and nails him to the ground through the throat. She nails spikes on either side of his lower spine. She starts to dance around him, swinging her hammer and yelling. Her yell becomes a roar and then a howl—the howl of an animal with its guts ripped out, dying alone at night. She uses the claws to rip out Dad's guts and dances with a streamer of the stuff hanging from her tool. I'm crying heavily, struggling to breathe. I see eyes—the eyes of a dying animal, sad, pain-filled, uncomprehending, alone.

Honey spits into what's left of Dad's face. She starts to wash her hammer but goes back and drives another spike into his back. Finally she washes the hammer, her boots and herself. She rejoins the others. . . .

Later it seemed obvious to me that the power of that session came from the changed image of Honey. It had finally allowed me to start putting my rage and hate on Dad, where it belonged. At the time, though, all I had were images and emotions, no theories. I remembered a taped lecture that talked about how emotions can come up separately from cognition when an amnesia is lifted or a repression breaks. Sometimes the emotion returns before the memory and sometimes after. This seemed to be the case with me.

Later still I had an "Aha!" experience when I read about Dr. Bennett G. Braun's BASK model. BASK is an acronym for behavior, affect, sensation, and knowledge. Braun's hypothesis is that these aspects of a traumatic experience can dissociate, as ego states do, and return to memory in any order. Sometimes I would experience physical feelings before a memory emerged; this was sensation returning before knowledge. Sometimes I would have an emotional crisis for no apparent reason, and then a memory would return; this was affect returning before knowledge. Sometimes I would remember a horrible event with emotional numbness; this was knowledge returning alone.

Young One holds the tiny being. It's dark skinned and looks both premature and very old. Its eyes are still closed. It's hard to feed because of the memory of being given a penis to suckle instead of a tit. Angry Red is proud to be a guard. Ill Red wants to hold the baby. He's healing fast, but he admits he's still too weak. He gets up and joins the circle around the baby, leaning on Young One. Robert is sad and

tired. The string in Bear's wound now looks like a military medal on a
ribbon hanging from his chest. Big Honey starts to dance and roar
and howl, but she is too tired to go on. We agree not to try to dissolve
Dad's corpse until she's done.

I wrote a short account for the group of how Dad trained me to accept his abuse. As a rehearsal I read it to Linda. I cried and stammered
my way through; it was too hard to read, even to her. Instead, I wrote
about Dad and Hugh threatening my eye with the burning stick.

In group I was tense and nervous. I told them I was a little hurt by
their lack of response the last time I'd talked. They told me they'd
been tearful and shocked, but my disciplined, almost clinical presentation made it easier not to respond. I read my account, trembling and
crying. This time some of them let me see (and therefore feel) their
emotional response. Almost the whole session was focused on me. I
felt connected and supported.

Nan and I discussed Mom. We both recognized that I had a ton of
unfinished business with her, but I didn't seem enmeshed. I had
strong containment boundaries; she wasn't allowed in my home
without a specific invitation. I didn't codependently enable her dysfunctional behavior by pandering to her hypochondria, and I didn't
feel her emotions. Wendy, the group leader, had recommended strongly
that I not confront her. Nan said it was my decision to make, but Mom
seemed to her to be on the border of real mental illness. Part of me—
the part that wanted Mom dead—resented any care I gave her, but
part of me hoped that some relationship might be salvaged. The way I
was acting seemed like an acceptable compromise. Was she a victim?
She was weak, and her identity was a tangle of lies.

I found what could have been a description of Mom in Jane
Middelton-Moz's *Children of Trauma*. Middelton-Moz says that
splits in families allow parents to project disowned characteristics
onto their children and then punish them. For example, a parent like
Mom, who is terrified of her anger, will have a raging, out-of-control
child who is then punished for being angry, often by the other parent.
The tantrums I had as a child were sometimes used by my father as
"reasons" for the abuse. Parents often unconsciously use their children to communicate and express the emotions they have difficulty
with. This is called triangulation, and it's one of the basic and perni-
cious patterns of communication in dysfunctional family systems.

The child is placed between the parents (forming the triangle) and used as a pawn in their relationship struggles.

GRACE, THE SEXUALLY NEEDY

Bear appears relieved and proud of his medal. Robert is weepy. A female part of him has appeared, someone I've never met before. She is graceful and beautiful and wants to be attractive. The baby is sitting on Young One's lap. He has grown much bigger. His head is still swollen, but his eyes are open, calm and knowing. Guard Red is okay. Ill Red is grumpy and irritable, but his stomach wound looks largely healed. I look for Dream Woman; she points back to the others. Little Honey is there with hugs. Big Honey takes the baby and holds him. He likes it; he wants to suckle. Image of a tit turns into a cock. Flesh is not safe for the baby. We give him a bottle. He holds it and feeds. It too turns into Dad's cock. Sadness. Tears. In the distance is anger, but up close all is sadness and the baby's unnamed feelings. Big Honey wants to get at Dad, so Robert and his female counterpart take the baby. Big Honey smashes Dad's dick with her hammer. She rips his face with the claws, blinding him. Like a horror-movie monster, he still lives. She takes him where the other beaten Dad is and nails him to the ground. She skins his dick with a potato peeler: He won't be sticking that in a baby's face again. There is fear that we can't seem to kill Dad off. Big Honey brilliantly reframes this: she's glad Dad won't die; she'll have the opportunity to really get him.

The insiders' mutability was confusing. I was continually struggling to interpret these new figures. I understood what was happening; the "stacking," or "splitting" of ego states is a fairly common phenomenon in therapy. It isn't really a new splitting but a revelation of a previously hidden complexity. Sometimes whole families of ego states emerge, as if they had been hiding behind an initial unified figure or contained within it. The two Reds were there all along; likewise the dual aspects of Robert and Honey. Only when I was seen as safe did the more vulnerable parts let themselves be seen as separate entities.

It would have been neat and logical if the insiders had stayed fixed, but much later I realized that the changes were actually signs of health. The more rigid internal boundaries are, the more powerful and impermeable the dissociation is, and the more difficult it is to heal.

The baby wants food. Robert starts to feed her (him?) with a bottle. Robert's female version uses her tit. Dad is trying to get in, but Big Honey keeps him away with her hammer. Bear helps her take Dad back and nail him through the head. The baby eats its fill and belches. The belch makes me happy. I realize with a pleased "Aha!" that Robert's female half is named Grace. As in Amazing. . . .

When I was about Robert's age, I abandoned all attempts to look good. Being sexually attractive carried too much pain. That female part of Robert, the "grace" and poise, was denied and buried all these years. I could remember only one occasion as an adolescent that I'd liked my looks. I was returning from an all-night drug party in Greenwich Village, and I saw my reflection in the window of a subway train. I was haggard, crazed and dangerous looking, dressed in an old army fatigue jacket. ("Real survivor stuff," Nan commented.)

Grace doesn't want to hold the baby anymore. She's angry and frustrated. Young One takes the baby. I sternly warn Grace that she won't be allowed to hurt it. I try to find out what her needs are, why she is frustrated. Does she need to be feminine, beautiful, dressed up, admired, pampered, loved? Does she need passive sex? Does she need to dance?

The baby has his head forced back, his neck hurting, choking on dad's dick. Panic: difficulty breathing and a need to scream that can't be fulfilled because dad's dick is filling my mouth. After he comes, he puts me down and gives me a bottle. . . . Young One has the baby now, with Bear as a guard. Grace is exposing her genitals: swollen, horny, raw. She is sinking into exhaustion from the tension of her burning desire and her inability to act on it. I try to reassure her that it's good to communicate this stuff, but that sex with the other parts is not okay. Her deepening exhaustion is transforming her anger into sadness. She now has her own room with a door she can lock from the inside. Robert has a swollen, painful erection. He feels some shame at his condition but mostly anger and sadness. Robert, like me, would like to masturbate to lessen the pressure, but his cock is too painful to touch.

The weird sex energy returned. Some part(s?) of me wanted passive sex; other part(s?) found this disgusting and shameful. Nan had commented, "It would be too bad if your father ruined all physical pleasure for you." I tried to stay with this idea, but I jacked off repeatedly just to get relief. My neck and shoulders were cramped up despite massage, hot pads, and stretching. At times I got so antsy I couldn't sit still; at other times I was so hate-filled I worried about maintaining control. I wanted to smash Nan's office and scare the shit out of her.

Something was building up. Was it the approaching anniversary of my brother's death? I'd remind myself that "The way out is through," and try to stay with whatever emotions I was feeling.

On August 15, I cried in Nan's office as I told her how the week had gone. Then I lay down and tranced out.

Bear shows up first with sympathetic eyes. The baby looks like a starving Ethiopian. I feed him and try to soothe his neck. I'm crying. Close-up image of Young One's eye with a big tear. As I back away I see that it's a black eye. Young One is very hurt, but this feeling turns to anger and he becomes cold and distant. Little Honey is scared and runs to me for hugs. Big Honey circles Dad's remains, waving her hammer. She is splattered with gore. Dad's corpse is a pool of gore, but a huge erection is sticking up from the middle. My inability to kill him off once and for all scares and angers me. I try to stay with Big Honey's reframing and use it as an opportunity to express my rage. Young One takes a machete and splits dad's penis vertically into fourths. He takes a rifle and shoots a few rounds into Dad, watching the flesh jump. Horrifyingly, what's left of Dad rolls over and gets up on his hands and knees: "Come on, Young One, why don't you fuck me with that gun barrel; I'd like that." Big Honey smashes him down and uses the claws of her hammer to remove his eyes.

Robert is sick, holding his stomach. He has a swollen, red erection. Sexual arousal and sickness don't belong together. ("Except in abused children," Nan introjects.) Robert keeps saying, "I want to die. I want to die. . . ." Images of cutting off his own dick or shooting himself in the head. Intense waves of shame. We get him a poncho and blanket to cover himself. Grace is on her hands and knees, presenting her swollen genitals. She looks around and says, "Kiss it, lick it, big boy!"

Then she collapses in tears. Dream Woman and Little Honey try to comfort her.

The pain and tension in my neck get worse. A memory of being fucked in the mouth with my arms held behind my back and my head pulled backward. I'm very small, maybe two or three years old. Dad's dick forces my scream back into my throat. I vomit, but Dad keeps fucking my mouth, cramming the vomit down. Suffocation—terror—on the edge of passing out. Pain in throat and neck.

Guard Red doesn't want to guard anymore. He's sick and leans against Young One. Ill Red pats his stomach, looks at what he's given birth to, then turns green and vomits. . . .

After the session and a massage I felt some relief. That night I had three drinks and slept for twelve hours.

I knew that most of the material in this trance was not "real." Except for being fucked in the mouth, it all felt like imagery. It was nightmare stuff, the value and reality of which lay in how much emotion it freed and processed.

The relief did not last long. Within a day my neck and throat were tightening down painfully again, and I was once again filling up with violent anger. I controlled it with long walks, yoga, relaxation exercises, and hot baths.

That weekend, getting up to pee in the middle of the night, I asked myself, "Is there any part of me that still doubts or denies that Dad sexually abused me?"

The answer was silence. There was no part that still doubted.

I poked at my internal image of Dad—a pile of gore and body parts with an erection sticking up. There was no response. Was the battle of denial truly over? Or would a counterattack come later?

Robert is tired and hurt. He's sitting against a wall, covered with a poncho for privacy. We try to imagine a place where he can sleep safe from Dad, but we can't. Bear agrees to keep watch and wake him if Dad comes near. Grace lies naked on the ground, too out-of-it to care. We give her blankets and pillows. Young One needs to lie down and rest. Everyone needs rest.

Had I reached the point where exploration was ending and closure could begin? So many times I had hoped or believed that therapy might be coming to an end and I could get on with my life. Each time I had been completely wrong. I was beginning to realize that the key lay with the ever-evolving inner figures. Therapy would not be over until the insiders said it was.

Chapter 7

Earthquakes, Within and Without

September-November 1989

Robert is tired and hurt, but his eyes are happy. He enjoys the warmth of the blanket, the softness of the pillow. He's testing them tentatively, barely able to believe that a bed can be a safe place. Bear is alert and cheerful. Grace is almost comatose. I try to put a blanket over her, but she refuses to be covered. She spreads her legs and points: "Look at my genitals." She is worried that she's scarred, callused. There is a flap of scar tissue that looks like a shark's fin. I try to comfort her. . . . My small-boy's ass being fucked by Dad: fusion of pain and stimulation. Will Grace ever be able to enjoy gentle touch?

Young One is angry and eagle eyed. It looks as though he's been crying, but he's fiercely intent on something and doesn't want us to stop looking. There is an image of female genitals. He stares at it and nods his head. Was it Mom? God, I hope not, not a whole new level of abuse! I promise Young One we'll keep looking.

Guard Red is frightened by Young One's fierceness; he and Ill Red huddle together. Big Honey guards Dad's remains. There is movement in the pile of gore, but he's held down by four nails through his dick, which is split lengthwise into quarters.

The baby has changed. There now appear to be two of them—or perhaps two aspects—one light and one dark. They both seem to be in good shape. Little Honey's been doing a great job. I take her in my lap and give her a big hug. She says she doesn't need her pillow to feel safe anymore. Me: "Well maybe I'll keep the pillow." Nan: "Why? You've been totally appropriate with the kids." She reassures me that I've been scrupulous in keeping the boundaries, but I still feel bad and guilty. Has there ever been a time when I was abuser? . . .

I had to learn to listen to the insiders. Going in with a presupposition or agenda proved repeatedly to be useless, even counterproductive. The trance state was like looking through a thick fog, and the insiders often needed patience and reassurance to let themselves be seen. If meaningful work was to take place, I had to respect their boundaries and not try to force them into my theories. Sometimes all that was possible was to check in, see how they were doing, and accept their "weather reports" as evidence of their slow process. They were not symbols or metaphors; they were split-off aspects of myself. Martin Buber (1947) was famous for his proposition that all human relationships must be "I-Thou" relationships. There are grave, deleterious consequences when you treat another as an "it." The insiders, shattered fragments that they were (and are), were "Thous," just as I am. They did not stand for anything; they just were. They did not need to be interpreted; they needed to be related to.

I kept my promise to Young One, though I wondered whether the female genitals he was staring at had to do with Mom or with the feminine side of my sexuality, my need to receive love. The female part of me was sexually the most wounded part. It had been made to feel secretive and whorelike. If I was going to heal my sexuality, I had to help Grace bring this to the surface, not add to her shame. I apologized for having tried to cover her. I thanked her for having the courage to show her wounds.

Grace wants long, hot baths. She wants to care for herself and make herself pretty. . . . She remembers Dad fucking her/me from behind while he holds her/me by the throat. He chokes me to keep me from squirming away as he penetrates me. My face moves rhythmically on the sheets as he fucks me. Vague and distant memories of sensation from my butt. . . .

The memories stop. Big Honey removes Dad. Grace rolls over and covers herself. A triangular piece of scar tissue near her genitals. . . . Now a close-up of a cunt. I'm a child between a woman's knees. Licking her cunt. I ask Grace, "Was a woman involved?" She nods. "Was it Mom?" Grace nods.

I don't want to believe this or even hear it. Nan: "How do you know it's Mom?" Grace: images of me as a child lying next to a woman's body. Robert nods: Yes, this happened. Young One, eagle-eyed, nods. Little Honey hugs me and nods. Nan asks, "Was Dad in-

volved?" *A memory of Dad's hand forcing my face down into the cunt. Big Honey takes time off from guarding Dad and talks gravely with me, but I don't ask her. The two Reds look serious. Guard Red hides behind Ill Red. The baby's okay.*

We chain and nail this stuff inside a trunk and place it behind doors until next time. I'm crying silently. I feel dizzy and blanched. I promise the kids I won't abandon them; we'll return and clean out the trunk. I tell Grace I love and value her no matter what message she needs to tell me.

I got drunk and stoned that night and went to bed before eight. I avoided seeing Mom. The next day, I bought a stuffed animal to represent Grace, a very soft and floppy bear. I held the bear and cried. I spent most of the week distracting myself. This stuff seemed to call for real-world action—like getting Mom out of the house next door.

When I arrived at Nan's for the next session, I found I'd forgotten to bring the obsidian rock.

Grace appears: an image of her being anally fucked by Dad. Robert looks okay but worried. Bear is being choked by a collar around his neck; we struggle to remove it. Young One: determined. Guard Red: scared. Ill Red wants a blanket. Little Honey: very tired. She needs help with the babies, who are now clearly two separate beings, one white and one black.

We open the doors, get the trunk out, open it and wait. . . . Image of my face between a woman's legs. She's on her back with her knees up and spread open. Dad is there; it feels like he's shoved his thumb up my ass, and his fingers have closed down on my genitals. The woman rolls over and I lick her asshole. Now she holds me on my back. Kneels on my arms and squats over my face while Dad fucks me. Fragments: naked, lying on top of a naked woman, my face shoved into a cunt; being held under the arms and pulled over a woman's supine body. A very clear memory of Mom as a young woman with her hair long and a braid across her head, the way she wore it when I was little. Cold, formal, and beautiful.

I ask Big Honey if it was Mom. She nods. I ask Dream Woman if it was Mom. She nods. I ask Big Honey if it was some other woman. She shakes her head. A voice comes up and denies it all: "This is just what your father wants you to believe."

We nail the trunk shut and lock it behind the doors. A distant sense of anger; an image of smashing Mom's head with a hammer. Notwithstanding the violence of this image, I feel emotionally numb.

ANOTHER GROUP, ANOTHER PERP

Group had reconvened after a long summer break. I'd wanted to talk about my sexuality at the first meeting, but the thought of discussing the weird things that aroused me filled me with shame. This reaction made me aware of how much work I still needed to do.

Now I was determined to tell the group about Mom. Group met Thursday in the late afternoon. All that day I was trying to get my courage up. I felt ill, but I was ready to do it.

I never got the chance.

Two new men were there. I was surprised because Wendy had said the group was closed. Now she told us that one of the new men was a perpetrator, a child molester.

From the start we'd had a firm rule: No perpetrators allowed. I had made an issue of it. I'd told Wendy how hurt and enraged I'd been by the presence of a perpetrator in Roseanne's group. Wendy had said she did not think perpetrators belonged in survivors' groups; she didn't even like them sharing a waiting room. Now she told us there was "something special" about this perpetrator; she had him come to a meeting to see if we'd let him in.

Wendy had called everyone to tell them about the newcomers except me. She said she'd copied my phone number incorrectly.

The admitted perpetrator talked. He was a semiprofessional actor, and he was a smooth talker. He said he'd been molested at age fourteen by an older male. He admitted to having molested a twelve-year-old girl when he was seventeen. He expressed contrition, but he didn't take responsibility: He "hadn't gone looking for it"; the girl had come to him.

Our group had adopted a definition of molestation which included any sexual contact with someone under eighteen when there is more than four years age difference. (This is one of several standard definitions used in statistical studies of abuse.) Now the second newcomer openly described having had sex with a fourteen-year-old when he was in his mid-twenties. He, too, was a child molester, and he had gotten by Wendy's "careful intake interview" without her knowing it.

Wendy pressed for a decision on admitting the new men while they were still there. She kissed the group's ass: "Your healing is so inspiring that I just wanted to share it with others." I was numb. I'd sat through the meeting with little comment, but now I refused to make a decision. I said I'd decide tomorrow what I was going to do. I think Wendy wanted a majority vote, but two of the guys said they wouldn't let the new men in if it meant I left. The meeting broke up without a decision.

The one thing I'd insisted on for my feeling of safety was no perpetrators, and now, with no warning, there were two of them. As I drove home, somewhat erratically, I felt more and more upset. At home I kept trying to call Linda, but there was no answer. I drank. I cried. I curled up in a corner behind my favorite chair, banged my head repeatedly into the floor, and bit my forearm. Lola ran out and hid in the yard in the rain. I had a big headache and feared that I might have given myself a concussion, but the physical pain made me feel emotionally better. I went into the room with the stuffed animals and asked for help. Finally, after crying myself out, I went to bed.

The next morning I remembered that while pounding my head into the floor, supposedly distraught about group, I had repeatedly cried out, "Mommy, why did you do that to me?"

By Sunday I'd bounced back strongly. I'd made notes about Wendy's assault. I was preparing in a rational, perhaps hyperrational way, to let the bitch have it.

I spent the next session with Nan talking about Wendy's crap. I was pissed that just when I needed the group to talk about Mom, I had to deal with this betrayal instead. I reviewed the comments I planned to make and the questions I planned to ask at the next meeting. In her usual nondirective way, Nan got me to make two commitments: to show how hurt I was, and not to become violent.

I talked to three of the guys in the group, and felt I had some support. Nevertheless, the day of the meeting I was tense and sweating; I had shoulder cramps and a bad headache.

I felt better once I started talking. I did not get violent or insult Wendy. I admitted the incident had hurt me, but I didn't want to be vulnerable; I wanted to counterattack. Looking Wendy in the eyes, I used the nicest words I could find for her behavior: "inappropriate, unprofessional, incompetent." I went through my list of issues like a prosecuting attorney. She had broken her most important promise to us. She had accepted the new man's statement that he'd abused only once, and she expected us to believe it, too, despite her repeated admonition, "Never accept the self-report of a sex offender." She had botched her intake interview of the other man. She had offered me no support during the last session, when I was so upset. (I thanked the guys for their support.) She had tried to manipulate the group into admitting the two new men immediately.

By this time Wendy was chewing the ice from her iced tea. I told her I was out $150 for extra time with my therapist in order to deal with this, and I expected her to pay for it. I said that none of us should have to pay for the last group session, this session, or any session until we were finished dealing with this issue.

I gave her a chance to respond. Crying, she gave a disconnected defense of herself. She admitted she'd made a mistake and seemed to agree to my monetary demands, but she distracted attention from the big issues. She had not reported either of the perpetrators to CPS. She had not discussed admitting them to the group with her supervisor. I asked her what procedure I would use to register a formal complaint to block her licensure. She claimed she didn't know.

At this point I said the magic word—malpractice—and threatened her with legal action. I pointed out that her behavior could in no way be seen as rational, conscious, or logical. I theorized aloud about her behavior: It seemed likely to me that women who haven't dealt adequately with their own abuse issues are drawn to working with male survivors for some very dark reasons. They get to appear caring and supportive on the surface, while satisfying their sexualized hate for men by seeing them in great pain over the same issues.

Wendy was crying quietly and unable to talk. One of the men suggested a five-minute break. While Wendy was gone, we agreed to keep working together as a group, to start looking for another therapist to take it over, and to meet again next week with Wendy and her supervisor. I felt pretty good about how I'd acted. I'd said some things I probably shouldn't have, but I hadn't become abusive, and I had put my thoughts and feelings out loud and clear.

Wendy returned after having phoned her supervisor. She assumed I was going to go after her license. "No, that depends on how you act now," I said. She agreed to meet with us and her supervisor the following week.

Nan and I had scheduled an extra session the next day. She thought I'd handled the confrontation well, but we didn't spend much time talking about it. Instead I lay down and tranced out.

Bear and Young One are being choked from behind with rope or wire. They're trying to pull it from their necks. Big Honey comes and takes Dad away. They cut his hands off and lock him in a trunk. The rope keeps trying to come back. Bear wants to put a board in front of his throat to protect it. Young One suggests a metal neck brace or medieval armor. Little Honey is doing a good job caring for the babies. She gives me lots of hugs. Robert doesn't appear. Guard Red is still scared. He's hiding behind Ill Red. I tell him he's done well. Ill Red's stomach is distended and painful. Big Honey appears with her hammer splashed with gore. I ask her for a hug, but she wants to wash first. I tell her she doesn't need to. We hug. Two separate, confusing images of Grace: one naked, exposing her swollen genitals, one covered with a blanket, holding a stuffed animal. Much crying.

Nan asks if I need anything. I tell her I want the cramps and tension in my shoulder to go away. Somehow it starts loosening. I cry more and more. Overwhelming grief. I let it tighten back up. I ask for as little tension as is needed to contain the emotion. I promise the kids I'll be back, and we'll take all the time they need to deal with this stuff.

Nan said I was in a crisis both in memory recall and in the real world. She told me to be gentle with myself.

I'd received an unexpected gift from an old friend, Ken; a beautiful oriental rug. I'd sent him a card saying thanks; it came at a time when I needed support. He called that weekend, and I told him what had been going on the last two years. I cried and struggled to talk. He repeatedly told me he loved me, that I was valuable and special. We scheduled a time for him to visit.

TORTURE

Bear has that rope-like thing choking him, but he is able to get free of it. It seems to be connected to Dad and anger. I go looking for Robert in the porch swing. Dad is there, looking smug. I ask him if he has anything to say before I let Big Honey drag him off. He says, "I got you. I had my pleasure. You'll never know what it's like to fuck a young boy." Keeps talking; gloating without even a trace of remorse.

Finally I see Robert. He appears as his stuffed animal. Head down, sad, ashamed. Doesn't want to be anywhere near the swing. It was hard for him to express vulnerability with Wendy; that's why he hid. Surge of sadness and tears. I tell him I'm glad he's back.

Young One also has a rope around his neck. . . . Dad is holding me down, pulling me backward with the rope. Angry; yelling. He hog-ties me so tightly that I'm choking. Leaves me alone. Comes back and pushes me on my side. Plays with my cock and balls. My cock gets hard. He flicks the tip of it with his fingernail. It hurts. I'm all wet or oily. He pries my knees apart and shoves something up my ass. The choking is worse. He's yelling: "You'll never do that again. Will you? Will you?" He moves in front of me. He unties me, and I suck him just the way he wants. I feel him come and I swallow it just like he told me. He leaves. We are in the basement of the house on West 87th Street, the room with the wrestling mats. I wait there. Later I follow him upstairs. There's no place else to go.

Young One nods: Yes, this happened. Little emotion. Numb. I keep thinking the word "torture," but I don't want to say it. Finally I say, "I don't want to be melodramatic, but the word is . . . uh . . . torment and . . . uh . . . torture." Nan: "That's not melodramatic." Me: "I have no idea why I'm getting this memory now." At once I think of an animal being trained to perform on command. It wasn't a rope, it was the dog's leash.

That night I had nightmares about being attacked and badly mauled by cats.

My right shoulder was all cramped up. My stomach hurt, and it felt like I was getting the flu. I scratched my balls and ass bloody at night. I had a chronic headache and fever.

I became afraid I had AIDS. A fatal, hidden sexual disease; a perfect symbolic fear. I'd been tested twice and so had Linda; we'd been monogamous for years, but rational knowledge didn't stop the fear. My doctor agreed to give me one more test to put my mind at ease.

Apart from this fear I didn't feel much emotion. I'd often been concerned that I didn't remember my abusers' orgasms. Now this aspect had returned in detail, and the milestone just slipped by me. I wasn't aware of it until I reviewed my journal months later. Same thing with the memories of physical pain: This blind spot had also been removed, and I hadn't even noted it.

I felt like shit physically, but I was going to the group meeting with Wendy and her supervisor if it killed me. At the meeting I apologized for mentioning lawyers and added that I'd never sued anyone in my life. I tried to focus my attention on the big issue. She'd knowingly broken her most important promise to us: no abusers in the group.

Wendy's supervisor made some comments about mistakes, but she seemed wimpy. She and Wendy agreed to write us apologies, and Wendy agreed to refund the money I demanded. We guys agreed to meet at one man's home the next week.

So it was resolved, but unsatisfyingly at best. I'd been badly hurt. The group had wasted a lot of time on these issues with Wendy, and I'd been physically ill for two weeks.

I felt better immediately after the meeting.

That night I woke at 3:00 a.m. with my mind rehashing the confrontation. I thanked that part of me for doing a good job, but I also wanted it to be quiet. It was entirely appropriate to feel betrayed, and I wanted to comfort the part of me that felt those things. I was glad I'd reacted strongly; but there had been a delay before I became clear about my feelings, and then they had come out through my body. I wanted to be able to deal with them immediately, and to deal with them as emotions.

LOMA PRIETA

I read Beverly Engel's *The Right to Innocence,* a book about survivors of sexual abuse. She wrote about emotionally separating from parents. It made me feel better to realize that by Engel's criteria, I'd been emotionally separate from Mom for years. She didn't control what I thought or did. I got no emotional support from her. I didn't have any intimacy with her. I didn't carry or express her feelings. I didn't give her any power to influence my attitudes (except for a slight tendency to do the opposite of whatever she'd suggest).

Using Engel's ideas, I made catalogues of my primary childhood role models, potentially more positive role models. I also catalogued my positive and negative personality characteristics, and messages from my childhood. This cognitive stuff was easy; it was a relief from dealing with the feelings. The messages from my childhood were: Don't trust. Don't be open. Don't ask for help. Be closed. Say what's convenient, not what's true. Get drunk or high. Go for immediate gratification ("imgrat"). Be sarcastic and cutting. Don't consider the needs of others. Rely only on yourself. Don't feel. You're fat and ugly. You're a reject. You're bad. Nobody wants you. You're not lovable. You're a freak.

In therapy on October 17, Nan and I talked about Wendy. I felt that I had done enough for there to be some kind of closure. I read over the cognitive stuff I'd done. Nan warned me that my separation was incomplete, that there was still a connection between Mom and the child within.

On this thought I went into trance.

Dad is in the swing ranting and yelling: "I got you! I got you and you liked it! You got hard. You're chicken, or you'd do it too. . . ." It goes on. Painful to hear. Little Honey comes up for her hugs and tries to whisper in my ear. I ask her if it can wait, but she seems disappointed. I stay with her, but I can't hear her. I ask for a picture. Image of an outrageously long cock about to fuck a little boy's ass. A memory of it entering my ass and me screaming and squirming. I can't believe how far in it goes or how much it hurts. . . . I say goodbye to Little Honey and greet Young One. Back to memories of being hog-tied and tortured, being trained to suck dick; memories of the urge to bite, berserk anger, struggling to hide tears. . . . Ill Red's swollen stomach bursts and a grayish box comes out. We store it behind the doors.

Grace: an image of an inflamed cunt zooms quickly toward my face. Image of a woman squatting over my face. Grace as a girl lying down, covered with a blanket. Big Honey reports that Dad's sexual part is controlled and safely nailed down, but the other parts have not yet been retrieved. She feels that with all the internal boundaries I've been tearing down, it's understandable that Dad got free. The babies are okay.

That afternoon at 5:04 the great quake of 1989 hit. I was just sitting down with a beer in front of the tube when the house started shaking. Lola ran under my chair, and the TV jumped forward into my lap. I couldn't get up. All the books and kitchen stuff flew around. Broken glass lay everywhere.

The shaking lasted only fifteen seconds. I took Lola out and put her in my truck. I checked to see if Mom was okay and quickly looked at my other two neighboring buildings. Neither had any major visible structural damage. The gas lines seemed okay, so I left them on. The power was out, the phones didn't work, and there was no water.

I went back inside to clean up the broken glass and get a radio going. I used the remaining daylight to clean up my place enough so that I could move around. I pushed stuff against the walls and made pathways through the house.

Where was Linda? As darkness fell I kept thinking, I don't care if the homes up there are gone, please let Linda be okay.

There was no dial tone on my phone, but early in the evening my friend John got through. He lived in the house next to Linda's. Everyone up there was okay, but he said there was major damage to my rental properties. The house that Linda rented was about three feet off its foundation, lying at an angle in the dirt. The duplex was leaning and broken in pieces. A landslide had taken away the driveway. The mains in my private water system had broken, and the 5,000-gallon storage tank had drained away. All the people were gathered in a field away from buildings and power lines. They had a fire going and enough water and food. The only working phone was in the leaning duplex. Every time an aftershock occurred (and these were frequent), John would drop the phone and run for safety.

I couldn't do much after dark. I tried eating but had no appetite. That night there were aftershocks about every twenty minutes. Some were powerful enough to be earthquakes in their own right. Each one startled me into heart-pounding alertness. Lola was terrified; for the first time ever I let her sleep in the bedroom with me.

The next day I rummaged through piles of overturned furniture, files, and books and found my insurance policies. My heart sank and I felt sick to my stomach when I read that they had all expired four days earlier. That was a bad moment. When my phone would finally make outgoing calls, I talked to my friend Ken, the one who sent me the oriental rug. He is an actuary, an insurance expert. He said that under California law I was probably still covered. I got through to a lawyer, and he agreed. I wrote a check for the insurance premium for which I had not yet been billed and sent it off by registered mail.

Linda came to stay at my place with her dog and two cats. We had to keep her aggressive dog separated from Lola at all times. We joked that it had taken a major natural disaster to get us to live together.

I spent most of that day trying to make calls on the intermittently working phone system. I needed plumbers, structural engineers, builders, geotechnical engineers, people to help me evaluate the damage, people to help me deal with the planning department and other government agencies—the same sorts of people everybody else now needed. Using contacts and skills I'd gathered in over ten years of building experience, I found help to start repairs and plan the rebuilding.

It wasn't until late Thursday afternoon that I was able to check out the property. It looked bad. John's house had big cracks in the foundation, but it seemed essentially okay. The woodstove chimney was questionable, and John had wisely foregone using their only source of heat.

Linda's home was a total loss. It was in one piece, but it was tilted about fifteen degrees off its foundation. We loaded up the truck with Linda's stuff and moved on. The duplex was a 1903 farmhouse that had been expanded over the years. With a lot of work, I'd turned it into two attractive and comfortable rustic homes. It, too, looked like a total loss. The U-shaped building had broken into three parts that were leaning on each other. The two-story wing was bent by the weight of the other sections. The road to the duplex looked irreparable. There had been a landslide under it, and half of it had fallen away. What remained of the roadbed was filled with six-inch cracks that ran for fifty yards.

I worked all weekend taking care of the emergency stuff. Emotionally I was doing fairly well. The worst part was the nighttime aftershocks. There were dozens of them that were strong enough to wake me, and each time I woke with a pounding heart. The shocks tapered off, but it was hard to function without rest. I got irritable and jumpy when I heard creaking noises. I cried a lot, but that was okay. The homes in the country had been the most beautiful thing I ever made. They represented years of work with my hands and brain. I often joked that I had houses instead of children. As I walked through the ruins every room held memories of hours of labor, countless small decisions, and doing it right.

LISTENING TO THE INSIDERS
... AND A FEW BUREAUCRATS

The next session with Nan was a week after the quake.

Robert and Bear are happy; they seem pleased at how they've handled things. Young One and Red look sad and tired. They thought they'd been abandoned and forgotten again. I promise them I won't do that. Little Honey needs hugs. Big Honey is tired, with bags under her eyes. She's sad that she needs to devote so much effort to containing Dad. Bear takes over her guard duty. She gives him her hammer and rests. We put extra bars on the internal doors. The babies are okay. Grace exposes her swollen genitals, but she reappears covered with a blanket when I ask her to.

I drifted a lot in the trance and had many flashes of tasks I needed to do. Afterward I felt sleepy. It was hard to reorient.

Most of my waking efforts were devoted to dealing with the aftermath of the quake. The insurance company would not confirm that my policy was in force. The local planning department, a notoriously inefficient and arrogant bureaucracy, was already causing problems. There was an unending stream of small, immediate repairs and cleanup.

Bear is exhausted from guarding Dad. Big Honey takes her hammer back and relieves him. Robert helps clean Bear, feed him chicken soup, and put him to bed. Robert likes being businesslike and effective; it's easier than dealing with incest. Young One appears dirty. He's ashamed of it and tries to clean himself. Big Honey is angry about having to guard Dad's stinking corpse, but she's determined to keep at it as long as necessary. Little Honey fears abandonment and aftershocks at night. Being startled awake set off old fears of Dad coming to get me in my bed. Grace gets on her hands and knees, and her swollen genitals zoom toward my face. I block them out before contact. I invite Little Honey and Young One to be with me as I work, if they want to. I assure them I won't forget them; I'll keep at the work of recovery.

My friend Ken, the actuary, came down and examined the damage and my insurance policy. We decided to present a claim to the insurance company and not wait for them to make an offer. It was surprisingly complex. We separated out the repair categories to maximize the coverage; then I started the months-long process of getting bids and documenting previous repairs and current damage. The claim turned out to be almost two hundred pages long.

When therapy time rolled around again, I didn't want to go. Working on earthquake recovery left me feeling like I'd drunk too much coffee. Nan and I talked about the dreams I'd had throughout therapy of remodeling homes and of homes being knocked off their foundations. These had seemed very apt metaphors for my personality in recovery. What had happened to me psychologically felt like an earthquake. Now real life had synchronistically recreated these images. We jokingly agreed that quake damage was a much more desirable symbolic expression than getting AIDS.

Robert and Bear seem happy. They like having the responsibility of a big job. Young One is basically okay, but his butt hurts. . . . Memory of being raped: Dad with his elbow in the back of his neck, yelling, "You won't be bad again!" Forced to suck Dad clean. Little Honey: tears; she wants her hugs. Her memory: trying to avoid sucking Dad's dick by turning my face aside, but he gets it in my mouth anyway. Fear of choking as he shoves it in. Afraid to bite. He comes and makes me swallow it. Little Honey is afraid that her mouth is foul and horrid. I let her kiss my cheek, and I tell her how wonderful she is. Nan tries to tell her she's not dirtied, but she won't believe it.

Ill Red looks almost dead. Guard Red appears lost, wandering. I offer them chicken soup. Big Honey is doing a difficult job well. The babies look okay. The doors seem secure, but I reinforce them. I almost forget Grace. Again the image of swollen female genitals coming toward my face. Is this about Mom or something else? Reorienting: I promise the insiders again that I will not abandon them.

I was getting upset and worried about the repairs. The people at FEMA, the federal disaster assistance group, were unbelievably difficult, even for government bureaucrats. The insurance company was trying to deny my claim. The county planning department was driving me crazy with jargon, technicalities, and their refusals to allow repair or reconstructive work. My lifelong inability to tolerate authority figures was largely a legacy of Dad's abuse, but even a saint would have hated the county planners. Useless jerks sitting around in their dry, warm offices making a bad situation worse. I got a lawyer who had been a county planner himself for more than ten years. He had a team of people to handle the bureaucrats.

I had to set priorities and stick to them. Sometimes one little thing would go wrong on top of everything else, and I'd sink into feeling horrible. It helped to focus on the hassles. If I avoided dealing with them, I only felt worse.

Linda and I had been getting on well together, despite the stress and despite our both being used to living alone. That Sunday, trying to be loving, she grabbed me from behind and wouldn't let go. I hated it. Panicked and on the edge of violence, I told her harshly to release me. She cried. I took a long hot bath, and when I got out she was still crying. She said she wasn't upset just because of me; it was cumulative. Sometimes she just needed to cry. I felt somewhat reconciled, but I thought the real reason she was upset was due to our poor sex life.

The insiders were restless. They were concerned that my preoccupation with quake-repair issues was causing me to neglect them. They (I) missed walking on the beach, writing in my journal, and processing memories.

I was keeping up with my reading, however. I found Evangeline Kane's *Recovering from Incest* a disappointment. It was a Jungian book, containing generalizations about gods, fairy tales, souls, and culture—windy obfuscation. Kane would rather talk about anything else than the ugly, personal realities of sexual abuse. She did follow Masson's devastating critique of Freud's cowardice, but she glossed over Jung's own refusal to acknowledge the existence of child abuse. Jung himself was sexually abused as a child, yet only once in his voluminous writings did he ever refer to it. This was in a 1907 letter to his mentor, Freud:

> My veneration for you has something of the character of a "religious" crush. Though it does not really bother me, I still feel it is disgusting and ridiculous because of its undeniable erotic undertone. This abominable feeling comes from the fact that when I was a boy I was the victim of a sexual assault by a man I once worshiped. Even in Vienna, the [flirtatious remarks of women] sickened me, although the reason for it was not clear at the time.
>
> This feeling, which I still have not quite got rid of, hampers me considerably. . . .(Bollingen, 1974)

Jung knew he had been abused; he admitted that the experience had had a major psychological impact on him; yet he never again mentioned it, and he never once mentioned childhood sexual abuse as a significant factor for any of his clients. What colossal denial! Like Freud, he ended up building a complex and sometimes beautiful psychological theory that was based on a lie.

For years I'd considered myself a Jungian. Now the Jungians' pretensions to wisdom seemed preposterous, and their vague yammerings about myth and culture repelled me. They were seductive distractions from the real, hard work of recovery. The way to money and power and reputation in psychotherapy today is to help people avoid working on their core issues while stroking their egos. People will often rather ignore the flesh-and-blood wounding of abuse and engage instead in self-righteous, sociocultural theorizing. Getting people to face deep wounds is hard, and supporting them through the process is difficult. Getting them to talk about human potential and how spiritually evolved they are is easier and more lucrative.

It was Thanksgiving week. Hate was rising within me, filling me. I wanted to hurt someone. I didn't want to be so vulnerable anymore. I didn't want to go back to Nan's.

Robert has a whip that he's using to keep the other kids in line. Eventually we get him to give it to Bear. Young One is eagle eyed and angry. Little Honey comes up looking determined. She spits in my face; then she hides. This makes me feel like I'm in Dad's place. My first response: "Fuck you, bitch, I'll kill you and never see you again!" Hiding, she says, "You can't get rid of me. You tried that for thirty years." She won't say why she's angry. Nan tries to draw limits while allowing the feelings. She tells Little Honey it's okay to be angry but not to spit. I check briefly to make sure the others are there. I feel tired, out-of-it, but as I reorient I feel myself putting the anger back on.

That night there were images of Robert's whip striking out and hitting Little Honey. I was tired of being the good boy who patiently works on his stuff day in and day out.

Thanksgiving morning I was up around 4:00 a.m. feeling not a bit thankful. I walked down to the ocean at first light and started crying. I got home and cried with Linda. I took a long bath and lay down.

Linda went out and had dinner with friends. I couldn't (wouldn't) face them. Instead, I read Sukie Colegrave's *By Way of Pain*. It was similar to Kane's book in its Jungian airheadedness but was much more substantial. Colegrave talks about the despotism of the ego and the necessity of listening for the Self. I translated this into dysfunctional family/recovery language: ego equals false self; Self equals real self. Robert, in some sense, has been a despot, but he did help me survive. Colegrave states that death is necessary for growth, but I don't want to let Robert, or any other part, die if I can help it. I feel that it's inappropriate and counterproductive to try to kill off, exorcise, or otherwise remove parts of the psyche.

The process Colegrave describes of turning inward toward the Self sounds like the process I'd used to find the insiders. Colegrave saw the Self as the gateway to numinous mystical experience. My opening inward had been the gateway to wounded children and powerful emotions. Was there a religious experience beyond? Was this more bullshit, more denial? Or was it a level beyond where I was working?

Chapter 8

Q: The Memory of Pain

December 1989-April 1990

Little Honey pantomimes spitting in my face but doesn't do it. Finally she agrees to sit on my lap with two pillows and no hugs. Bear has the whip; he's whipping the outside world. Robert is fearful of doing the wrong thing. Big Honey is doing well controlling Dad. She is holding her hammer and is splashed with gore. She comes over to comfort Little Honey, but Little Honey says she's dirty and smells bad. Big Honey: "Yes, sometimes work makes you dirty." Young One is withdrawn, bent over with his arms wrapped around himself. He's used to being alone. Ill Red too seems all but shut down. Guard Red is sad and lonely. He tries to play by himself to keep from being afraid. . . .

By December business hassles had become so intrusive I was finding it hard to settle down and go inside. The county planners were classifying my buildings as "existing nonconforming." If they determined that my buildings were more than 50 percent destroyed, I would not be allowed to repair them. The county could legally force me to demolish Linda's house and convert the duplex into a single-family dwelling. My lawyer advised me to repair what was there and put it back just the way it was, even if this cost more than rebuilding. The catch was that the insurance adjustor who had previously assessed the buildings as total losses had gone back on his word. He said he needed to reinspect them.

I was beyond irate. I couldn't get it out of my mind. I couldn't sleep. We were already into the winter rainy season. If we had a major storm before I started working on the repairs, it would vastly compound the problem.

A big, swollen, red dick is sticking up between Little Honey's legs. It isn't possible to hug or cuddle her without sexual contact. . . . Very early memories: crawling around Dad's naked body, playing with his erection, being sucked and enjoying it. Young One seems almost co-matose, fearful of abandonment and preparing to hibernate again, but I sense that he's watching like a hawk. Grace's genitals and ass appear with memories of licking. Bear finds a way to pat Little Honey's head so that she can be touched without sexual contact. Rob-ert: worried, helpless. The two Reds: okay but very tired. Me: ex-hausted, drained of energy. The insiders' needs for care and attention feel overwhelming. I don't want to make the effort. I need gratifica-tion and relief myself.

Sometimes I wondered whether I had made any progress at all. That weekend, in a book of short pieces by people who'd been abused, I came across an account by a man who was gang-raped in a Washington, D.C. jail—brutally raped in the mouth and ass and pissed on and humiliated. It turned me on. My dick got hard, and yet I was filled with shame. After all this therapy, my sexuality was still weird and conflicted.

I could not talk about this in group. I still felt that they'd throw me out if they knew the bad stuff—the weird fantasies, the violent hate, the amounts of pot and wine I used, the grosser incidents of abuse. We had a new leader, a locally prominent therapist named Charles. I was glad we'd found someone to take over the group, but I didn't care for Charles. He seemed weak, and he gave sanctimonious advice; a Boy Scout with a merit badge in psychobabble. I happened to know that he was gay, and it bothered me that he did not reveal his sexual orientation to the group. I put up with him in order to be with the other guys.

The week before Christmas I took the obsidian to Nan's for the first time in months. The insiders "rewarded" me with more memory.

Little Honey sits on Dad's lap, playing with his huge erection. We call it Dad's lollipop. A later memory, strong and detailed: on hands and knees being fucked simultaneously in mouth and ass. Dad and Hugh. The thrusts into my ass push the cock deeper into my mouth and visa versa. Clear sensations of moving and twisting. Some arousal. Dad's voice: "You wanted it; you'll never get so much atten-tion again!" . . .

Despite two years of such memories, I reacted to this one with denial: *This has to be fantasy!* Yet why couldn't they both have used me for sex at the same time?

Group was painful that week. I wanted to express my fear that the other guys would be revolted if they really knew me. There were only five minutes left when Charles encouraged me to start talking. I had hardly begun when Rick, one of the holdovers from Roseanne's group, attacked me verbally. He started ranting about how I "bluster" and pretend, and how he discounted what I said anyway—I had all the words and theories, but I didn't seem real.

I tried to stay open and take it in, but when I replied he said he did not care what I thought. I felt misunderstood and confused. Rick was somewhere between passive-aggressive and just plain aggressive. I'd been trying to talk about my fears and vulnerability, and he'd attacked me. Perhaps Rick, who was usually codependent and placating, was somehow trying to prove his manhood at my expense. Michael commented usefully, "Why don't you ask us what we think?" That's what I'd been trying to do in an oblique way, but I foolishly dismissed Michael's offer. Charles was no help at all. He just told us that time was up, and we all left.

I felt unfinished. My usual response would have been either to attack both Rick and Charles with anger and vicious insults, or to cut them off emotionally and stop participating. I knew that neither of these responses would do me any good.

Nan agreed. She almost never gave advice, but when we talked about what had happened, she said she didn't want me to get pushed into reiterative patterns of behavior.

Little Honey has clear, almost physical memories of being penetrated for the first time. Images of a small ass and a huge dick; sensation memories of gentle, patient stretching and the rubbing of my ass with oil. A dick prods my asshole and then penetrates. Confusion; numbness. Pleasure at the oily rubbing, deep shame and self-hate about the pleasure, about wanting to feel pleasure. . . .

I had liked the attention, the sexual excitement, the feeling of being part of something special and secret. I had a foggy memory of being praised when it was over for being a "big boy," for "taking it."

It was the New Year. I started one of my periodic forty-day get-in shape plans. Instead of being a ruthless disciplinarian, I tried to emphasize the pleasure of being straight and healthy.

With the fast came a new rush of memories. The abuse was getting ever more painful and vicious: anal and oral rape, choking on Dad's penis; Dad yelling and ranting as he hit me. There were layers of memories of sex turning angry and sadistic. They stopped before there was any memory of pain. There was an image of Little Honey as a long-toothed nocturnal animal, perhaps a cornered rat. We applauded her for using whatever strength she could find. Red was irritable and groggy; he slapped away attempts to approach him. He suffered from being straight and on a diet. Young One was okay but disliked Red's attitude. Robert was worried. Grace was there with her swollen genitals, but usually she just wanted to hide. Dream Woman appeared holding the handle of a hunting knife. The knife began descending toward something round.

LOOKING FOR STRUCTURE AMONG THE INSIDERS

It was impossible for me to connect most of my behaviors to specific inner figures. I wondered if this inability meant that there were more parts yet to be discovered.

I read John O. Beahrs's excellent book, *Unity and Multiplicity.* He states that there are two main types of metaphors for psychological splitting—horizontal and vertical. Freud's idea of splitting in the form of repression, is a horizontal metaphor. The repressed material is forced down across a barrier into the unconscious, like a balloon held underwater. The metaphor suggested by multiple personalities is a vertical division, brought about by trauma. Consciousness, volition, identity, the dissociated memories, and emotions all split off together, forming an alter. This vertical splitting is clearly the case with full-blown MPD and is also a much better description of what went on in my own mind.

I also liked Beahrs's image of healing the various parts instead of trying to impose integration on them. He says that splitting is normal and beneficial to some degree and that trying to force unity is often perceived by the parts as a mortal threat. Beahrs proposes the metaphor of a musical group playing together. This pleasing idea preserves each part's independence and creativity while indicating that together they can achieve something greater than any of them could accomplish alone.

Beahrs's book also discusses Ralph Allison's concept of the "internal self-helper," or "ISH." Allison hypothesized that all or most multiples have an ISH, an alter which is benign and is not limited by the amnesias that the other parts experience. For Allison, accessing the ISH was an important part of therapy.

Was Dream Woman an ISH? She seemed to know a lot, but she was remote and refused to take an active role. She would only point. I wondered about her mysterious gesture with the knife. What the hell did it mean? Why couldn't the message be clear? As Beahrs puts it, "[T]he challenge presented by the ISH is whether it can be activated and given power" (p. 110).

I tried to see if I could find any meaningful structure to my parts. They seemed to form pairs. Red and Grace held urges. I was coming to think that Grace had the difficult task of holding all the sexual stimulation I felt during the abuse.

Robert and Young One seemed to hold ego, or executive self. I saw Robert as the part of me that dealt with rising, adolescent sexual energies and gave me a stable, but amnestic, identity. Young One resembled me at age six or so. His facial wounds had healed, and he was now willing to come out of the shadows and be with me. Lately he often appeared watchful and intent.

The two Honeys were clearly a pair. They seemed to have collectively replaced that sexy, hard-drinking black woman I'd first met in a dream a quarter-century earlier. Big Honey was the powerful part of me that kept Dad's image locked up. Little Honey was innocent and loving.

Bear and Dream Woman seemed to be internal self-helpers. Bear was strong, silent, protective, and always seemed to be where he was needed. Dream Woman was elusive. She often appeared as a draped, shadowy form and sometimes was hard to see at all. The babies were minor, transitory figures, but they too were a pair.

I didn't know what, if anything, any of this meant. This stuff didn't come with labels.

When group met again I told them how I felt about the last session. I repeated back to Rick his offensive comments and said, "The nicest thing I can say about you is that your mind was on vacation, and your mouth was working overtime." He sort of apologized, saying that what I'd heard was not what he meant to say. I told Charles that his asking me to talk at the last minute had been a mistake, and I should have refused.

Some of the other guys encouraged me to specify what I wanted or needed from the group. I had thought about this. I wanted to reduce my sense of shame and my need to hide; I wanted them to open up more about their own stuff; and I wanted real emotional contact among us.

After I told them, I felt better about the group. I wondered whether photocopying part of my manuscript for them to read might not be a way of revealing some of the stuff I felt uncomfortable talking about. Nan didn't think this was such a bad idea, and this encouraged me. I decided to do it. We spent a lot of time talking about it at our next session, before I went into trance.

Little Honey's ass appears. Zoom into a close-up of her asshole. . . . Images of her ass being fucked. This goes on for some time. . . . Nan suggests that I ask how best to use the time. Image of the internal doors. I open them and see the gray box that came out of Red's stomach. It's a jack-in-the-box. It pops up; looks like a penis with prominent veins and a human head. Dream Woman is there with her knife. Clear memory: I'm spread-eagled, face down with my feet and arms tied. Something is in my mouth, and a gag is tied tightly over it. Hugh (maybe Dad) is sitting at my head facing me. His legs are under me, and the toes of his shoes are pushing into my crotch, forcing my ass up. I feel the hard leather of his shoes against my cock and balls. It seems like I am held in this position for a long time. . . . I'm being fucked. . . . My ass and genitals are greased and rubbed. I'm very excited. . . .

Something sharp pokes my ass and legs. A deer-skinning knife. The point is stuck in and drawn slowly, very slowly, from under my balls to my asshole. Then up toward my lower back. A shallow cut or deep scratch. Dad grabs my ass and pulls the cut apart. Licks the cut and my asshole. Holds the tip of the knife in my asshole. Rubs my dick with grease. Moves the tip of the blade to where my leg joins my torso and slowly pushes me down onto it. Twists the knife in the wound. . . . More shallow cuts, some radiating from my asshole, almost as though they are carving a design. Slow, calm, deliberate. At one point they hold the blade against my genitals and threaten me.

Fear? Terror? These don't describe how I feel. I am frozen, a para-
lyzed rabbit. Pain, helplessness, and extreme excitement. Immobi-
lized. I want them to fuck me and get it over with. . . . As I reorient I
carefully put the jack-in-the-box behind the doors, lock them, and
hose down the area.

Denial rushed in—even Dad and Hugh wouldn't do that—but I
didn't want to shove this back down. I made no commitment to myself about belief or disbelief, but I did promise that I'd try to take gentle, respectful care of myself that week.

I left Nan's feeling dazed and shaky. The rest of the day I was exhausted and near tears. The body memory of being held immobile in
that position stayed vivid. In the days that followed, I had multiple
physical discomforts, but no strong emotions.

I was beginning to acknowledge that the bad physical feelings—
allergies, muscle tension, shakiness, itching balls, and all the rest—
were how I experienced fear. I felt some of these same sensations the
following week when I handed out copies of my manuscript to the
group. Regarding Pia Mellody's emotional triangle, I'd had an abun-
dance of sadness and anger, but fear had been largely missing. I
seemed only to experience it as nervous, self-conscious "shyness"
projected onto others and reflected back in my fantasy of their opinion of me.

I was starting to realize that I didn't feel fear, the way a fish doesn't
feel water. I was immersed in it and knew nothing else. I had phobic
behaviors so ingrained that I couldn't begin to feel the fears behind
them. I avoided fear by limiting myself so that I didn't get in situations that would trigger it. I avoided shame by not going out much in
public. I avoided rejection by not reaching out for love. These were
not conscious decisions, but they were rigid patterns that ruled my
behavior and limited my life.

I asked the insiders which of them held the fear, but I got no answer.

MEMORIES IN AND OUT OF TIME

Memories of sadistic abuse continued to rush in every time I
opened the imaginal doors and took out the jack-in-the-box. They

made little razor cuts on my penis and then sucked it. One man sat on the back of my head and held my arms while the other fucked me. They whipped my bare ass with a belt. They tied my hands above my head and used the rope to pull me off the ground. They slapped my face as I hung there, threatened me with the knife, squeezed and hurt my nipples. Sometimes they just left me hanging. Sometimes one of them would grab my feet and lift up my legs, then lower me butt-first onto the other man's cock. I feared that this deep, out-of-control penetration would kill me.

There were memories of their caressing me gently after the violence. There were memories of my cooperating with them, of licking their genitals and assholes, and giving them blow jobs. There was a memory of Dad putting his hand on my shoulder in a grotesque parody of fatherly reassurance.

There was a lot that slipped immediately back into amnesia.

At the end of each trance we carefully put the jack-in-the-box behind the doors, locked and barred them, and hosed down the area. I told the insiders, "I'll be back. Dad is dead; this will never happen again. Thank you for trusting me with the memories."

My research was bringing me more insight into the nature of my memories. One lecturer maintained that trauma memories that have been in amnesia need to be reinserted into the time line of personal history. Dissociated memories are timeless and unfading. They will retain their power until they are placed back in the flow of ordinary memory, where they become part of history, no longer immortal. This theory suggested that I would need to pay more attention to how each episode of abuse began and ended.

Some memories came stored in groups of similar context without much regard for time. Sylvia Fraser's book, *My Father's House,* describes such experiences. Memories that happened in one developmental era (i.e., to one ego state) often appear stacked up. As a memory returns, a story line will unfold and then appear to split into two or more parts.

This stacking phenomenon seemed to imply something about how the brain stores traumatic memory. It was three years later that I read Renee Frederickson's *Repressed Memories* and discovered her concept of accordion memory: "Accordion memory occurs when a young child collapses two or more memories into one, so that the composite memory has elements from more than one incident. When the retrieval process is started, the memory expands like an accordion file, exposing an entire set of related memories" (p. 164).

Before the next therapy session I thought about what I wanted to happen. Did I want more memories and/or emotions? I wanted the emotions so that they wouldn't have to keep coming out through my body, but what "I" wanted wasn't important. I needed to ask Bear, Dream Woman, the "higher power" what would help me heal most deeply. I had to be open to whatever came. I had to listen and watch, to let myself feel and remember.

Hands and knees. They're fucking me simultaneously in ass and mouth. They switch ends. Clear memory: one of them has a hard time getting his dick up my ass and the other holds my head down and pulls my cheeks apart. . . . Hog-tied. Elbows tied together tightly behind my back. . . . Held while one of them pokes at my genitals and lower stomach with a knife. He's saying something threatening. They release me and tell me to eat a piece of shit off the floor. I do it. I lick their assholes. Dad comes at me naked. I stare at his hard-on, fascinated. I suck him. . . . Dad slowly wraps his belt around his hand, getting ready to whip me. I want to run, but I can't. I'm frozen, staring. . . . Hugh calmly puts a knife down on a table in front of me. I stare at the blade. Sucking Hugh's dick; each time I gag he pokes me with the knife. They pee on me. Piss hitting my face. Shame. Can barely tell Nan. Many fragmentary memories. More than two men there? . . .

Bear and Robert are taking care of Guard Red. I apologize to him and promise to do my best to protect him. Dream Woman indicates that the red "X" that appears on her pointing hand refers to the "X"s they cut over my anus.

Except for shame, there was little or no emotion. The insiders didn't want feelings. Somehow, having my shoulders pulled up and together with my neck scrunched down broke the connection between head and heart. It helped keep the feelings out of consciousness.

That Saturday I was very depressed. (Beahrs states that dissociation always causes depression because contact with life energy is cut off, along with the traumatic material.) I sat in a chair doing nothing. Occasionally tears would roll down my face. Nothing seemed worth doing.

I told Linda about the new memories. She said she was glad that I told her, and I did feel relieved afterward. On the whole, however, our relationship was doing poorly. My allergies were now clearly traced to her cats. (I found it ironic that I was allergic to her "pussies.") She talked about moving out; it was apparently more important for her to live with her cats than with me. I felt unlovable and couldn't imagine anyone wanting to be with me. I continually suspected Linda of unconsciously, passive-aggressively sabotaging our relationship. She hated it when I'd say this. Talking helped. Reading parts of Janet Woititz's excellent *Struggle for Intimacy* out loud to her helped us communicate.

The next time group met I was tense and uncomfortable while waiting to start, wondering how they had responded to my manuscript. One of the guys had decided to quit and returned it without comment, saying he'd read very little. Michael said he'd read it all in two days and numbed out. After reading one chunk, he went out to buy food wearing his slippers and without taking any money. Laughing his nervous laugh, he said that some of it had turned him on. He mentioned my distinction between reiterative and nonreiterative sex and said that for him all sex seemed reiterative. He was shocked at Dad's cruelty; certain scenes kept coming back to him. His dreams had been affected by reading the manuscript.

Rick's response was quite different. He could only bring himself to read little bits at a time. He'd space out at the descriptions of abuse, "like looking through the wrong end of a telescope," and preferred the more analytical sections. His dreams, too, had been affected. Both Michael and Rick appeared to be remotivated to continue working on themselves and to continue group.

Charles's response was vague.

As they talked, I felt relieved. Hearing Michael talk about Dad's cruelty brought tears to my eyes, but nobody mentioned any concrete details, and this helped me keep my emotions under control.

Afterward I wished I'd been able to let out more feeling. It took me a while to realize how relieved I was. Nobody found me repulsive. I felt closer to Michael and Rick. As I started feeling less vulnerable over the next few days, I felt more resentment toward Charles. He was a weak leader, but I continued to put up with him to be with the guys.

That week I got good news on my insurance claim. The company had approved a settlement close to the amount I had asked. I could now start scheduling the major repair jobs. I could save both buildings and repair them to utilitarian rental standards, acting as my own contractor. It would be the biggest construction project of my career, but I might actually make money on the quake.

I open the interior doors and wait for what comes. . . . I'm in the bathroom. Dad's washing me off under scalding running water. He uses a brush on my face and hair. . . . He fucks me; makes me suck him clean. My eye is swollen shut. . . . He leaves. I try to sleep, but my face is so sore. . . . The memory becomes coherent now: he was molesting me, and I became afraid and shit. He got angry and pushed my face in it and made me eat it. I puked. He hit me and slapped me. . . . The insiders seem tired and sore.

Silent tears were running down my face, and my jaw and shoulders were aching with tension. This memory was about pain and fear; it was hardly sexual at all. Nan noticed my tension and asked about it. I realized it was the effort of not crying and not screaming. She said that I might want to make noise. I let out a couple of the tiniest moans or sighs. This felt weird and shameful, and I stopped it by giggling nervously.

Group had dwindled to just Michael, Rick, and me. That week Charles said he couldn't work with just three people. I objected to him saying "I can't work with just three of you" instead of "I won't." I confronted him with my resentments. I told him I'd known all along that he was gay, and I resented his keeping his sexual secrets from the group.

Charles was somewhat defensive, but he agreed to discuss the issues with his supervision group. He said he felt angry about my outing him, but he wanted to continue working with us. Michael, who was openly gay, had also known that Charles was homosexual. He said Charles's keeping himself in the closet had made it impossible for him to discuss sexual issues. Charles was so wrapped up in his own stuff that he showed no concern about the negative effects that keeping his secret might have on us. The next meeting, a week later, was emotional and productive. The focus was back where it belonged, on us and not on the therapist.

We untie the child and try to comfort him. He seems drugged, semi-conscious. . . . My face repeatedly, rhythmically bangs into the floor. Dad is fucking me. My arms are tied behind my back. (This seemed to be the completion of a memory fragment I'd had early in therapy of a baseboard, table legs, and a bit of flooring.). . .

Red has a pus-filled sore on his face. Young One's back is rounded over in pain. He's somehow holding a lot of pain, containing it, keeping it cut off. His memories seem drugged or drunken. Grace appears again with swollen genitals.

HITTING BOTTOM WITH LINDA

That week I received the big checks from the insurance adjuster. I had a moment of joy as I drove to the bank. No one would bid on the repair work—it was too "iffy"—but I'd found a contractor who would let me hire his crew by the hour. He had a lead carpenter whom I knew and trusted. I lined up a house mover, an engineer, and permits.

Then the pipes in the water system I had just repaired burst in an unexpected frost. My accountant told me that the insurance settlement was probably taxable. The I-wish-I-was-dead voice had returned. I could hear it at quiet times. I couldn't tell what part was speaking. After a month and a half without alcohol, I started having wine before dinner again.

Even with pills my allergies were still bad. My doctor insisted I get rid of the cats. I talked this over with Linda, and after much crying and sulking she agreed to move them into a cabin next to my garage. I tried to comfort her, but I felt pissed off. My struggles with allergies didn't trouble her, but now that her cats had to move she was nothing but tears. This started a strange pattern that increased the distance between us. Every night after dinner Linda would go out to the cabin, make a fire in the wood stove, and spend a couple of hours watching TV with her cats.

Our sex life continued to be desultory. I found myself attracted to people I didn't even like, male and female. It seemed my sexual energy wanted to go anywhere but to Linda. I wondered if she were gay. I wondered if this were a projection; if *I* were really gay. Or was it only my old pattern of becoming bored with my lover?

"Do you talk to Linda about it?" Nan asked that week. I said no. If I couldn't, Nan said, Linda and I would need help—couples therapy. We both had codependent patterns of relating that didn't work and needed to be changed. These comments were unwelcome, but I admitted they were true.

Bear is okay. Big Honey is reticent but okay. Red has images of being tied by his hands pulled up overhead. "Hung out to dry"; "twisting in the wind." Swollen, puffy face; red erection. I take him down, hold him, then put him to bed. He seems semiconscious. Young One: bent over and hurting. Images of a young boy's ass being pulled open, a young boy screaming. Dream Woman helps Young One. Robert: Anhedonia. Fluctuates between boredom and worry. Even the insurance money brought only a few moments of good feeling. He wants to cuddle Little Honey but is afraid he might get an erection. I hear Dad's laughter in the background. Grace: swollen genitals. She seems to wish that she could be asexual.

"I want to reclaim my ass," I told Nan. I wanted to let the physical sensations come back, particularly the anal sensations. I didn't know whether this was important, and I didn't want to do anything that would be reabusive, but I didn't want to be stuck in unfinished numbness. I focused on this idea in trance, but it was a frustrating session. Some sensation memories emerged, but they were fragmentary. They faded out immediately after penetration or were so dissociated it was like watching a film. Again I had failed to consult the insiders.

I tried to figure out what my most pressing tasks were. The most immediate internal need seemed to be freeing Big Honey. It was necessary to deal somehow with the Dad introject so that she didn't have to guard his image and could move on to other things. The biggest external problem was that I didn't enjoy sex.

I've missed Robert; it's been a long time since we've spent time with him. He seems to indicate that there is much more that I've forgotten, that I was older when it ended. Little Honey comes up and plays distractedly. More ass-fuck images, but she pretends that nothing is happening.
There seem to be two versions of Young One. The older of the two, the one with the fierce, glittering eyes who seems cunning and resis-

tant, like Little Honey in her ferret-like aspect. He caves in when beaten badly, but he comes back more determined than ever. There's a monstrousness about him, like Quasimodo in The Hunchback of Notre Dame. *Grace, with her swollen genitals, is the gratification I'm not getting. Ill Red is eating too much as a substitute gratification. Big Honey wants a rest. Her work is important, and she's proud of it, but there is more to life than that. She wants to be clean and well dressed.*

Robert's comment about the end of the abuse seemed important. Early in therapy when I asked about this, I had seen a hand draw a figure eight. I'd assumed this meant that the abuse ended when I was eight years old. This was comforting to believe; such a young child has no responsibility, and the blame lies entirely on the parents. Now I wondered whether the number might not have referred to the eighth grade.

Linda and I hit bottom. First she made a big point of quitting drinking. She stopped; I didn't. I made a point of doing nice things for her, hoping we could get to where we could talk about our lousy sex life, but she responded with indifference. Then she got angry at me for being sullen. She never said anything; she just acted like a passive-aggressive bitch.

I was depressed and angry. I didn't want to be loving and understanding. I wanted to hurt her back. I had the usual fantasies of getting her out of my life and preparing to live alone. At work I had to struggle not to cry.

I was in despair over ever really healing. I tried to ignore my despair by staying busy or high. All the insiders seemed angry, wounded, needy. Some parts wanted me to quit all use of pot and wine while other parts refused. I told Nan I thought I was worse off than when I started therapy. I was angry at her; I wanted to leave and never come back. She asked if I seriously wanted to stop therapy. I told her no; I felt so bad that if I didn't have at least the hope of change, I would kill myself.

My birthday was approaching again.

I felt less sexual than at any time since puberty. There had been times in therapy when the idea of sex with another person was repellant, but I'd jacked off to deaden desire. For the last five weeks I had not even wanted to masturbate. Thoughts of sex brought on fear, hate, and the phrase "I'd rather stick my dick in a meat grinder." I had cramps in my groin. I had difficulty urinating. I wanted to hide, to curl up in a ball and disappear.

I was back at Nan's the day before my birthday.

I'm on my back. Dad is sitting on my chest and face, holding my ankles in the air. My knees are bent, my legs forced apart. Hugh starts sticking something sharp into my ass. Then he fucks me. I scream. I keep screaming. There seem to be other men in the room. Dad-voice: "You'd love to shove your dick into someone until they scream, too." Later: a young boy's ass held open and covered with blood and shit. Nan: "Oh, no!" "Oh, Bob!" Her expressions of sympathy piss me off. She asks, "What would you do if you walked into a room where this was going on?" Me: "I'd freeze in fear and disbelief." Dad: "You'd get in line and wait your turn." I imagine attacking and beating the abusers. I'm crying uncontrollably.

That evening Linda asked me several times if I was ready to feel really depressed on my birthday. I guess she was trying to joke, but it hurt me terribly. I told her to stop. She apologized, but it still felt horrible.

The morning of my birthday I woke up crying and ashamed. I did not want Linda to see me; I didn't want to be in the same room with her, but I couldn't hide all day. I told her in a quiet, tear-choked voice that it was "horrible and unfair" of her to make fun of my emotional problems.

She brought home a good take-out dinner that evening and gave me a gift, but things started to fall apart almost at once. She bitched at me because I didn't want to drink the champagne she'd brought and because I didn't like the pie. After dinner she went and pouted in the living room. I could feel my defenses going up, the hate rising. It felt like Linda was a last chance for me. I couldn't imagine starting over, making an effort to be honestly intimate with anyone else. I could imagine getting hard, bitter, and small.

When Linda came to bed, I said I was sorry we'd both had such a miserable day and apologized for not thanking her enough for the dinner. Things will get better, I assured her, and we hugged a little. Even as I was making this non-blaming, non-judgmental effort at reconciliation, part of me was rehashing Linda's errors and exposing how our problems were all her fault. Another distinct part was gleefully and angrily planning to take a hammer and smash the unwanted present she'd given me, mash the broken pieces together with the unwanted pie, pour the unwanted champagne over the mess, and leave the house.

We talked that Sunday. She said it had been a month and a half since we'd had sex: "My needs aren't getting met. If it goes on too long, I'll leave." My emotional reaction was, "Fuck you, bitch! Leave now!" but I kept silent.

FEELING Q'S PAIN

There was definitively another part, "Quasimodo," under or behind Young One. He had a grimace of exquisite, skinned-alive pain. His glittering-eyed cunning was defiance in the face of this pain. I kept seeing his grimace in daydreams—his lips and face pulled back, his teeth exposed in the acceleration of pain. It was the face of a burn victim. Quasimodo seemed to have a history which was revealed to me in a progression of images: a baby burn victim, a skinned-alive child, a silent scream, a glittering-eyed grimace.

He knows his pain is repulsive to others. He is lonely and can't go out to play. He watches through windows. Many moments of overwhelming pain and sexual stimulation. It didn't stop at the intolerable level. It kept accelerating, intensifying, until the world disappeared in a white-out of pain.

One conscious reason why I didn't want children was that I feared they might be crippled or retarded. The crippled child I'd feared so long was within me. He was horribly disfigured by pain. Who could love him? Who could even stand to look at him?

Quasimodo has an erection. His arms are tied down; there is a strap across his forehead; he can't move and he can't turn his head to see what they are doing. He is filled with fear. Dad has a pair of pliers and another clipping device. With the pliers he grabs small folds of flesh from my ass and pulls and squeezes them. I hear a child's voice screaming over and over. Dad grabs my genitals with the pliers and threatens to rip them off. He waves the pliers in my face while screaming threats. . . .

I giggle in a horrible, nervous way. This is too bizarre; I'll never be able to tell anyone or integrate this. It somehow seems more shameful than anything else I've remembered. But Quasimodo's screams, and the waves of tears, make this concern seem trivial. I try to reassure him that the shame and responsibility were Dad's. I welcome him; I tell him I'm glad he's revealed himself, but I don't think he believes me. He keeps screaming, resting, then screaming again. I am crying profusely. I promise him I'll be back and I'll give him all the time and care he needs.

It takes me a long time to calm down. The insiders are distraught. Little Honey is almost in shock. . . .

I got the idea that this was done to me on my birthday, or the night before my birthday.

At some point during the trance, Quasimodo had indicated that he'd rather just be called "Q." Early the next morning I checked inside and spent time with Q.

He's tied, immobile. The thing he's strapped to looks like one of those outdoor aluminum chaise lounges with some of the webbing removed. I offer him comfort. I loosen his bonds and free his hands so he'll have control. His crotch becomes the focus: He wants me to look at his genitals. I'm uncomfortable with this, afraid of being sexual. I wonder if he's really worried about damage to his genitals or if he's testing me. He has an erection. I look closely and see no signs of permanent damage. I reassure him. Before I leave, I cover him with a blanket.

I couldn't talk about this in group. I felt immense shame about the pliers. I made helpful comments about the other guys' stuff and showed no emotion. I didn't tell Linda anything either. I'd lost trust in her. I was alone with my feelings and memories. Often I'd hear a child screaming in unbearable pain. Sometimes it seemed that the pain and the screams were all that existed.

I took a long hot bath that weekend and checked inside. There seemed to be an angry, fast-moving, violent side of Q that ran out and hit me in the groin. That imaginal blow paralleled the cramps and urinary difficulty I'd been having. The hyperactive, angry Q seemed to balance the immobilized, crippled Q. During the bath there were many weird fantasies about sex with almost anyone except Linda. Most of the fantasies had sadomasochistic overtones.

The next session with Nan we talked a lot about Linda. This let me postpone going into trance and seeing what was there.

Little Honey comes running up for a hug. She's scared. Q is still strapped in the chair. His eyes are bugging out of his head, and he's gesticulating wildly. I feel some fear of him. Now a succession of memories of letting them fuck me, of sucking them. Docile. They play with my dick until it gets hard. They make little razor cuts around the head and suck it. . . . Dad shakes the pliers in my face, scolding and threatening me. He sticks them up my ass and opens them. He squeezes little folds of flesh flat. He grabs big chunks and twists. He waves the shit-covered pliers in my face and jams them up under my upper lip. I keep my teeth clenched. He taps on my teeth with the pliers. Harder and harder. I give up and open my mouth and lick the pliers clean. . . . Something blunt is shoved up my ass. Sudden pain, on off, on off, on off. Electrical shock. A dildo-like thing with wires coming off it. They shock me other places. I lose control and shit and piss. Convulsions. They tell me to lick it up, and I do. They make me suck the electrode clean.

We get Q out of the chair and into a bed. Bear stands guard with Little Honey and Big Honey nearby. Q is very tired but seems to like the bed and blanket. I ask him, "Is there more?" He nods.

Torture. It was torture. No other word would do. Deliberate sexual torture, planned sessions, and special implements. Bondage and conditioning, mixing sexual stimulation with pain.

That night Linda told me how all these people were leaning on her for support—a guy whose lover was HIV positive, a woman whose mother had Alzheimer's. She talked about how tired she was and then asked, "How was Nan's?" I told her nothing.

Chapter 9

Frankie: Befriending the Monster

May-October 1990

I have a dog's leash around my neck. Half a dozen or more men are in the room. I go around giving blow jobs to them all. They have a device with a bit that holds my head immobile. Some of them lick and suck me. Some of them fuck me. Some of them make me lick their assholes. They laugh at me, a trained, performing animal. If I suck them well enough, maybe they won't hurt me. . . .

Through the spring and early summer, Q's memories of group sex, bondage, and sadism came in a flood every time I entered trance.

They had a device that was a combination gag and blindfold. The blindfold had protrusions that pushed against my eyes. Leather straps came off both sides of the device like reins. Sometimes they'd pull on them while they were fucking me. Sometimes they'd nail them to the floor on both sides of my head so that my nose was inches from the ground. Sometimes they'd tie me up and leave me hanging by the leash.

They had ropes or straps that fit around my genitals and held something shoved up my ass. They'd tie me in straps with sharp metal studs. They had a metal ring with sharp points on the outside. They'd push this between the cheeks of my ass to keep it spread open. They'd attach my penis to a board with a leather thong and nails and threaten to squash it with a hammer.

Little Honey and Big Honey are holding hands. Robert is confused and worried. Grace wants sex with a straight male friend of mine. Red dislikes Grace's sexuality. Bear guards Q, who is in bed with a stuffed animal. Freeing him from the device with the restraints was

*difficult. As much as he hated it, he was afraid he'd be unable to sup-
port himself without it, like a quadriplegic removed from his wheelchair. He likes Bear holding him. Fur is safer than skin. . . .*

Sometimes they'd put me in high lace-up boots. It felt as if pieces
of broken glass or sharp pebbles were in them. They'd tie the boots on
and fuck me. They'd pull the boots sideways until I thought my
crotch would be ripped apart. They'd hit and slap my face and whip
me with belts. They'd step on me, kick me, and make me kiss their
shoes. They'd hang me up by straps tied to my legs and arms and
lower me onto someone's cock. Sometimes (and this terrified me)
they'd shove something up my penis.

Frequently they'd tie me by the ankles. Sometimes they'd only tie
one foot. (I remembered Dad saying, "It's better when he squirms a
little.") This made me think of the third monster from that dream tied
by one foot in the street, and of the unexplained foot pain I'd had then.

Once I was gagged and tied up, lying on my back with my feet in
the air. I was squirming. Hugh stuck the point of a knife under my
balls, and I froze. Another time Hugh told me to go lick a man's
asshole. I did. He told me to push his cheeks apart and lick deeper. I
did. He told me to get up on the ass and start humping. I did. I don't
know how old I was, but when I stood up the top of my head was on a
level with the men's waists or navels.

I wondered if Dad and Hugh got paid for this. Many of the men
were strangers. Some of them I never saw. Was it prostitution?
Sadomasochistic child prostitution? They probably got big bucks.
Having a young boy who'd give blow jobs, lick assholes, and submit
to torture probably gave Dad status and a bargaining chip among his
"friends."

I kept thinking of a story I'd heard about a "blow pig," a girl who
gave all the boys in her neighborhood blow jobs.

I wrote Q a letter thanking him for telling us what he knew. I promised that Nan and I would keep coming back and give him all the time
he needed. I asked him to let me know if anything could help him feel
safer or more comfortable. Even though the events were horrible, the
emotions were so powerful that I knew I couldn't be faking them. I
felt no denial, no doubt at all that the memories were true. There
could be no possible secondary gain from such memories. They made
my history so bizarre as to invite isolation.

Was this batch of memories the third monster? Had I reached the bottom of the barrel; was memory work drawing to a close? If so, when could I resume a normal life? What did I do with the sexual energy that kept pulling me toward men, women, anyone other than Linda?

Grace shows her swollen genitals. She wants a gentle, kind lover. It doesn't have to be a man. Grace's longing and yearning used to be channeled into anger and hatred for her genitals and violent masturbation. Now it's near despair. Robert is protective of her. Grace is hopeful I'll have sex with someone who can satisfy her.

TALKING ABOUT SEX—AND ENJOYING SOME

Linda and I talked cautiously about sexuality. I told her I was very confused about sex now. I specifically mentioned homosexuality. I told her I was basically hiding; I needed a place to hide out. We talked about her moving out but agreed to wait at least until her teaching was over for the year.

Linda had apologized for the way she acted on my birthday. She acknowledged that she'd been passive-aggressive. This seemed like a major positive change to me. We had begun making love again. At my suggestion we were giving each other sexual massages. This was an improvement, but we still had not talked frankly about sex, and our sex life still wasn't satisfying to either of us. I continued to be bothered by the thought that I hadn't been able to give her an orgasm since she'd read my account of the abuse. Despite her denials, I still suspected that she found me sexually disgusting and untrustworthy. I also suspected that there were sexual issues from her own past she wasn't dealing with. She had made vague references to abuse episodes and "weird sex." Part of me projected that there was an unconscious, vicious part of Linda that was happier when we weren't sexual. I wondered if she maneuvered to minimize our sexual contact in a way that made it seem as if it was my fault, my "illness." I thought of a statement I'd heard a therapist say: If you show me a couple who come to sex therapy with one as the identified patient, I can almost guarantee that the other one has the problem.

Grace is angry and bitter. Her frustration and resentment are turning into desires to lash out and kill people and to mutilate her own genitals. Q is in pain. He has been ignored lately. Young One, Robert, and Little Honey feel hopeless, scared, alone. The I-wish-I-was-dead voice is starting to make noise again. I think it may be Grace.

I wrote a short statement about the sadistic group sex and read it in group. I got through it without breaking down. When I finished I held myself, shaking, and sweating, and staring blankly. I was proud that I'd read it, even though there were details I chose not to mention.

There was silence at first. Then the guys reassured me that I wasn't a monster, that Dad and Hugh were the monsters. One guy was disgusted: "How could they find that many men who wanted to torture boys?" Charles said that people like that tended to gather in "sex clubs." That seemed to fit better than prostitution.

Group had become very helpful. We'd begun to speak the truth and let our emotions show; but now it was coming to an end. Charles said he needed a long vacation. My fear of abandonment was stirred up.

"I'm so depressed and upset nobody wants to be in a room with me unless I pay them," I told Nan irritably.

She tugged at my sleeve and said, "You couldn't pay me enough."

"So I won't pay you."

Q is back in that torture chair with his head strapped down. He is angry at me for being weak; calls me a wimp. He wants to strike out and hurt me. Bear is badly wounded. His wounds look infected, repulsive, but he's trying to be good-humored. Grace appears to have split her head, shoulders, and arms off from the rest of her. She wants to die, to leave her red and lumpy body behind. Nan calls her back, and she agrees to wait. Dream Woman helps her. Robert feels like an inadequate failure. Just before we leave trance Little Honey comes running up terrified and shaking.

As I drove to my massage after therapy, I realized I *had* forgotten to pay Nan. I felt bad; then I laughed about it. I had unloaded on Nan and given her zero positive feedback. I began once again to fear that she would disappear or abandon me.

I told Linda I wanted to experiment with ways to make our sex life better. She said she liked the massage and would possibly be willing to try some sex toys. Unfortunately, I kept going. I said I'd like to try a ménage à trois. She got agitated. She said that what I really wanted was her okay to have affairs. She said she felt rejected and abandoned; she wouldn't live with me if I had affairs. It took a lot of patient talk from me to convince her that this wasn't what I was asking for. What I wanted was an exciting and healthy sex life with her.

It's an old idea in family therapy that when one person in a system changes, it forces the others to change, too. Because these changes are often difficult, the family system usually ends up resisting or undermining the individual's change no matter how positive it is. I worried about Linda in this regard. I wondered why she stuck with me through all the pain. Sometimes she seemed like a life-saving companion, almost too good to be true. Did she prefer this almost asexual caretaking role? Would she resist major changes in me? Middelton-Moz talks about "unconscious contracts" between couples. They might agree, for example, "You be abusive, I'll be a victim; you be hysterical, I'll be calm; you be drunk, I'll be codependent." Did Linda and I have such a contract?

There are two distinct versions of Q. One looks like a feral animal trapped by the foot, lips curled back in a grimace. I cut the chain and give him food. He gnaws it hungrily in the corner. I cut the laces of the boot that's restraining him and wash his bruised and bloody foot. He thinks I want sex with him, that I have some weird foot fetish. He walks a little, limping. The other Q is in a wheelchair and needs to be strapped in to sit up. He does not feel safe.

Grace is also split in two. Her head, arms and shoulders are separated from the rest of her and no longer have feeling. She looks at the rest of her body: on hands and knees, red, skinned alive. The swollen anus and vagina are like mouths of fish out of water, gulping at the air. She feels like a failure, pulled apart by forces beyond her control. I fear it means she has given up.

Red, tough and needless, smokes a cigar. Robert seems better. Bear's wound is healing, but he is sad.

The night after this session I lay in Linda's arms and cried as she sang softly to me.

I read *Subpersonalities,* by a British psychologist, John Rowan. He treats dissociation as a normal, functional adaptation. He makes the critical point that the inner part you ignore will turn against you and destroy you: "Whatever energy we disown, life brings to us, exactly as we have disowned it. . . . The God or Goddess whom you ignored became the one who turned against you and destroyed you. So it was with the Trojan War. So it is with consciousness work."

Or, as Pia Mellody has said, "Embrace your demons, or they'll bite you in the ass."

Bear and the wild Q are protecting the Q in the wheelchair. Wheelchair Q seems a little stronger; he can lift his head and move his arms a little. Distinct sensation memories of my head held immobile in one of their devices while they abuse me. I cry in tired sadness. Little Honey appears, bothered by a cock and balls that pursue her like a persistent wasp. Probably Dad's. I hug her and give her a board to sit on so that nothing can get at her bottom. Robert is strained and crying but agrees to try to help Little Honey. Big Honey defends her with her hammer. Grace is too tired to help; she has no resources left. The normal containment images, the locked and barred doors and the safe, aren't working anymore.

Linda was out of town for a few days in July. When she returned it was a pleasure to see her. We didn't talk about our issues, but the lovemaking was good. We agreed to talk at a later time, to try to work things out ourselves instead of seeing "a goddamn couples counselor." Nan suggested it might help if I emphasized my vulnerability and feelings to Linda when we talked.

Bear and Active Q appear happy. I go and see Wheelchair Q. He gets up and takes a couple of steps. I cry silently. After asking permission, I shake his hand and hug him. He is aware that we both have genitals. I assure him that there will never be sex between us. This is a tearful celebration.

Grace is lying down, covered with a blanket. Big Honey, Little Honey, and Robert guard her. She is barely conscious, too tired to be bothered by sexual urges. She lets me stroke her hair. Little Honey, who now often sits on a board or pillow to protect her ass, is in some ways the opposite of Grace, whose genitals are often maximally exposed.

A WORKSHOP ON EGO-STATE THERAPY

That weekend I attended a two-day psychology workshop at the University of California at Berkeley. Before therapy started stirring up my feelings of shame and vulnerability, I had gone to dozens of workshops and seminars, but this was the first I'd attended in over three years.

The workshop was conducted by John and Helen Watkins of the University of Montana. He was an emeritus professor of psychology; she had been a counselor for many years at a university clinic. John Watkins had developed ego-state therapy, which I found to be the best model of trauma, dissociation, and healing. It was a well-researched and consistent framework that fit my situation well.

Ego-state therapy is based on the idea that everyone dissociates to some degree. There is a continuum with normal dissociation at one end and polyfragmented multiple personalities at the other. In the middle are ego states—semiautonomous psychic entities, like my insiders. Ego states may be created by normal differentiation, introjection (especially of parents), or trauma. They are often best accessed with hypnosis. All ego states should be befriended, even the hostile ones—those which, for example, cause a client to self-mutilate or attempt suicide. They all have positive, protective functions, and it's one of the therapist's jobs to help them fulfill these functions more powerfully. The Watkinses maintain that ego states created by trauma often require hypnotic abreaction in order to heal. An abreaction is the cathartic revivification of an emotionally disturbing experience which releases the bound-up emotions. The Watkinses have described in detail how both the therapist and client can handle the intense emotions that arise and use them for healing.

The workshop was excellent. There were no exercises that required me to expose myself or interact on a deep level. The Watkinses showed videotapes of abreactions they had done with clients. This was hard for me. I had to use every trick I knew (breathing deeply, counting, looking away) to keep from crying.

The Watkinses sometimes saw clients in Montana for two or three days of intensive therapy. I wrote Helen Watkins asking if I might have such a session with them. She phoned back, and we arranged for a weekend in October.

Little Honey leads me by the hand to Grace, who is calmly sitting up. She wants food. I give her chicken soup. I cry when I think about how hurt she has been. She finishes eating and stands up. She becomes dizzy. Robert and I grab her arms to help her. She doesn't like this at all. We let go of her slowly. She takes a couple of shaky steps, then lies back down and goes to sleep.

Little Honey leads me to Q and Bear. Bear is happy to see her. The active Q is proud to be guarding. The hurt Q is languid and thin but able to stand, sit, and move around. We give him food and leave him to rest.

Dream Woman holds a metal device, like a key ring, shaped like the classic alchemical sign for woman. I ask, "Does this mean Mom was part of the abuse?" She nods. "Is this what we should do next session?" She nods. To check her veracity I ask, "Am I an orangutang?" She laughs and nods. I don't know what to believe.

Big Honey looks bigger than ever. She holds the hammer, and there are no penises or Dad images bothering Little Honey or Grace. At the very end of trance there are a couple of glimpses of me as a young boy in the head harness and tied by my foot. This sets off waves of sadness.

The two forms of Q that were developing, one an invalid, the other a guard, paralleled the split in Red the previous year. I resisted the temptation to theorize about this intriguing subject, focusing instead on listening and observing.

The injured Q seems to be standing: calm and civilized. Probably gay. I realize suddenly that this is a construct he has made to please me and hide his pain. I can see the real injured Q still paralyzed, strapped in the chair. Sinking heart; silent tears: I've let him down. Injured Q hates Mom. He wants to kill her. Living next to her is intolerable for him, a betrayal and denial. I thank Q for communicating with me and for trying to make it easier on me. I apologize for failing him.

Grace is lying down with a half smile. She doesn't need to show me again that she can stand on her own two feet. I ask her about Mom. I get no direct answer, but I remember Grace's swollen genitals and the feeling that they represent not only my damaged female part but also a female abuser.

CONFRONT MY MOTHER? THE INSIDERS SAY NO

I returned to the idea of confronting Mom about what Dad and Hugh had done. Nan noted that my continuing hope for Mom's confirmation made me vulnerable. At her suggestion, I considered Mom's possible reactions to a confrontation and traced the chain of events that could arise from each. Would any response force me to take action I was not ready for? I also checked into emergency mental health care so that I wouldn't feel the need to help her if she had another psychotic episode.

In trance I asked the insiders how they felt about it.

Injured Q is sad and frightened, curled up facing the wall. He does not want to move, does not want change. Little Honey comforts him. Guard Q is dispirited, sitting with his head down holding his knees. He keeps thinking, sadly, "Why doesn't Mom just die?" I ask Grace about confrontation. She says, "You know she molested you, don't you?" Me: "No." Grace, quibbling: ". . . was sexually inappropriate with you?"

Bear, Robert, and Grace seem ready. The two Q's are opposed, the two Honeys unsure. Do I need more memory before I confront her? I feel pressure to do it anyway. . . .

I vacillated. A confrontation might heal the shame I felt about living next door to Mom. Was I enmeshed with her? At best she had been a guard in a concentration camp, enabling Dad and Hugh to maintain the façade and continue the abuse.

When I checked inside that week, I could not clearly see the injured Q. There seemed to have been a fire or explosion. Had I pushed too hard? For Q's sake, I decided against a confrontation.

I started looking into PhD programs in psychology. It excited me to feel that I was moving on and doing something. Yet at the same time it depressed me because I didn't know clearly what I wanted. I realized that a major, and perhaps unhealthy, aspect of my motivation was a need to be part of a class or group, a need to belong.

I wrote lists of the projects I might do, but none of them gave me pleasure. Anhedonia again. The urges to confront Mom, buy a home and move, and get a PhD, all made me profoundly nervous, and yet somehow I didn't feel it directly.

"Fear, the emotion I don't feel, rules my life," I wrote in my journal. "I eliminate the things that might frighten me. Then I sit home bored and lonely."

It was now almost certain that I would make enough money on the earthquake repairs to buy a new home. Linda and I agreed to look for a house together. I liked where I was living and didn't want to feel that I'd run from my own home to get away from Mom.

Injured Q: just his face, no more, strapped down. Memories emerge from the head: penises, asses, a screaming mouth shoved into Q's immobile face. Now Dad and Hugh are tying and gagging me. Raping me. I'm grabbed by the hair. My face is forced into someone's ass. I'm made to lick it. Smell and taste of shit. This is the first distinct, coherent, detailed memory I've had in a long time, the first time smell and taste have been a direct part of memory. I have been in retreat from memory, focused outward.

I ask Q if this is what he needs to do: release more memories. His reply is to get up dance around. I apologize to him for trying to be finished too quickly.

I had been in a rush to escape Q's pain: escaping outward by dealing with Linda, worrying about Mom, obsessing about real estate, thinking about what to do when therapy was over. I wanted to be okay while avoiding what I really felt inside. This is what an earlier generation of therapists used to call a "flight into health." I realized that my overwhelming sense of isolation and despair was insignificant compared with what Q had experienced as a child. I wondered to what extent those feelings were Q's old emotions leaking through.

Once again, the insiders had let me know, not gently, that my life was still on hold.

ALL EGO STATES HAVE A POSITIVE FUNCTION

Injured Q has a scared, nauseated grin. He appears to be floating just under the ceiling as he looks down on the scene below. Dad is raping me. My feet are tied with leather straps with sharp metal studs turned inward. I am bent over a green, canvas, duffel bag. My arms are tied behind my back and my face is banging rhythmically into the floor. I have an erection. The rough canvas of the duffel bag chafes against my penis. As usual when Dad is done he makes me suck him clean. He whips me with a belt. . . .

Q feels guilty about abandoning the young boy. He's worried that some conscious part has been left in the body. I cry quietly throughout the trance. I have a huge urge to pull Dad off the child, kick his face in, and stomp his genitals. I try to help the child clean his mouth out, brush his teeth, and take a bath.

My understanding of Q's guilty feelings changed over the next several days. They weren't about Q abandoning the child, they were about me abandoning Q. He needed to tell his story; needed to share his pain and his memories.

Grace is a beautiful, sexy dancer. Now she's a bloody wound. She feels trapped by desires she cannot satisfy. She retreats to her depressed position with her head in her hands. We offer comfort and companionship.

Guard Q is withdrawn and depressed. Injured Q's face is puffy and teary-eyed, but I feel no emotion. Memories: being fucked; my jaw stretching while I suck them. Kneeling with feet tied, blindfolded and gagged, pushed forward over the duffel bag, greased up, raped. . . .

I read about Pierre Janet (van der Hart and Friedman, 1989), the great French psychologist of the nineteenth century. With a different vocabulary he seemed to have come to many of the same conclusions about post-traumatic stress as the modern theorists. He described post-traumatic decline as "degeneration of the will. . . indolence, hesitancy, indecision, impotence to act or focus," accompanied by withdrawal and a hypochondriacal preoccupation with the body. He described how people who used dissociation as a defense in childhood become addicted to it and use it chronically. Unfortunately most of Janet's insights were buried in the avalanche of Freudian hogwash.

Injured Q's face is puffy from crying. He points to scenes of me being raped, tied up, and bent over the duffel bag. Watching Dad and Hugh fuck each other and then being forced to lick and suck them clean. . . . A hypodermic needle and an injection: Now I have an idiot grin on my face. Somebody fucks me. I can feel the greasy object going in and out; the first time I've had clear sensation memories from my ass. No pain. I pee. They get mad and push my face in it, but I don't much care. . . . My elbows are tied together behind my back. A gag is tied tightly in my mouth. They tie the back of the gag to my elbows with a strap, pulling my head and arms back painfully. . . .

I went with Michael to a meeting of SIA—Survivors of Incest Anonymous, a twelve-step group. There were only three men among twenty or thirty women. Michael hated it and left early. I was nervous and emotional. I'd felt uneasy about going, but it felt good to say to a roomful of strangers, "Hi, I'm Bob; I'm a survivor of incest." I liked the group feeling, but it was too female. I didn't feel like I belonged.

By the broad definition of incest that SIA uses, there were a couple of times I might have been a perpetrator. As a young man I'd had affairs with two distant cousins. In both cases the sex was consensual; in neither were there significant age differences. I'd never felt that I'd done anything wrong, but now the thought that these experiences might make me an incest perpetrator in anybody's way of thinking filled me with shame and self-hate. SIA specifically bans offenders from their meetings; this stance had attracted me to them, but now I felt uncomfortable about going back. Would anyone there consider me an offender? Would I have to tell them about the affairs and ask their judgment?

Q's face is still puffy and swollen. He's covered with dirt, shit, come. He sits rhythmically rocking and banging his head into the wall until he passes out. Robert is brokenhearted; I can't tell why. He has a bloody wound from his neck to his navel. He is irritated by Nan's invasive offers of support. He has to lie down and be alone. Little Honey is worried about Robert. Eventually she and Bear go over and sit with him. Grace is horny. She wants to get laid or masturbate, but this seems inappropriate and shameful considering the pain of Q and Robert.

In a few weeks I'd be going to Montana to work with the Watkinses. John Watkins, PhD, and Helen Watkins, MA, often work together. John is the originator of ego state therapy. Helen is a licensed psychologyst. They are pioneers in working with trauma and dissociation. I listened to a tape of them doing an abreaction. The client's cries and screams affected me powerfully. I hoped that working with the Watkinses would be a big leap forward in my healing, even if it was difficult. I prepared a written summary of my therapy to send them, and Nan and I reviewed it together.

Robert is embarrassed to be the first focus of attention. He still has a huge wound splitting open his front. Image of Dad's finger poking into the wound. His voice jeering: "Whenever you have sex you'll

*know I was there first." Big Honey has to come with her hammer and
drag Dad away. Robert stabs at his own genitals. I feel the assault as
cramps in my groin. Robert wants to get up and pretend he's not hurt.
His chronic position is to be ready for attack. He wants to hide his
pain because showing it leaves him vulnerable and gives Dad something else he can use, but he stays prone and does not hide.*

    *Grace is frustrated and filled with hate for Robert. She blames him
for keeping her hidden and controlled. Now she shifts to suicidal despair. Q is sitting up with a swollen face and a big headache. He's
afraid that I want to finish therapy and get rid of him. He's also afraid
of seeing the Watkinses. I reassure him that I want to be closer to him,
not to get rid of him, and that he can numb out at the Watkinses if he
needs to.*

All the newer literature on MPD agreed in essence with the
Watkins' contention that all alters have a positive, self-protective
function and that none should be weakened or exorcised. Frank
Putnam's *Diagnosis and Treatment of Multiple Personality Disorder,*
to give one example, states clearly that abuser introjects are a type of
persecutor-alter that need to be integrated, not destroyed. I tried to list
the possible positives of the Dad introject in my head: It stated the
most painful things; it had power; it enjoyed confrontation, and it was
glib. But it told me vile things about myself ("If you weren't such a
coward you'd fuck children too"), laughed at my deepest pain, and
bothered the inner children whenever they were most vulnerable. Big
Honey had to put all her energy into keeping it contained. If I was going to heal, I had to find some way to integrate it, to identify and focus
on its positive function.

    *Robert sits holding his wound closed with crossed arms; Dream
Woman stands behind him. He's pissed off: "I'm strong, I can function even if all of you think I'm the bad guy." He gives the finger to offers of support: "Even now I don't need help, and I'm proud of it."
Grace stabs at her genitals with a knife. She wants to cut them off. She
blames Robert. She gives up in despair and goes numb. I ask her for
the knife and for a promise that she won't hurt herself. She sees the
extreme parts of her sexuality as masochistic. This gives her a huge
advantage over the sadist when pain and sex are tied together: she's
not an abuser of others. I realize that the release of the healthy parts*

of her sexuality—her vulnerability, receptivity and gentleness—might also necessarily release huge amounts of childhood pain.

Little Honey is lonely but okay. Q has a whole "can of worms" that he doesn't want to open just now.

I felt invaded and shaky after that session, the next to last one before I was to leave for Montana. That week was all distilled dreadfulness: anger, hate, nightmares, an infected cyst on my penis, a boil on my ass, a bloody rash in my crotch. There was no release, no escape, just unremitting shit and the fear that I was going insane. Some of the hate was directed at Nan, with the usual fantasies of destroying her office. Nevertheless, I needed to prepare the insiders—and myself—for the trip.

Little Honey comes up first. We hug. Q has a huge can of worms with a lid on it. Grace is lying under a blanket. She pulls it away and reveals a young, sexy body without any swelling or redness. Dad's voice: "She's just a slut." Grace is hurt. She doesn't want to be attractive anymore. She has a knife. She promises to use it on Dad, not on herself. She gets a volume-control knob to turn Dad's voice down. She's afraid the Watkinses might let him loose. Two distinct images of Robert: one standing with crossed arms looking strong, the other an invalid lying under a sheet. He's afraid of nightmares and out-of-control panic, but he wants to go.

WORKING WITH JACK AND HELEN WATKINS

I was nervous the day of the trip. I had to change planes in Salt Lake City and go on from there in a small plane. The flight was so bumpy that one passenger screamed a few times. I arrived at the hotel in Missoula at three p.m. I was tired even before the work started, but I spent two hours with the Watkinses in their office.

John ("Jack") and Helen Watkins were both in their sixties or early seventies; straight-laced and middle class. I was immediately impressed with Helen. She seemed warm and devoid of pretense. Jack struck me as an absentminded professor type, but in retrospect this impression might have been due to my unfamiliarity with working with a male therapist. They asked about my history, and I told them. I felt shaky and close to tears. We agreed to start the next morning at nine o'clock.

That night I had a vivid dream of being fucked by Dad. There was intense sensation in my asshole. Much as I loathed to admit it, it was mostly pleasurable. I woke up with a big erection and jacked off. I wished I hadn't had that dream. It left me sick with self-hate. I felt I'd have to tell the Watkinses about it.

At their office, there were few preliminaries before they asked me to go into trance. I was not comfortable sitting up, so I lay down on the floor.

They want to talk to Dream Woman and Bear. They ask about my earliest memory (being sucked as an infant). Then they ask about the earliest negative memory (when the greased prodding of my butt started to get painful). They ask Dream Woman what we should work on. Surprisingly a memory fragment I hadn't thought about for a long time came up: the back of my head banging rhythmically into a wall. That and last night's dream are what Dream Woman wants to deal with.

They ask me first to go through the memory dissociated, like watching a movie. . . . Dad and I are at Lake George. We're in bathing suits. He's taking me upstairs, holding me by the upper arm. In my bedroom I retreat against a wall. Dad takes off his bathing suit. He comes at me with an erection. I open my mouth. He threatens me with horrible things if I bite him. He starts fucking my mouth. The back of my head bangs repeatedly into the wall. I arch back and press my head against the wall so that it won't bang. I try to use my tongue to keep his dick from gagging me. When he finishes he threatens me again. Then he leaves.

I don't understand why my unconscious chose this memory; it was fairly ordinary for my childhood. Now Helen and Jack want me to go through it again, this time associated, experiencing it as the child did. They are forceful, aggressive in their suggestions that I feel exactly what is happening. Again and again they say things like, "You can really feel your head hurting as it hits the wall." This is very different from Nan's technique, but it's okay.

After I complete the memory the second time they say, "We're with you now, go back and do whatever you want." I go back and see Dad on the stairs as he's taking the child to the bedroom. I grab him and throw him down the stairs, but there's no pleasure in it; it feels like a duty. I just want to leave. I feel very sad. I'm crying and twitching. I have a tremendous need for a father, for a good parent of either sex. Killing Dad is like having to shoot a beloved dog that has rabies, but Jack and Helen encourage me strenuously. I repeatedly ram the fireplace poker into his heart, his eyes, his mouth. It feels like killing a vampire. I keep going at him as Jack and Helen urge me on. I split him in half and smash his genitals and face to a bloody pulp. He's squirming like a worm on a hook. Jack: "Keep killing him until you can safely turn your back on him." I smash at him until he's hamburger; then I mix the meat with ashes and burn it in the fireplace. Deep sadness. No satisfaction or anger. I want a daddy or a mommy so badly.

Finally I tell Jack that I'm completely able to turn my back on Dad. He says that if I look up at the top of the stairs, I'll see something new, a positive, father-like part. I see a figure that looks vaguely Egyptian with a headdress or towel on its head. Now the image changes until it looks like Groucho Marx.

There's a short lull. Now Helen asks the critical Dad-like voice in my head when it first appeared. It replies with an image of a photograph of me at five or six. I'm dressed in a heavy winter coat and wearing a leather flyer's cap. With a serious and determined look on my face, I'm taking what is obviously too big a step up the front stairs of our new home.

The Dad introject says he was there "to harden Bobby, to make him tough and hard to fool." Helen calls the Dad-introject, "The Bully." The Bully apologizes for being clumsy and not helping as well as he might have. He told Bobby some good and useful things. Bobby wants to trust him, but that won't happen right away.

Now Helen asks Bobby to go inside the house and ask Mom for help. He finds her at her office desk. She's "too busy" to talk. Now she's upstairs in her darkened bedroom with a migraine—"too sick." Bobby stands there in his heavy coat and flyer's cap. His posture is almost military. Tears are streaming silently down his face as he looks at Mom. She just wants him to leave her alone.

At this point I got up and sat on the couch, and we talked a little. Helen had been crying. She said what moved her was the image of the little boy standing beside the mother who wouldn't help. She and Jack had made some minor misinterpretations of things I'd said in trance, and I used this time to clarify them. They talked about finding good things for the Bully to tell Bobby.

I lay back down on the floor. This time Helen used an eye-roll induction to help me into trance. We had to deal with last night's dream. Again they had me go through the experience twice, but this time they wanted me to do it associated first.

It becomes immediately clear that the dream was about a drugged experience. Jack and Helen keep asserting strongly that the body responds; that healthy bodies respond. Jack asks me to divide into two parts: one that liked it and one that felt hate and shame and guilt. There is some dialogue, but the one-that-liked-it is too out of it to talk much. He just grins, drugged and stuporous, and cooperates with Dad.

We go to a memory of the morning after. My butt is sore. I feel confused; worried that I'm "one of them." The memory of feeling dirty is so intense that I cry. Jack keeps at his positive messages: "It's not bad to want touch"; "You weren't guilty"; "It's okay to want a father." He and Helen ask me to forgive my genitals and anus for responding, to forgive myself for wanting to be held, for needing human touch, for wanting to be close to Dad. The sense that I am not "one of them" grows within me. I am not like Dad. It has been a long and costly war, but I have won.

The rest I forgot very quickly. I might have forgotten it all if I had not forced myself to make extensive notes as soon as I returned to the hotel. It had been a very emotional five hours, and I was exhausted.

Late that afternoon I took a long walk around the university campus turning the session over in my mind. The subjects we'd worked on were unexpected; they were not my conscious choice. They'd been chosen by my dream and by Dream Woman and Bear.

Jack was usually the theoretician of the pair, Helen the clinician. She said she'd chosen to have Jack there so that I'd have some sort of positive male role model. I realized that there were no positive male authority figures in my life.

I worried about being drugged in that homoerotic dream. I didn't want to blame my compliance on the drugs. What did this say about my current homosexual fantasies?

I hated killing Dad. I'd never before let myself be aware of how badly I needed a father. Killing him off was a sad necessity. I realized that the birth of the Dad introject was the start of my isolation and self-sufficiency. I quit expecting love or respect; I was ready to deal with contempt and degradation.

I realized how useless Mom had been emotionally and how this had exacerbated my need for a father. Helen pointed out that I was now doing to Mom what she'd done to me: providing for her financial security while ignoring her emotionally.

Helen also remarked that I had been consistently depressed; that I knew nothing else. I thought it might be more accurate to say that I'd been consistently afraid and knew nothing else. My rigid, fear-induced habit patterns had so severely limited me.

That night, as often happened when therapy was intense, I slept a good eleven hours. I dreamed I was returning from a digging job carrying a pickaxe, a shovel, and other tools over my shoulder. I had a couple of stacks of redwood pieces I wanted to bring back, but I was having trouble carrying them. The emotional tone was positive accomplishment followed by mild frustration.

I woke on the verge of tears. One meaning of the dream was immediately clear: I needed to tie things up into a bundle so I could take them home with me. I worried that the Bully might revert to his old pain-causing behavior. I didn't yet have a clear visual image associated with him; I thought that if I did, it might be more fixed and less likely to change back. The appearance of the Bully from behind Dad's image reminded me of *The Wizard of Oz,* when Dorothy and the others discover the man at the controls of the mechanism that produced the scary images and sounds of the wizard. This metaphor made it clear why my previous attempts to destroy the Dad introject had failed: I'd been attacking a projected image, something that could never be defeated or killed. I wondered how Big Honey, who had done most of the work of attacking and containing the Dad introject, was going to react.

At the Watkinses office we again talked only briefly before they asked me to go into trance.

THE DAD INTROJECT BECOMES FRANKIE

The Bully comes up first. He prefers the name "Frankie," short for Frankenstein. He likes that name because Dad is the worst monster he knows. Frankie goes to Bear, and Bear holds him. Frankie loves being able to feel something alive and warm, with a heartbeat. He's been starved for such contact. He's been absolutely alone all his life. He was born to deal with isolation. He's so grateful, but he also feels exposed, sad. I'm crying a lot and having trouble breathing. Helen covers me with a blanket, and I feel more secure.

We ask Dream Woman if it's okay to go to a really bad memory. She indicates yes. We go to Hugh making cuts on my ass and penis and stretching and licking the wounds while I'm held immobilized in restraints. Again the Watkinses are aggressive in telling me that I should feel exactly what is happening to me. Now Helen asks for Big Honey to come get Hugh and Dad. Big Honey comes with her hammer. She smashes them. She pops their balls, eyes, and skulls like rotten eggs. Helen and Jack encourage her. They cheer her rage. She burns their remains using gasoline and the wood from last night's dream. She tends the fire with tools from the dream.

We free the child. Little Honey and a dog lead him toward Bear and Frankie. He is contorted in pain. His neck is twisted and spasmed from struggling against the restraints. We get him into a hospital bed. Dream Woman comes over and put her hands under his neck and lower back.

Helen asks if we are done. The image of the pliers comes up, with a feeling of fear. We go back to relive that memory. I'm in the same room, tied down in the restraints, and Dad is torturing me with pliers. Sometimes he rages in anger and sometimes he laughs at my pain. Again the Watkinses suggest that I sense and feel it all. Big Honey comes in and does her job again. She uses her hammer to rip out Dad's collarbone and ribs, then pounds them in like stakes. She rips out his spine and smashes each vertebra with her hammer. She smashes his balls, his eyeballs, and his skull as Jack and Helen urge her on. She is thorough and complete. She burns the remains. I do not feel the immense sadness I experienced yesterday, nor is there any screaming anger or savage joy. I feel determined. Again we free the child and take it to a hospital bed. He's cramped with pain. I hear a dog howling and feel very sad.

I got up and sat on the couch. Jack said that what we'd done was like lancing a boil. It hurt, but it would help the infection heal. He said there may be more pockets of memory left, but he felt I could deal with them if I didn't push them down. I had to let myself reexperience them fully, then master the memory and protect the child.

Helen gave me the same message: Memories must be let back fully. "You can't fight an enemy you can't see." Simply recalling the memories is reabusive, she said. It was necessary to fight back, to achieve some mastery, to go back with adult resources and perhaps a therapist. This is how they had worked with me. They had urged me to feel and sense the memory completely, and then they encouraged and celebrated Big Honey's devastating attack.

Helen added, "You have so many good parts inside."

I collected my stuff at the hotel and headed for the airport. During the trip home, fragments of what we'd done over the weekend kept coming back. I avoided thinking about the most intense parts because I didn't want to cry in public, but I was able to reflect on the ten-and-a-half hours of therapy and draw some conclusions.

When Jack or Helen wanted one of the insiders, they asked for it to say, "I'm here" and for the most part talked with it directly. Nan, in contrast, always asked me to tell her what was happening. The difference is significant. One way increases dissociation and gives more autonomy to the parts, while the other emphasizes the central role of the executive ego and increases intrapsychic communication. Later when I asked Nan about this, she said she was aware of the difference, and her way of proceeding was the result of a considered and deliberate decision.

The exception to the Watkins' direct communication was with Dream Woman. When they asked for her, I replied "She's here" and relayed her messages to them. One time in trance I called Big Honey Dream Woman by mistake. Later, when Helen said something about Dream Woman not being able to be there until I did the work of expelling Dad and Hugh, Dream Woman said, "Yes, but I snuck in a little through Big Honey." I felt love and pride for Big Honey. It seemed significant that her weapon of choice, a hammer, was primarily a construction tool.

Another thing the Watkinses did differently from Nan was to ask a part, "When did you first appear?" This often was a very fruitful question. Asking the Dad introject when he had first appeared quickly led to my understanding of his positive function.

The transformation of the Dad introject into the Bully and then into Frankie felt solid and irreversible. I had left him with Bear and offered him what comfort and welcome I could.

Both of my dreams had been useful and important. I noted that Q, who himself was split in two, divided his work into two sections—the knife and the pliers. I remembered that the Watkinses had repeatedly suggested that my muscles could begin to relax and let go as I healed. I must have looked tense and cramped to them. I felt that Q could now enter a period of convalescence.

I had a long layover in Salt Lake City. I avoided the airport crowds and watched the sunset through plate-glass windows. It was sunset in the inner world, too. Seeing it simultaneously in both realms had a calm, timeless quality.

Big Honey is still tending the fire with the dog by her side. The dog howls by the dying fire: a mood of ending or graduation. In the last daylight Big Honey douses the embers with water. The dog pees in the wet ashes. Big Honey comes indoors, washes and lies on a pad on the floor near Q's hospital bed.

Monday night I had a long, good talk with Linda. I had really missed her hugs and presence in Montana, and I told her so. I cried as I told her what had gone on, and she was warm and supportive.

Frankie sits with Bear and Little Honey. He is afraid, especially of Big Honey. He seems to want to go back to the way he was. Big Honey leaves her hammer with Q and tries to approach Frankie. He's not comfortable, so she steps back. After some negotiating she builds Frankie a combination fort and playground. She promises never to go there without Frankie's permission unless there is an emergency. Frankie seems happier. Dream Woman again puts her hands on Q's neck and lower back. This simple act moves me to tears. Big Honey checks the place where the fire was. It's dead out.

Chapter 10

Male at Risk

October 1990-April 1991

When I saw Nan that Tuesday, I grinned at her—a shy, boyish, self-conscious grin. Telling her about what happened in Montana was more emotional than telling Linda, but I had a genuine sense of accomplishment. All seemed well inside.

Q looks burned and contorted in his hospital bed. He can move his lips a little and drink through a straw. Dream Woman again puts her hands under Q's neck and lower back. Big Honey and the dog go out to the field where we burned Dad's and Hugh's remains. The dog pees in the ashes. Big Honey spreads grass seed. She leaves her hammer behind and goes to see Frankie and Bear. Frankie sucks at one of Bear's black, hairy tits, oblivious to the world. Robert and Grace do not appear until Nan asks for them. Robert is watchful, his arms crossed over his chest. Grace feels that her problems are related to that dream of enjoying being fucked.

I checked inside frequently that week, most often while soaking in the tub. Frankie reminded me of myself as a child. His bullying behavior and rough play alienated Little Honey. He bit Bear's tit, which caused Bear to withdraw from him. Nan and I focused on helping him feel safe. I told him he was not allowed to hurt others; I tried to give him firm boundaries without being punitive. Sometimes he retreated into isolation, but I knew he loved the warm physical contact he'd recently come to know. He made no movement toward shifting back into the Dad introject.

When a rape memory came up, I dealt with it as Helen and Jack had suggested: I let Dad and Hugh in fully and then attacked them.

Big Honey led the assault, smashing them with her hammer and burning the remains. Frankie helped her. His fear of Big Honey was vanishing; they were on the same team now. Q did not take part in the attack, but he appeared to be healing. As I reoriented I told myself, "I forgive my anus and genitals for responding. I forgive myself for wanting touch, skin contact, to be held. I forgive myself for wanting a daddy or a mommy."

One evening my mood darkened with no apparent cause. I got a headache and my vision was blurred. I checked inside to try to see what happened. There was movement in the ash pit. We got pitchforks and fishhooks and dragged out piece after living piece. All the insiders except the invalid Q helped to smash them, one by one.

The work went on whenever I checked in. Grace was sickened by it and returned to Q's bedside to care for him, but the others kept at it, determined and methodical. I was worried that this might go on indefinitely, but I wanted to keep the boil open and let it drain. I reminded myself that Dad and Hugh were dead, there was a finite amount of abuse, and I was stronger and more unified than I'd ever been. Richard Kluft, a leading theoretician on dissociation, says that the best prediction of therapeutic success is neither the severity of abuse nor the degree of dissociation but the level of cooperation among alters. This gave me encouragement and a sense of direction.

I asked Linda how I seemed since returning from Montana. She said that I'd been open, sweet, and vulnerable. I'd told her I loved her more times that week than in the previous year. She also thought I'd sunk into bad feelings the last two days.

Grace is tired and confused. She leans against Q's bed. Robert wants to let go of his wound and let his guts spill out, but he's strapped himself together to help destroy the last of Dad. Big Honey and Little Honey are at work in the killing field. Little Honey is happy to be part of it. Frankie is happy in Bear's arms. They help too, fishing pieces out of the ashes and crushing them. Grace and Q bring firewood. Everyone walks or dances around the fire. A periscope emerges from the ash pit and looks around. We pull it out and destroy it, but it pops out again. . . .

After six months of bureaucratic delay, I'd finally gotten the permit for the last big earthquake-reconstruction project. That week I signed a contract for the job. I should have felt relief, but I didn't. The builder

I'd been using was proving to be dishonest and unreliable. One day he casually told me his estimate on one job had changed from sixty-five to eighty-five dollars per square foot. I squashed my reaction. I didn't realize I was angry until later, just as when Roseanne and Wendy had let the perpetrators into their groups. I created lacunae, negative hallucinations, in my perceptual field.

This was part of an old pattern of not feeling my feelings, a psychic defense mechanism that derived from a deep belief that I was a freak. I felt that it was part of the system Robert had engineered to help me survive my childhood and adolescence. I asked him to let me feel a little more. I didn't necessarily want to show my emotions in such situations, but I wanted at least to react enough to ask challenging questions.

My sense of smell was changing. I had heard and read about strong male crotch odors and the smell of semen, but as an adult I had never been aware of them. Now I was able to sense those odors. My guess was that I'd blocked them out because they would have been strong memory triggers that would have broken the amnesia.

Little Honey hugs me and bites my neck. She's angry and needy: Frankie is taking Bear's attention from her. There is a reconciliation. Bear ends up holding them both, one in each arm. Q is split in two again. One part is still in his bed, badly burned; the other part stands guard over him. Dream Woman comes and picks up Burned Q. Big Honey is still out by the ash pit, pulling out chunks of the abusers. Grace is curled up, sleepy and sad. . . .

GRACE'S SEXUALITY—AND MINE

Grace's stuff was prominent. The masochistic flavor of her sexuality both turned her on and filled her with self-hate. When I let myself think of what Grace wanted sexually, my dick got hard. Knowing that other survivors experienced the same feelings and hated themselves for it didn't help much. Any fantasy of passive sex stimulated Grace, especially when it involved asses. But her sexuality was somehow tied to abuse, and this left her feeling dirty and confused. For as long as she could remember, she'd been stuck with powerful desires she couldn't act on. The way she usually appeared, lying on her back displaying her red and swollen genitals, was an expression of this dilemma. I offered comfort, but I had no solutions for her. She was not averse to the idea that her desires might change, but if they didn't, she wanted to act on them.

Little Honey, Frankie, and Bear are together and happy. Their reconciliation is holding. Grace is clear about what she wants: to have sex with a gentle, understanding but dominant man; to experience intense but not painful sexual sensations. To be penetrated. The others, in turn, shake their heads "No" to the idea. Guard Q indicates that even thinking about it while Burned Q is hurting so badly is out of place. Maybe when he is healed it will be okay. Dream Woman seems to agree. This gives Grace a ray of hope and increases her involvement in Q's healing. She has the power to sabotage my sex life through impotence or premature ejaculation; but as long as she has hope, she won't do it.

Nan asks Grace when she first appeared. Grace has two answers: around age six and around age twelve or thirteen. Her function was to hold all the pleasurable aspects of the stimulation from abuse and then to encapsulate it and wall it off when I entered adolescence.

The depression that usually set in around Thanksgiving seemed, refreshingly, to be staying away. All the insiders but Grace seemed to be healing or content. Nan told me she'd never seen me happier; it was the first time I'd really looked okay. I backed off from dealing with my stuff. I smoked a little pot and drank moderately. Linda and I had pleasant and playful sex.

I read *Males at Risk* by Frank Bolton, Larry Morris, and Anne MacEachron, a book that offered plans for sexual healing. Most of them were aimed at sex offenders and dealt with reducing deviant responses through behavioral conditioning. The text recognized that some people cannot become aroused or reach orgasm without deviant fantasies. It suggested as an exercise that one masturbate to a deviant fantasy until "orgasmic inevitability" is reached, then switch to an acceptable fantasy and have the orgasm. This didn't seem great, but at least it was a concrete plan to deal with abusive arousal. I've often thought that masturbatory fantasies and imagery were keys to understanding an individual's sexuality, and I was pleased to see this view in print. A problem for me was that this technique presupposed a clear boundary between deviant and nondeviant fantasies. In the past, I'd always thought that anything two consenting adults chose to do with each other was okay; but now I knew that, for me, certain acts and fantasies were reiterative of abuse. Did this make them bad and unhealthy? Was any part of my sexuality free of contamination? Because I still didn't know what kind of sex was okay for me, Grace was in pain.

Little Honey takes us over to Bear and Frankie. Frankie has an erection; he feels ashamed or shy about it. We talk about it: It's fine to feel sexual and experience pleasure, but it's not okay to be sexual with the other insiders; and it's never okay to force sex on anyone. Grace seems okay, sleepy, and stretching. Her genitals seem less red and swollen. We ask Dream Woman, "Will Grace be satisfied after Q is healed?" Dream Woman nods. "Does this mean I'll have a male lover?" She nods. This is by far the most explicit Dream Woman has ever been. It scares me a little. Am I misreading her somehow? Her answers make Robert uncomfortable; he'd rather be asexual. His idea of sensuality is a warm, soft bed.

Big Honey stands by the ash pit with her hammer. Some Dad carcasses are still coming up. She wants to use her hammer to build something.

I declared my vacation over after Thanksgiving weekend. It was time once again to stop indulging myself, time to start working harder at therapy.

Little Honey is wet, bedraggled, and upset. Frankie has peed on her. He's defiant, almost gleeful. We put him in a "time-out chair" in a room by himself. After trying to talk with him for a while, I lose patience. I tell him I don't want to take care of an obnoxious brat. . . . Image of myself as a child, alone and isolated, trying to play. Deep sadness. Now Frankie apologizes. Bear takes him back, but Little Honey is not completely reconciled.

Burned Q looks shrunken. He appears to be dying in Dream Woman's hands. Dream Woman nods: "Yes, he will die." Grace: "See? I won't get laid. The promises were a trick." Guard Q is angry at Dream Woman. He takes Burned Q from her and holds him in his arms. There is still some life in him.

Little Honey goes to the ash pit to be with Big Honey. She doesn't want to go back to Bear and Frankie.

I attended another workshop, after overcoming a case of last-minute jitters. It was given by a recognized expert in imagery and hypnosis. I went with positive expectations, but he turned out to be a lame and boring fool who was inordinately full of himself. He said that the reality of abuse in a client's past was unknowable and irrelevant. I found this offensive; a polite cover for massive denial. It may be unknowable from a philosophical standpoint, but this argument invalidates memory and reduces human motivation to psychotic autism. A lot of neo-Freudians have retreated to this position. Faced with incontrovertible evidence of the prevalence and pathogenic nature of child sexual abuse, they can no longer claim that people's memories are just fantasies or wish fulfillment so now the truth is unknowable.

I had the same response to Leonard Shengold's *Soul Murder.* Shengold amends the Freudian tradition of denial and blame-the-victim with a few lukewarm modifications to allow for the evidence of child abuse. I feel sorry for any survivor who falls into the hands of the Freudians. There are a few exceptions. Alice Miller has written several wonderful books, but she has explicitly repudiated her Freudian background. John Watkins continues to honor Freud, but his ego-state therapy is valuable in spite of Freud's theories, not because of them.

Guard Q is holding Burned Q. When Guard Q looks down at him, I'm filled with intense sorrow and fear that Burned Q will die. When Guard Q looks up, I'm filled with savage, protective, tear-your-throat-out rage. My childhood screams ring in my ears, and with them comes a sickening sensation of being unable to escape or stop the pain. Guard Q is desperate for sleep, but he's afraid a cock and balls will attack Burned Q; afraid they might be his own. Nan discounts this fear, but I think it might be justified. Dad and Hugh tried to condition me to sadomasochistic child abuse. Part of me gets aroused against my will. Was Guard Q's vigilance what saved me from becoming an offender?

Little Honey and Robert agree to stand watch, and Guard Q allows himself to sleep.

MORE DEPRESSION, MORE THEORY, MORE DENIAL . . . LESS SEX

The holiday depression proved only to be a little late in arriving. The triggering event was Linda's announcement that she was going to

spend part of her Christmas vacation at her brother's home at Lake
Tahoe. I told her this made me feel bad; I knew I wasn't much fun at
holiday time, but I wanted her company. When she got mopey and
stared silently at me, I flipped over to my get-the-hell-away-from-me
mode. I had cracked an old rigid pattern and admitted dependence
and need. Now I felt deeply ashamed that I'd let her see my neediness. I
wanted to tell her to stay away for the whole damn vacation. Over the
next few days came smashing, killing rages followed by insistent,
kinky sex fantasies.

Nan said I'd experienced "a massive shame attack." I'd expressed
vulnerability and been slapped for my trouble. It felt good to have a
name for the sudden mood shift. It *felt* like shame. When I was angry
I wanted to be alone so that nobody would see me.

What happened in trance that day was unexpected.

*Little Honey comes up reluctantly for a hug. Everyone else stays
away. There is growing anger inside. Guard Q and Robert especially
are pissed off: "You're a jerk, a fool. You've made things worse and
more painful."*

*They hate me. They want to leave therapy and never go back. I
can't get past this or get any more information.*

I was angry and confused. I wanted to hide. What was going on?
How had I made things worse? Was I afraid of something? Vulnera-
bility? Appearing lonely or weak? Confronting Mom? Sex with
Linda? Being gay? Was I afraid of Christmas itself?

I was tense all that week, unable to check inside. I got some pot and
planned to be numb at Christmas. I was constantly angry at Nan. Before I started therapy it had been as though I was walking around with
a beaker full of acid inside of me. Now the acid was pouring out, and I
was feeling it burn. Nan had suggested that I'd entered therapy because the beaker was beginning to fail, as symbolized by my back injury. This idea was neat, plausible, and wrong. Before therapy I'd
been doing everything I could to break into the beaker—studying
psychology, recording my dreams, doing hypnosis. It didn't fail on its
own.

Intellectually, I knew that my negative feelings about Nan were
largely irrational. They were the opposite of the usual transference in
which the client thinks he's in love with the therapist, but knowing

that didn't keep me from feeling the feelings. Our next scheduled session was the last before the holidays. I was so pissed at Nan I didn't know if I'd go. Somehow I got there; somehow I was able to trance out.

Little Honey comes up for hugs. Guard Q appears with a sword doing martial-arts forms. He is angry, desperate. He feels that things are closing in on him. He's been hurt over and over; it's time to strike back. He hates the whole course of therapy. Being sensitive and open to pain seems stupid to him. He wants to be Spartan. He's ready to sever things: relationships, his own right hand. He and Grace are angry at each other. She feels abandoned. Robert is struggling to contain the hate and not be violent.

Burned Q looks dirty. Pieces of charred flesh hang off him. I wash and reclothe him. Grace and Little Honey take over caring for him; Guard Q is too disturbed to handle a hurt child. Big Honey is thin and exhausted. Bear is mangy and tired. Only Frankie is energetic, throwing rocks at the Dad-fragments in the ash pit.

I left hating Nan. Some of the insiders would miss her, but I was glad I wouldn't be seeing the bitch for a while.

That night I cried as I talked with Linda. It was a relief. Tears were easier than the constant grinding hatred.

I numbed myself as much as I could, partly by reading abuse books and listening to taped lectures. Janet Woititz said that victims often perceive the termination of their abuse as traumatic. Since abuse is often the only close contact they know, termination can feel like abandonment. I still had no idea how my abuse ended, and Woititz's comment reaffirmed my suspicion that there might be another trauma there to uncover. Usually I disliked slogans, but Woititz reminded me of an old twelve-step saying that fit: When what you want is not what you need, you'll never get enough.

Jane Middelton-Moz suggested in one of her lectures that being a family scapegoat is a form of caretaking. This was a shocking idea. I was the bad child in the family. I was the problem. I got blamed. Had I been caretaking the others? It had certainly made their lives easier.

Alice Miller's *The Untouched Key* also raised questions. She hypothesizes that the difference between abused children who grow up to be monsters and those who don't is that the latter had at least one person with whom they could express their emotions and reality. I had not become a child molester, an ax murderer, or a Hitler, but I couldn't identify my childhood confidant. Could it have been Gloria, the black woman who took care of me? Dr. Bixby, the school psychologist I'd seen from third through fifth grades? Had I, in some sick way, leaned on Mom and received support from her?

I couldn't stay numb. I was filled with night terrors, shame-filled dreams, and black depression. I was scratching my ass and balls bloody in my sleep again. When I checked inside I found Burned Q growing and healing under the care of Grace and Little Honey. They were tired. Frankie was manic, like a hyperactive kid bouncing off the walls. The others didn't show.

The morning before my next appointment with Nan, I had to take my dog Lola to the vet. All her life her favorite thing had been riding in the truck. Now she was too old and feeble to get in. She tried once and fell. She panicked and wouldn't try again. Bleeding from the nose, she ran back to the house. This episode upset me deeply.

I felt great resistance returning to therapy, but I knew it would be self-destructive not to. Nan told me I had been so angry last time that she hadn't been sure I would come back.

Little Honey comes up for hugs. Now Grace appears. She has been helping care for Burned Q, but she gets down on her hands and knees and displays her genitals. She is painfully aroused, unsatisfied, tired of denying her desires.

Guard Q refuses to appear. Robert acts as an intermediary. Guard Q has withdrawn; he doesn't want to be vulnerable or have anyone see him as lonely or helpless. Robert agrees with him but knows there is no fun or joy in such a life. Robert can't imagine having fun; he can only see himself as an outsider watching other people have fun. Big Honey tends the fire at evening, sad and lonely. Frankie is hyperactive, birdlike, moving very fast.

During the trance there were many images of Lola struggling to get into the truck, her eyes fearful and lost. I identified strongly with her and didn't understand why. Nan suggested it might be Lola's helplessness that moved me so.

Afterward I felt better and was glad I had gone.

As the earthquake repair work wound down, I had a big but pleasant decision to worry over. I'd done such a frugal repair job that I had a substantial amount of insurance money left over. I had to reinvest it in real property or it would be taxed as income. Linda had long wanted to buy a house as an investment. I decided to look for one for us to buy together.

When I told Nan about this decision, she asked me if I'd told Mom. I hadn't. I was still thinking about confronting her. Now Nan suggested that it might be better to wait until after we moved.

The Watkinses believed unequivocally that confronting abusers externally was useless at best; it was internal confrontation that mattered. Nan had no such rule; she felt that confrontation was an individual decision. This individual, however, was conscious of being made up of parts who were in disagreement with one another. Confronting Mom would be a casting off of secrecy and a rejection of shame. It would affirm that I was exploring every avenue toward healing, including healing my relationship with her. Yet if any part of me needed her confirmation of my reality, I was setting myself up to be badly hurt.

There could be other negative consequences. She might have a breakdown and require care. Living near her was barely tolerable; with everything out in the open it could get even worse. Money was also an issue. If I confronted her, she could write me out of her will. I was reasonably well off without her money, but it complicated things. I wasn't sure whether this issue robbed me of my power or whether it just a screen for my neediness.

At the Watkinses the child inside had turned away from Mom and given up. Could this symbolic act be turned into mastery? What would mastery look like? Anger? Finding a different mother figure? Internal confrontation?

Little Honey has a splinter deep in the ball of her foot. We remove it, but it leaves a hole. We try to comfort her. She indicates that it has to do with something Dad did. Bear, Big Honey, Little Honey, and Grace gather around Burned Q. He no longer looks burned; he looks like a large, healthy baby. Grace is not happy. She displays her needy genitals but states clearly that she won't be sexual with Q.

Robert and Guard Q are off by themselves. Guard Q wants a clear task. He agrees to help guard the ash pit. Frankie is still enjoying his freedom, moving so fast that he is a blur. He will help Guard Q. Big Honey will get rest.

Nan compared Guard Q to a veteran who's returned from the war and doesn't know what to do.

That week I dreamed I was fishing, using big, bloody hunks of meat for bait, hooking a huge fish and continually losing it. This dream fit with the foreboding feeling I had that somehow I was blowing it, missing a big chance.

I seemed to be missing something with Linda too. None of our issues had gone away. A planned romantic getaway had ended in fiasco. We'd all but stopped having sex again, and I felt she was responding with passive-aggression instead of open, honest communication. This in turn left me hostile and irritated. She was diagnosed with endometriosis, a gynecological condition that would require surgery. I had the irrational but painful idea that my sexuality was so poisoned that it rotted my lover's genitals.

Guard Q is in a castle or bomb shelter. He is angry at Mom, Linda, and everyone else. He sees my relationships as an entangling octopus. He wants to strike out and hurt, to slash and cut his way free of all connections, but he fears loneliness. He's exhausted and wants to die. I check with the other insiders and find myself hating them all. A nasty bunch of self-centered assholes. Guilt, exhaustion, desperation: I'm way too irritable to relax. . . .

Linda's brother, Grant, and his thirteen-month-old son, Gabe, came to stay with us for four days. Grant is a builder; he looked at a home Linda and I were interested in buying. At one point Gabe reached out to me to pick him up and hold him. This broke my heart, but I didn't let it show. His bright eyes and trusting smile made me afraid and sad. When I held him I was aware of his crotch against me and of my own genitals. I was hypervigilant for any sign of arousal. Thank God I didn't feel any. It would have been proof to me that I was still deeply contaminated. I realized that as an adult I'd never picked up a little child and held it. I'd always avoided children; I especially avoided touching them.

When Grant and Gabe left, I talked with Linda. Crying, I told her how I felt being around a child. We got to talking about other issues. She mentioned her resentment at the failed vacation. I told her how hard expressing needs was for me; how it left me feeling vulnerable, unsafe, expecting to be humiliated and manipulated; how I retreated like a snail into its shell.

I apologize to each of the insiders for rejecting them last week. I'm not perfect. I make mistakes. Little Honey doesn't come running up for hugs, but eventually she lets me carry her around. She tells me she could disappear. I tell her I'd be lost and lonely without her and the others. Guard Q is building a tower with crenellated battlements. He thinks therapy is dangerous and foolish, but he can't stop us. All he can do is prepare a sanctuary for himself. He's willing to let the others share it if there's trouble. Bear and Robert offer him help. Grace is taking care of Burned Q. She doesn't expose herself. Frankie is the only one to reject my apology. He says flatly that he doesn't need me. Big Honey, somber and tired, conserves her strength.

Linda and I had set aside Sunday morning to talk about our issues. The first thing she said was that she didn't want to buy a house with me. I didn't react, but I was hurt. This was completely unexpected. We'd been looking for a home together. We had found one that was attractive and a solid investment. Her brother had okayed its structural soundness. We were ready to make an offer.

Then we talked about sex. Linda told me I was all wrong in my presumption that she'd stopped having orgasms because she felt my sexuality was tainted. Early in our relationship she'd faked orgasms; the change was that she'd quit faking. It had nothing to do with my abuse history or my manuscript.

I told her that sex had stopped being fun for me. It felt as though my needs and desires didn't matter; all we focused on was her orgasms. We talked without reaching a conclusion, without having sex. We ended up hugging and saying, "I love you."

As usual it took a couple days for my rancor to surface. I let out some of my frustration and resentment at Nan's. I talked a lot about Linda before I went into trance.

Little Honey comes up for hugs. We go over to Guard Q's tower with Bear and Robert. They have been helping Q. The idea that he finally has someone on his side starts me crying. Burned Q looks like a big, chubby baby who loves to eat. He doesn't move much.

We ask whether we need to do more memory work. Everyone seems to nod yes. I try to contact Dream Woman, who hasn't been present for some time. She seems to nod yes, but it's fuzzy and vague.

I asked Linda why she had decided not to buy the house with me. In essence she told me it was a "vote of no confidence" in me and in our relationship. She was depressed all that week, as bad as I'd ever seen her. She said she was upset by our talk Sunday, but that was only part of it. Due to the endometriosis she had extreme PMS with cramps that lasted a week or two each month. I comforted her, but beneath the surface I was irritated. She was the one who had rejected commitment, and yet I was the one who had to be supportive. She wouldn't call a friend or her therapist. I held her and told her that I loved her even on bad days, but inwardly I was ready to tear her apart.

Guard Q is raging. He wants to cut all emotional connections. They make him feel like he's caught in a spider web. He has a stainless-steel scalpel as big as an ax. Nan asks if he wants to kill Mom internally. He starts to split her head open but stops in fear. He's ready to cut Linda out. He insists on using the words "viciously passive-aggressive." He wants to cut free, to confront, "to force it down their throats," but he fears loneliness. Nan: "Am I a dangerous spider?" Guard Q, cuttingly: "You might be, if you were stronger and smarter." Now he's confused and sad. Nan: "You can be angry at me and I won't leave. I won't come closer unless you want it." The idea of human closeness releases a wave of sadness. Bear and the dog go over to Q to let him touch their fur and feel their warmth. This provides comfort, but it quickly turns into a memory of small hands in pubic hair and a big dick. Very sad. The need for warm, living touch stops the desire to wield the scalpel. Me: "Are there more memories?" Guard Q nods. . . .

I told Nan that I'd started again to doubt the torture and group sex memories. Denial, my old companion, was slipping back in as a counterpoint to my negative feelings about therapy.

In retrospect, I'm surprised I wasn't aware on a conscious level that something was terribly wrong. For a while after seeing the Watkinses I'd felt almost okay, but the relief hadn't lasted long. My rage at Nan and my resentment of the insiders, Q's tower building and

Frankie's hostility, were all ominous signs. Later I would recognize that they marked the start of my descent into the blackest, most immobilizing depression of my life.

Little Honey: "Don't try to take care of us; you're the one who needs care." She sits me down in a big, soft chair. Big Honey is grave. Grace wears a sack-like dress. Burned Q is a huge baby. They come over to me, and we look for Guard Q. He is in his tower flanked by Robert and Bear. He wants to kill Mom. He's cold, brutal, removed: Hitler speaking from his reviewing stand at Nuremberg. Guard Q could have gone in that direction. I want to go back to another SIA meeting, but he's not willing to. This angers me. I feel like I'm starting over again. I'm too tired and weak. I can't stop crying. I'm such a wimp and a failure.

Nan asks me if I feel suicidal. Yes, I do.

CHOOSING TO CONFRONT MOM

I focused on real estate. Linda had taken herself out of the home-buying picture; I reorganized my search to fit my goals as a solitary investor. Usually I loved this aspect of my business, examining property and making offers, but there was no joy in it now. It was just a way of staying numb.

Rick from group called. He'd confronted his abuser and gotten an out-of-court monetary settlement. It was good to hear from him; I'd been feeling so alone.

I'd always been able to feel okay if I sensed any movement in therapy, but just then I was walking in circles through deep mud. I was feeling ever more isolated and unhappy. I'd wake up at two or three in the morning and stay awake until dawn. I dreamed of giving my brother Eddie, a blow job. The dream was so explicit that it felt like a memory. I was tired and depressed all the time. I felt like a total failure. I was a hopeless mess. I wasn't talking to Linda. I smoked dope and drank almost every night.

I needed to do something, anything. What I decided to do was confront Mom. All the books I'd read advised that a confrontation with the abuser must be for the survivor's emotional well-being, not to achieve something else. I was thinking very hard about this idea. Regardless of any response Mom might make, confronting her might be what I needed to get myself moving again.

Little Honey comes up, and almost at once there's a commotion in the background. Guard Q indicates angrily that he wants to kill Mom, to suffocate her. He thinks confrontation is dangerous. He retreats into his tower. Robert is in favor of confrontation because not confronting is worse. Bear has no comment. Frankie is a hawk, flying around, refusing to settle anywhere. He wants freedom, not work or responsibility. Grace shows her ass. It's not a sexual gesture; it's more like "kiss my ass." She wants to say things to Mom that will really hurt: "You might as well have put a gun to Eddie's head and shot him. Dad had his lovers living in the house with us. He had sex with them in your bed. They molested your sons right under your nose and you didn't know?" Big Honey nods: Confront. She indicates that my repeated fantasy that Mom would die is really about wanting my emotional ties to her to die.

Burned Q looks big, sedentary, chubby and healthy. He loves to eat. His unwillingness to move makes him appear retarded; but he's really just afraid to risk the well-being he's achieved, afraid he'll be hurt. His fear makes me sad. Little Honey moves around, showing him a safe area. . . .

Nan gave me a homework assignment: to write out my scenario for the confrontation. I developed a plan over the next several days and spent another week refining it.

I planned to give Mom three messages up front. The first was to ask her if she had time to talk, and then to tell her I wanted to discuss a difficult and painful subject from childhood. The second was, "Starting from a time before we moved to West 87th Street, Dad sexually abused me repeatedly over a period of years." I would repeat this message twice, then add that the abuse was sadistic, that I had seen him abuse Eddie too, and that Hugh had also participated.

The third message was a request: "What I want from you is information about how the abuse ended. This is not a time for keeping secrets or making up stories. I don't remember everything about the abuse, but I think you and maybe Dr. Bixby had something to do with stopping it. What happened?" This message was something of a ruse. Mom loved to boast and take credit, even if none was due. I was inviting her to brag about ending the abuse as a face-saving way of acknowledging it. Every book I'd read that discussed confrontation strongly advised against asking for anything; it shows vulnerability and empowers the person being confronted. I was consciously choosing to go against this advice.

At this point I would stop and wait for Mom's response. I felt it could fall anywhere on a continuum from a sincere reply to strong denial. Once she displayed her attitude, I would speak to her own culpability: "You knew Dad's lovers were living in the house, in your bed. Both your sons were sadistically sexually abused on an ongoing basis right under your nose. The abuse killed Eddie and it damn near killed me.

"You have responsibility. You were often ill, and I used to think of you as one of Dad's victims, but you were an adult. You could have stopped him, but instead you abandoned your two young, defenseless sons to a sadistic molester."

Burned Q wants to get up. He tries getting on his hands and knees, but a penis comes at his butt. Then, with Big Honey and Bear behind him and Frankie scouting in the distance, he stands. He wants to do more. I'm worried about Guard Q in his tower, but Burned Q's standing is a happy occasion.

It was March 19, early in the morning before my appointment with Nan. I went next door to Mom's house. She was sitting at the table in her kitchen, and I stood leaning against the cabinets halfway across the room as I delivered my three messages.

Her response was "Oh, no!" but it was not an expression of denial or disbelief. She hadn't known, she said, but she had been afraid it might happen and had worried about it. She couldn't ask us if we were being molested. She sort of thanked me for telling her and said she hoped I'd feel better now. She stayed calm and didn't minimize. For the first time ever, she admitted that the frequent migraine headaches she'd had when I was a child were psychogenic. She acknowledged that she'd had psychotic episodes.

Dad kept all the money out of her hands, she told me. He stopped her from socializing with other mothers of young children. He would not let her bring them into the house. He tried to get her to take part in sex games with his friends.

We discussed Dad's homosexuality. He'd confessed it to her shortly after we moved to West 87th Street. She believed that his murder was caused by his homosexual activities. She told a long, distracting story about how one of Dad's friends had taken her to dinner after he was killed and told her he had introduced Dad to "the life" when she was in the hospital giving birth to Eddie. She bragged about how she had stormed out of the restaurant. I didn't believe the story. I had a strong intuition that Dad had been basically homosexual and sadistic far earlier than that.

Mom said that the molestation explained why Eddie was seeing a psychiatrist at the time of his death. I stated flatly that the abuse killed Eddie. She said that couldn't be proved. This was the closest she came to denial. She said that if she'd known about the abuse she'd probably have left. She'd thought of leaving, but money worries stopped her. I told her repeatedly that she should have left, that I'd have been better off in an orphanage.

I cried a little at her house and a lot when I got home. I wondered whether my anger was satisfied. Had I really put it in her face? She'd patted me on the back as I left. It was the closest she'd come to a show of affection in years, maybe ever. Overall it was a more positive response than I'd expected. I promised to get her a book or two on child abuse to read.

At Nan's we talked about the confrontation. Nan said that Mom had "wimped out" when I was a child. I wondered if I'd wimped out in the way I'd faced her down.

Little Honey comes up for her hugs. We go looking for the Qs but can't find them. Instead a new figure appears: a soldier, a grizzled man who looks like a member of the French Foreign Legion. We embrace and kiss both cheeks. He wants to leave; says that his work is done. Grace comes out of hiding. She doesn't want Mom to ever know that she exists. The soldier agrees to stay awhile. He goes out to the field where Big Honey burned Dad and Hugh. There's a timeless, lonely, dogs-howling-in-the-distance-at-evening feeling like I had returning from Montana.

When I picked up the mail that evening I found a note from Mom. She backed off her statement about having been worried Dad would molest us, saying rather that she'd been worried his friends might.

She called Dad a "sadistic, selfish bastard," and said she'd feared he and his friends might do something "drastic" if she confronted them. She admitted she'd let us down badly and offered to go to a therapy session with me if it would help.

SHUT DOWN

The next day I had a decision to make, and it had nothing to do with Mom. I found my dream house—a big two-bedroom, somewhat run-down, on two-and-a-half gorgeous acres. It was in an old olive orchard on a gentle, south-facing slope with panoramic ocean and mountain views. I made an all-cash offer of two thousand dollars more than the asking price to make sure I'd beat all other offers.

My offer was accepted. An escrow was opened. I now had ninety days to perform the necessary inspections and arrange for the loan. For tax reasons, I was purchasing the house as a rental investment, but I hoped eventually to live in it.

By my next session with Nan I was starting to doubt Mom's response. Was it a rehearsed story designed to absolve her of responsibility? Did I want to tell her more? Maybe I needed to tell her about the sadism. Maybe I needed to tell her how devastating the aftereffects had been—the shame, isolation, compulsivity, and loneliness. I did not want to tell her about the amnesia or the weird sexual arousal.

I can't see anything clearly. Little Honey is a mature woman. Now she's a child again. She pulls my hand, trying to lead me somewhere, but I can't see where we're going. The Legionnaire is waving a sword around. He seems to be drunk. Robert feels like he's accomplished a difficult task. . . . Little Honey isn't trying to lead me anywhere; she's trying to run away. Bear comforts her a little. I feel tremendous anger at Linda. Nan: "This is unclear and murky, and probably represents something about your mother." I look for Burned Q: multiple, unstable images. Guard Q is hiding in his tower. Frankie is flying around. Grace doesn't appear.

Nan asks if I can feel the grief. No, I can't. I'm too full of frustration and anger.

Linda showed no enthusiasm or joy about the house. She was obnoxious, sour, and contrary. I tried to pretend everything was okay, but eventually I asked her, "Are you pissed off at me?" She angrily replied, "No, how could you think that?" She said she was "preoccupied" but wouldn't say with what. She halfheartedly apologized for her lack of enthusiasm, but there was no warmth, no emotional connection.

The next session with Nan was April 2, two days before my birthday. She was going on vacation for three weeks, and I felt I had a lot to do.

None of the insiders appear. I feel shunned, abandoned. I try to be calm and loving and open, but I feel myself growing angrier and more frustrated. What have I done wrong? Finally I see Burned Q. He's crying. He, too, feels unjustly rejected. Little Honey comes up briefly. No one else.

I charged out of Nan's office halfway through our scheduled time. My emotional response was, "Well, fuck 'em if they don't want me, they can go to hell."

What had I done to drive them all away? Did I need more memories? I just didn't know. Something was very wrong.

I was amazed at the extent to which repressed fear had constricted my life. I forced myself to attend to my real estate business. I walked the same two-mile route every day and bought groceries at the same store. Shopping at a new store felt like an achievement. That was it. Now my inner world was closing down and getting smaller too.

There was one bright, clear spring day that threw me deeper into depression. I hid in my bedroom and cried. I wondered if this could go on forever. Were pain, anger, sadness, and fear all there was inside of me? Recovery seemed hopeless. I wanted to quit therapy, but I didn't want to abandon the insiders. I felt hate for Nan and didn't want to see her, but I was in a very bad place and knew I needed help. An inner voice shamed me for feeling so bad: "A lot of people would envy you. You're not crippled. You don't have cancer or AIDS. You're wealthy. You're buying a big new home. . . ." These thoughts only made me feel worse. I thought seriously about suicide and started rewriting my will.

Linda thought I'd been going downhill since Christmas. She said I seemed like an open sore. I'd never bounced back from my usual holiday depression; I just kept sinking. She was right.

188 A MAN'S RECOVERY FROM TRAUMATIC CHILDHOOD ABUSE

Lola no longer had the strength to climb up on her couch. I threw the couch away.

I had zero emotional strength. I was a raw, weak mess, so easily upset that I could barely function. Often I'd be awake for hours in the middle of the night when all I wanted to do was sleep round the clock. There were frequent bad dreams. I had a long dream about trying to take a shit in a filthy bathroom with people watching. I couldn't do it. This dream seemed to describe therapy. What was it I couldn't shit out?

I was struggling not to cry the next time I saw Nan. I told her I was there only because I was desperate; if I felt I had a choice, I wouldn't come anymore.

Nan said she'd been worrying about my shutting down. She said it looked like clinical depression and suggested medication. I refused. If I had a "biochemical problem," it would have been manifest all along. The nasty parts of me thought that Nan would rather see me drugged than admit her therapy was failing. Maybe it was me that was failing. Four years of working hard at therapy and now I need psychiatric medication? How much longer before I have to be locked up?

My emotions were leaking out everywhere. I found no joy in anything. I'd lost all sexual urges. My genitals were a source of pain. Nan said she'd call around to try to find another group and consult with other therapists. She asked my permission to consult with the Watkinses, and I gave it.

I hear the voice as soon as I start to go inside: "I want to die." Over and over and over. With that voice in the background, Burned Q appears, wrapped in a blanket like a Native American. He seems to be suffocating. There is a horrible smell—fart, menstrual fluid, infected pus. Is it really here, or is it memory or fantasy? Q is afraid he'll have to pay a huge price for warmth and affection. He struggles free of his blanket. He has a knife and is looking for someone to hurt. The dog comes over to give him comfort, and he stabs it in the ear. I take the knife away and tell him it's good to have some power but not okay to hurt others. The dog returns with a bandaged ear. Q apologizes. Q wants to apologize, but when Nan tells him he needs to he almost refuses. This time it's Guard Q, not Burned Q. They seem to be alternating or perhaps merging. Little Honey comes up briefly and shyly. One arm is badly hurt, like when I first met her. It looks crablike, metallic, almost as if it has turned into a big socket wrench.

I ask Little Honey if this means there are more memories that need to be worked on. She nods. . . .

Chapter 11

The "Oh, No!" Experience

May-November 1991

None of Nan's local colleagues had any useful advice. There were no new groups for male survivors, no new ideas. The Watkinses thought (and Nan agreed) that I needed to confront Mom internally.

I got the feeling that I'd failed kindergarten, and I didn't want to try again.

I had a powerful need to talk to someone about what was happening to me and what I was feeling, but talking honestly left me feeling vulnerable. I had long since given up on talking with any of my male friends. I organized a meeting with Rick and Michael. Maybe we could continue to have some sort of group with or without a therapist.

We met in a restaurant and I spoke about how depressed I was. Because I felt shame, I downplayed my feelings so much it bordered on self-betrayal. I really got down on myself afterward: "You're a failure. You're a coward. You're basically garbage and you'll never make it."

I had never felt more isolated. Fortunately, over the next few days, five old friends phoned me just to talk.

Linda returned from a trip loving and affectionate. I could detect no hostile undercurrent, though I was looking for one. A revealing incident happened: Linda was putting disinfectant on a sore on my back, and she was letting it run down my side. I asked her not to do that. She said, "Boy, if I do it now it'll really be passive-aggressive." As she was saying this, she poured the disinfectant down my side. We both laughed about it, but it was not an intentional joke.

Nan again told me she thought Linda and I would need couples counseling if we were to stay together. She suggested a few names but refused to work with us herself. She said she could not be my advocate and a neutral couples counselor at the same time; she could not be totally honest with Linda while maintaining the confidentiality I required for individual therapy. I agreed with her; I feel that all therapists should regard this boundary as an ethical standard.

Guard Q, unrepentant and hostile, plays with his knife. Burned Q hides under his blanket. Little Honey's arm still looks like a tool. She is sad and lopsided. I ask her if there are more memories. She opens a metal plate on her arm. . . . I'm in a bathtub with Eddie. We play sexually with each other, giggling, while Dad watches. A second memory: I'm tied down on the floor, face up. Dad is here. Eddie stands over me and pees in my face. He has a smile of triumph; he's one of the adults now. . . .

I felt nothing after recovering this memory. Of course this was what they'd do to prevent Eddie and me from helping each other. I kept expecting the associated emotions to surface during the week, but they didn't. I didn't even remember any nightmares.

If I'd been given the chance to escape the victim's role as Eddie had, I most likely would have jumped at it. Joining the adults must have felt like a victory to Eddie, but it was a dreadful moral defeat. He'd become a perpetrator. This would have made his healing all but impossible.

Little Honey looks very sad. Scary image: a turtle having its head ripped off with pliers. Seems like a memory. I had a pet turtle for a while. Did Dad do it? Did I?

Little Honey goes off with Bear. When I say goodbye to her, there's a strong, clear image of the turtle being crushed by pliers. It's Dad. He shakes the mangled body in my face. I'm relieved that Little Honey completed the memory; I would have worried that I might have done it. . . .

Eddie stands over me, peeing, smiling. I try to tell him that I forgive him, that I hope he can rest in peace.

I was concerned that my sympathy and quick forgiveness of Eddie might betray some part of me that had been hurt by what he had done to me. It must have represented a painful severing of my last family contact. If any of the insiders were angry at me for forgiving Eddie, they expressed it by not showing themselves.

Little Honey comes up with Bear. Her arm now looks like half a scissors. . . . Dad and Hugh are threatening me with scissors. Holding me down and poking. They threaten to cut off my penis. They snip a hot dog to pieces in front of my face. Terror. Cramps in my groin as though my genitals are trying to retreat inside my body. Hugh and Dad are yelling. I give them each a blow job eagerly, relieved that they've stopped with the scissors. . . .

Burned Q is inside his blanket. It stands like a teepee. He doesn't want to come out. He plays quietly alone, keeping his focus within that small area. Guard Q leans against the teepee, in shock, staring blankly. He stays still; any movement causes pain. This seems like progress: He is neither armed to the teeth nor unconscious. Waves of strong emotion as I focus on him. . . .

Escrow closed on the new house. Taking possession represented the culmination of fifteen years of prudent investments and hard work. I scheduled the first phase of work on the place and found some wonderful tenants. I even experienced pleasure as I worked on re-modeling plans.

The return of memories seemed to be lifting my depression some-what. There was still something important I was missing, but at least there was movement. I had a few terrifying nightmares and lots of cramps in my groin, but I was feeling surprisingly okay. Linda and I even had a few people over for dinner.

That Sunday she told me she was thinking of leaving me. She felt I'd abandoned her. Once again, as soon as I had begun to improve, she withdrew and became difficult. Who had abandoned whom? She was the one who worked fifty-hour weeks and who went out to the cabin every evening to be with her cats. She would not acknowledge that she could be passive-aggressive, yet now she was refusing to plan a vacation and resenting me for there being no plans. I insisted that lack of sex was a major problem between us, but she wouldn't talk about it.

The one good thing that came out of the discussion was that she agreed to see a couples counselor with me.

COUPLES THERAPY

The counselor we chose was an MFCC named Charlotte. She seemed okay, maybe a little wimpy. I wondered whether she'd be strong enough to deal with powerful emotions or client confrontations. At our first session she asked us about our personal histories. I cried a little as I recounted mine. She asked me directly about suicidal thoughts. I told her yes, I'd thought about it, but I'd never told Linda before because of her brother's suicide.

Linda had a few surprises for me too. I knew she'd been seeing Nan before we met, but I didn't know she had entered therapy because she was vomiting after sex. I knew she'd been molested as a child by a next-door neighbor, but it was news to me that she'd been examined by a doctor who found vaginal bruising but ignored it.

Linda told Charlotte that she was orgasmic; that her sexuality was "fine." I couldn't let this pass; it seemed like total denial to me. "Orgasmic with difficulty," I said. We discussed the issue. Charlotte said we'd need to work on communication before we worked on sex. She pointed out to Linda what a serious emotional blow her threat to leave me had been. We agreed to meet again.

After the session I found myself thinking about my fear that Linda was sabotaging my healing. It was an ugly thought; I hoped I was wrong. Yet she seemed to be happiest when I was hurting and she was caretaking. I was clearly improving now, climbing out of the abyss of the last six months. I listed the probable causes of the depression: failure to take healing out into the world, failure to face fear and terror, premature stopping of memory work, not enough grieving, and (possibly) Linda's sabotage.

Guard Q is cold. He wants to be held. This is a first! I pick him up, wrap him in a blanket and hug him for a long time. His eyes still hold shock and terror, but it feels great that he wants me to hold him. Frankie is no longer flying around, afraid to land. He's settled down with Big Honey.

I wasn't able to see the real reason until months later.

My anus had been bleeding intermittently. I feared for my health, even though I knew the condition was very likely connected with the recent memories. The idea of having a doctor examine it was as bad as living with the fear, but I made a appointment to get it checked. My doctor shoved a small metal thing up my ass. He couldn't find the source of the bleeding, but did tell me there was scarring inside my rectum.

Early in therapy I'd desperately wanted confirmation of my memories. Here at last was undeniable physical evidence that my ass had been traumatized; now that I had it, it had zero emotional impact.

The doctor told me I needed to have a sigmoidoscopy. I was going to have to let a specialist, a stranger, shove something eighteen inches long up my ass. I steeled myself for the procedure, convinced of its necessity.

Guard Q wants to be held and fed with a bottle. His eyes are panicked and staring, but he wants my comfort. . . . Memories: head immobilized, neck arched, "something bad being done down there." Convulsive pain with interludes of fear, unable to look, waiting for the next assault. . . .

Little Honey is fearful and sad. We ask her if she wants to "leave" during the sigmoidoscopy. She doesn't like the idea of leaving Linda, partying, having different sex partners. She feels rejected; she does not want to go back to the place where she'd been hidden for so many years. Maybe she can help protect the Qs.

Frankie is perched on Big Honey's shoulder. He looks like a falcon, tough and dangerous. Is this defensive? Maybe, but he's much better off than when he had to fly around to feel safe.

I had the sigmoidoscopy. There was no sign of a tumor or colitis. As I drove home I was near tears. No one in that office knew what an ordeal it was for me. I felt angry at my doctor for insisting on the test. I was more convinced than ever that the bleeding was psychogenic. Having the evidence of scarring was reassuring, but it was not worth enduring the procedure.

Linda had started going to ACA (Adult Children of Alcoholics) meetings, and I went to one with her. I have great respect for the twelve-step tradition, but I didn't get much out of the meeting. Several people talked about how they were hurt when they were children by being told they were dumb. I felt out of place.

Guard Q's arms are extended, reaching out (for a hug? for Mommy?) His eyes are wide open but unseeing. I try to comfort him but he doesn't seem to know he's being held. Bear comes over and we hold Q between us. He recognizes and likes the touch of fur. Little Honey comes over too. Q rests, sleeps; then starts suddenly, fully awake and terrified. Nan: "It's hard to tolerate terror or even be near it." She asks me to associate, to feel the feelings emotionally rather than through my body, but I can't. . . .

I came out of trance early, feeling that it was pointless. I got angry at Nan and said, "You're just another woman who can't help me."

"Yes, that's largely true," she said. "I can't take the pain away." Then, after a pause: "I'm so sorry."

We both cried. I struggled against the tears, later wishing I'd let them flow. I left feeling dazed. As I looked back at Nan, she appeared physically very small.

Linda and I went back to Charlotte. We were both in tears. Linda apologized for threatening to leave. She said she loved me and wanted to work things out. I said that my trust was damaged and only time would restore it. Charlotte asked me if I was resentful. I said no, it was lack of trust; but shortly after the session, I realized I was wrong about that.

Q is moving around, crying, his arms reaching out. Memories of helplessness, of hurting so much that pain was all there was, of lying in bed at night waiting, terrified. I offer comfort. Q responds with willingness for sex. He doesn't know there can be warmth and contact without it. He feels bad that he hid away for so many years. He's worried that the others don't like him and will hurt him. I acknowledge how hard it is to handle his feelings and tell him how he saved the others from extreme pain, night terrors, and isolation. Little Honey is mad at Mom for letting it happen. A voice yells, "It's time to burn the bitch." Two images of Frankie: a small bird on Big Honey's shoulder and a hawk circling high in the sky. Big Honey is sad and serious, funereal. Coming out of trance I feel a sense of accomplishment.

Q continued to reach out to be held every time I went inside. There were more memories of rape, degradation, torture. Once he appeared as a drooling monster on his hands and knees. He remembered Dad and Hugh laughing; Dad calling me "a little monster." I assured him that they were the monsters, not he; I thanked him for trusting us enough to let us know what happened. I reassured him that I wouldn't run away, that we'd keep at it until there were no more memories or until he said he was done.

There were memories of being fucked by a different man, someone gentler. He untied me. He sucked me. Sometimes he'd hold me between sex acts. He was another friend of Dad's, a physicist. I couldn't remember his name, but I remembered his explanation of fusion reactors. I really tried to please him. I wanted to be with him. I wanted to go away with him. I wanted him to rescue me. I felt guilt and shame about wanting him and about the sexual arousal. He touched my vast need for kindness and adult interest, but of course he abandoned me to Dad and Hugh.

I felt like a rejected whore.

Frankie couldn't stand this neediness. It only led to more hurt and self-hate. He wanted to squash the need for love. I told Q that he'd done right. It was healthy to reach out, so sad that only abusers were there to respond.

Where the hell was Mom?

Linda and I saw Charlotte every two weeks. We kept at working through old resentments: her reaction to reading my manuscript, her backing out of buying the house, my depression. We talked about how expressing resentments honestly and directly builds trust. With a hateful undertone, Linda talked about how "pathetic" I was when I was depressed. Her resentment spilled over onto other things because she (codependently) couldn't express it directly. Only now was it emerging into daylight.

ME AND MY SHADOW

I'd reserved a place in a workshop at Esalen scheduled for mid-August. As the date approached I grew fearful about it, but I ended up going after all. Esalen is a stunningly beautiful place. It's situated on a few acres of flat land in the steep Big Sur mountains, right above the Pacific. Esalen can house a few hundred people, and it has gardens, meeting rooms, a lodge, natural hot springs, and a swimming pool.

Instead of isolating myself in my room until the workshop started, I wandered around the grounds. As I rounded a corner by the pool, I saw about a dozen naked children laughing and playing in the water. One young boy, his body glistening with water, was beside the pool on his hands and knees with his butt up in the air. This sunny scene terrified me. I turned and quickly walked away feeling shame, fear, and discomfort. Soon these feelings turned to sadness that I could still have such a reaction. I berated myself, thinking that I'd never be able to have kids of my own; I was still such a mess.

The workshop was led by Paul Rebelliot. The subject was "Dealing with Your Shadow." The shadow is a Jungian term that has become popular in the human-potential movement. It refers to a person's disowned, negative parts. Paul told Robert Bly's story about how we take parts of ourselves we don't like and put them in a bag that we carry over our shoulder. By the time we're forty, this bag is big and requires a lot of energy to drag it around.

There were about twenty-five of us, and I quickly felt like part of the group. I found a couple of people I liked and could be open with. The group danced a few times, and I danced with them. This was something I'd always self-consciously hated to do.

At the Friday evening session we each were given a blank mask we were to paint and decorate to look like our shadow. As I worked on my mask, it became clear that it was Dad. The skin was pale green. There were big black rings around the eyes. The teeth were jagged and dripping blood. There were a large erect penis and balls on the forehead.

When we met after dinner on Saturday, Paul told us we were going to get into small groups, put on the masks, and "dance our shadow" in front of the others. I walked out—partly from selfconsciousness, but mainly because I refused to put on Dad's face. I felt bad about leaving, but I didn't retreat in isolation to my room. Instead I went down to the hot tubs and soaked in the moonlight. Soon other group members came down. They kidded me a little about chickening out, but I quickly felt like I belonged again. I decided to go to the next and last meeting Sunday morning and tell them why I had left.

As soon as we gathered, Paul asked me what had happened. I told them I'd had a psychopathic sadist for a father. The mask was his face and I refused to put it on. I used the Nazi-and-Jew parallel: Would Paul ask a Jew to put on a Nazi's mask and identify with it? I added that there must be other victims in the room and putting on the masks might hurt them, too.

I was on the edge of tears. Paul said he heard me, but he didn't say he agreed. Several people thanked me for talking and said I was brave.

I didn't feel so brave by the time I got home. My biggest failing was that I had not used the word "sexual" in reference to the abuse. I hadn't convinced Paul that what he was doing was a harmful error. I had stayed and talked. I had danced. I had connected with several people, and I'd had fun.

The fundamental problem with the shadow concept is that it does not fit well with a trauma-survivor model of therapy. It tells you that when you find ugly, hateful things inside, you should own them, take responsibility, and recognize them as part of yourself. The implicit message to a survivor is, "you're responsible for your abuse." This is perilously close to blaming the victim. I'm not responsible for what Dad and the others did to me. Anything that makes me identify the least bit with perpetrators scares and disgusts me. Of course there are ugly parts of our personalities that we need to recognize and own, and this fact provides a reasonable cover for denial; but asking me to put on that mask undermines my recovery.

Nan and I talked about the workshop. She felt that choice is necessary in a therapeutic environment, and that Paul's error was in not providing it.

THE INNER PERVERT:
CRYSTALLIZING MY SEXUAL CONFLICT

Little Honey is happy to see me. Q is upset but relieved that I didn't put the mask on. Frankie looks like an eagle and like Groucho Marx at the same time. He had a big role in my not putting on the mask. Fear of looking like a coward and social pressure almost got me to betray myself. In Little Honey's eyes it would have been a battle lost. Robert is back; he is studying the incident to see how he can better protect us.

Grace is back too. I say something to her like, "You're still a big problem." She gets very sad and hurt. I feel horrible. "I didn't mean it like that, Grace. Please don't go away or hide. Grace, I love you. You have performed a difficult and valuable function, keeping the hope of sex and physical love alive through almost impossible times. We'll find a way to work things out. Please don't give up on us."

Q threw out memories furiously, one after another, every time I went inside. Electric shocks. Suffocation. Threats. Giving blow jobs to a roomful of men and saying "Thank you" to each of them. Dad, laughing: "He'll do *anything*." One group-sex memory felt like a raffle or an auction. I wondered how many times this had happened.

Q seemed afraid he'd be rejected if he revealed more. There was guilt over snuggling up to the one "kind' abuser. Had I looked like a willing and eager sex partner? Was I blocking out incidents when I was abusive with a younger child? Dad would have tried to get me to do it, like he did with Eddie. I told Q, "Please tell me, let me know. I won't reject you. No matter what it is, we can face it together. I love you."

Grace comes up, gives me a nonsexual hug and goes back. I'm relieved she doesn't hate me for my clumsiness. Her sexuality is like masturbating with steel wool.

Linda said she was afraid that I was slipping back into depression. I told her that I felt different now than I had through the winter and spring. I was sad, but I no longer felt as stuck or despairing. More memories of extreme abuse were surfacing. I was looking unflinchingly at the possibility that I might, in some way, have been an abuser.

At Charlotte's we talked about Linda's hidden anger over my depression. At last she had begun to express some of it. I had to restrain myself from saying "I told you so." She had retreated behind a wall instead of communicating. She attributed her retreat to my drinking and pot smoking. There was some truth there, but there was also defensive blame-casting: "I cut myself off because you're a drunk." This conveniently made me the problem. I'd told Linda that I wanted to go to Esalen alone Christmas week. She encouraged this, but her message was, "You're so depressed at Christmas that I'll be happier with you gone." I wanted her to make her own festive plans. I feared that otherwise she would resent me. It was so much better to talk about it.

Kneeling. Tied by hands and feet, giving Dad and Hugh blow jobs. A dildo shoved up my ass. I have an erection. Dad: "Look at that. He likes it. He's a queer". . . .

Guard Q is lying on his back, too tired and hurt to move. As a guard he functions both as protector and as jailer to the other parts. The other Q—or is it a new insider?—is naked except for a black leather collar with silver studs. His beautiful young body shines with oil. He has on dark eye makeup. He radiates intense sexual energy. I think he resents being reborn in an overweight, middle-aged body. I tell him: "Q, or whatever name you choose, you are beautiful and sexy, but I will never be sexual with you. I love you and hope you find satisfaction. I want to make you feel safe and welcome, but there will be no sex between us. Please let me know what you need, as long as it's not sex. I think you may have had a big part in saving us from becoming a perpetrator and from killing ourselves like Eddie."

The new memories were crystallizing my sexual conflict. The part of me that liked weird, passive, and masochistic sex proudly identified himself as "the Pervert." There was another part who'd kept him restrained all these years, whom he called "the Puritan." The Pervert hated the Puritan for all the years of missing his kind of sex. He taunted the Puritan with images and arousal. The Puritan saw the Pervert as a contaminated remnant of the abuse. He was tired, but he said he'd kill them both before he'd let any weird sex happen. It was this long-standing stalemate that caused the shame and self-hate I felt about my sexuality.

Acknowledging the existence of "the Pervert" made me feel hugely vulnerable, but I was grateful that this part of me was passive and masochistic. It made me more likely to be revictimized than to become an abuser myself. Anything would be better than becoming "one of them."

It was long after the incident by the pool at Esalen that I realized its real significance. I had felt absolutely no desire or arousal. *None.* The intense emotion was only an impulse to shout a warning, to protect the children. I repeatedly reexamined my response, looking for any hint of weirdness. I was *not* "one of them." I was nothing like Dad or Hugh; I was not sexually aroused by children. Some adolescents seemed sexy to me, but around children I felt only fear. Though I continued to agonize over whether something ugly I had done in my past might still be buried in amnesia, my fear that some present part of me might be a perpetrator had been put to rest.

Q'S SEXUALITY—AND LINDA'S

After months of little or no sexual energy, there now was lots of it. In trance, the new Sexy Q appeared with many images: tied up, being fucked, sucking dick, being whipped, being choked unconscious while being fucked. In a bitchy tone he said, "At least I'm wanted, desired, the center of attention. You're isolated and alone." There was an image of Q's throbbing erection on the verge of orgasm but with no release, no satisfaction for years, for decades. This is what his life felt like. There were images of him taking off his collar and lying down deflated, tired and sad. Nan commented that none of this was his choice.

I read *Incest and Sexuality* by Wendy Maltz and Beverly Holman. The book offered a lot of information on sexual healing for survivors. I also found it depressing. It made sex seem like work. For me, I was realizing, sexual healing would mean reconciling the Puritan and the Pervert within me. Maltz's definition of abuse was very broad, but it didn't seem to include my youthful experiences with cousins.

Robert Johnson, a Jungian analyst and writer, developed an idea he called the Jericho technique: If faced with an impenetrable wall in the psyche, walk around the issue seven times, and the wall will fall down. He theorized that sustained attention is a powerful psychic force. I started regularly stating, "I want to know if there are any big memories of my being abusive that are still in amnesia. I want those memories."

Sexy Q says he's not the same as the Hurt Q. He's a little contemptuous of Hurt Q's weakness. . . . Choking memories: being held with the dog's choke collar and leash while being fucked; a scarf twisted and tied like a tourniquet around my neck. It has a stick in it so they can tighten or loosen it. They use it as a training device. A numb, zombie-like feeling. Hugh used the scarf to train me to say "please" and "thank you": "Please, may I suck you?" and "Thank you for fucking me," and "Please, let me kiss your feet," and "Please, fuck me." It got to where they'd just wave the scarf and I'd do anything. Intense shame. A flash of wanting to die rather than do these things. . . . Bear stands aside to let all this out while tears run down his face.

Peg, my massage therapist, worked on my chest and throat that week. She called the suffocation abuse "near-death experiences." This seemed true and gave me a new perspective. She was worried I might have breathing difficulties and panic attacks.

Michael and I went to an all-male Survivors of Incest Anonymous meeting. My anxiety left me once the meeting started. As before, it felt good to say "Hi, I'm Bob, a survivor of incest" to a roomful of people. There were about a dozen men there, and they seemed to know each other. We took turns reading the twelve steps and statements of the group's purpose. There was a clear announcement that offenders weren't welcome and should leave. Then each person spent about five minutes talking about his recovery. They used a lot of slogans: "Giving away your power," "Negative bonding to the perpetrator," and "You're at just the right place in your recovery." One slogan I particularly liked was, "The way out is the way through." Another slogan, referring to addictions, was, "Once is too many, and a million times are not enough."

Linda and I finally began to talk with Charlotte about sex. I said that sex had come to feel like a performance for me. I always initiated and put the energy into it, and it didn't seem to please Linda anyway. It had stopped being fun; I'd quit putting out the effort. Linda said that sex had become anxiety-producing and scary for her. Charlotte talked about making sex "safe" for Linda.

Linda had had surgery for her endometriosis. She had to take hormone injections. She still bled intermittently, and the hormones were jerking her around. Now she told Charlotte that she wanted to avoid sex for a while. We hadn't been having much sex at all. Her statement put it on a conscious level and put her in control. I kept quiet and didn't say the word "psychogenic." When she mentioned it herself as a possibility—"I wonder if I'm making myself ill to avoid the sex stuff?"— Charlotte told her that thinking that way didn't help. I was frustrated and angry, but I kept it to myself. I'd so often expressed my views about the psychogenic nature of most illness that she probably knew what I was thinking anyway.

That Sunday morning Linda and I lay down and cuddled and talked. It had been a long time since I last told her what was going on in trance. I told her about everything except Q's new hyperaroused, sexy appearance. I cried. It was a whole new release of shame, but it was good to talk and hug.

Another torrent from Q: arousal, sadness, sex images. Several men in the room. Being fucked in the ass and mouth. Sucking them clean after sex. Licking their assholes. A needle in the genitals. Licking stuff (come?) off the floor. Being choked unconscious while being fucked. Extreme, intense sensation: beyond pain and beyond struggle to a

*place where "they can't get me any more." When I stopped trying to
breathe I went to a calm state—calm and intense at the same time. I
didn't want to come back, and I resented being revived. The sensations are so real I can feel them in my body. Nameless, strange emotions. . . . Now a clear memory of a shot with a hypodermic needle. I
feel warm and fuzzy. Sex no longer hurts; it feels good to be fucked
while drugged. This is Sexy Q's kind of sex. Normal, vanilla sex seems
contemptibly bland to him. The center of his desire is the other-
worldly, calm intensity of suffocation sex. . . .*

*Q is angry at the other insiders. They left him alone to take the
worst of the abuse and have kept him locked up and hidden away ever
since. Defiantly he yells, "I liked it! I liked it! I liked being fucked! My
asshole liked it!" Hate. Hurt. Little Honey is shocked into regression.
Robert turns away sadly. It hurts him to be called a jailer. He's done
the best he could. The others pretend not to hear. Nan asks if Big
Honey can help. She is very tired, but she offers Q some comfort.*

At the next session with Charlotte I knew I had to talk about what I
saw as the psychogenic aspects of Linda's physical problems. I did
not feel, nor did I want to say, that Linda was solely (or more than
half) responsible for our lousy sex life, but it did seem to me that she
had deep-seated, unresolved, unconscious sexual difficulty. I needed
to voice my resentment that our sex life (when we had one) seemed
entirely focused on whether or not she'd have an orgasm. Now that
we were trying to reestablish a sex life, her sexual organs were constantly ill.

My typical strategy in this kind of situation was to organize my argument rationally and hammer home my points like a prosecuting attorney. This didn't work in intimate relations, no matter how right I
was. Charlotte and Linda had been working on me to rephrase my
ideas as questions, not assertions. This seemingly small shift made a
big difference. I asked Linda if there might be some psychological
meaning to her physical problems. I asked her if there were any parts
of her that would rather not have sex. She admitted that there was a
part of her that didn't feel sexual at all. I encouraged her to listen to
that part and see what it wanted. Without arguing, without blaming, I
made my major point: Linda's body was telling us something.

So was mine. At the doctor that week I found I weighed 235
pounds. Ever since my back injury ended athletics for me, I'd been

gaining five to eight pounds per year. I knew I needed to turn this around, but I had no energy or self-discipline available.

Little Honey is with Bear. She won't hug me. Images of erect penises come at her. She hates it when the warm cuddles she loves turn sexual. When Linda and I make love, she goes off with Bear. She doesn't want Q turned loose. Finally she gives me a short hug and returns to Bear.

Q is excited about a female hitchhiker we saw: young and sexy, wearing boots and black leather. Q feels she's like him. He has fantasies about kinky sex with her. Nan: "Do you realize you were hurt by Dad and the others?" Q doesn't want to think about it. He wants excitement and satisfaction but is near despair about getting it. Seeing that hitchhiker gives him hope.

I ask Q if he liked the homosexual encounters I had as an adult. Does he like being penetrated? He doesn't know. When the sex started, I went numb. Later, when I tried to remember what it felt like, I became amnestic.

Robert is crying, his arms crossed over his chest. He's worked with effort and discipline to make an adjustment. The results of his labor are dissatisfaction and deep splits. He apologizes for Q's being locked away all those years. Q is no longer angry at Robert, but he is extremely frustrated.

Grace identifies with the female hitchhiker. She looked like that once. She is sinking into despair because she feels old, fat, and ugly. Frankie flies around, afraid to land. He does settle on my shoulder briefly, and I thank him for trusting me.

Big Honey is still in the killing field. The dogs-howling-by-moonlight sound comes up. Big Honey is ashen, depleted. I give her a quilt. She needs protection so she can rest. Bear, Little Honey, Red, and Frankie all help her. I feel bad. I haven't realized how much she needs help. She's always seemed so strong.

Something was stirring. I hadn't seen Red in almost a year and a half, since shortly after Q had appeared. At home in the evenings I felt sad in that eerie, timeless way. I was bothered by allergies and nightmares, such as often prefigured a new rush of memories. Some of the dreams were about aliens attacking. Some were explicit scenes of sexual abuse.

Several times that week I checked in with Big Honey and comforted her. A detached penis and balls seemed to be pursuing her. She said they were *her* penis and balls. She said she'd had to cut them off; that she'd done a good job of it. I didn't understand. Did severing the genitals help prevent me from becoming an active, sadistic perpetrator like Dad? Did it allow Big Honey to be strong without being abusive or scary?

It was the week before Thanksgiving. Mom was to be one of our dinner guests.

At Nan's:

Little Honey and Bear appear first. We go to see Big Honey. "She" appears male! She looks like a thin man in his twenties. There is stubble on her face. She looks haggard and ill, but she's sitting up and wants to proceed. The scene is formal, dignified. Little Honey approaches the new man and greets him with a kiss on each cheek. It is a greeting fit for a diplomat, a castaway rescued from a desert island, an exile returned. The new man's eyes brim with tears. He winces as if the light is too bright. Bear greets him with similar gravity. His emotions are almost overwhelmed by the contact with warm fur. Q and Grace give him similar greetings. Robert, too. Robert has some fear that he'll be resented, like an officer who has sent another on a near-suicidal mission. There is no resentment. Frankie is scared that the new man might hate him, but they receive each other warmly.

Everyone sits down to a meal together. Where is Big Honey? She doesn't seem to be dead. We invite her over from the killing field. She greets the new man with a sensuous kiss on the lips. She lies back on the table and pushes her crotch in the air. She arches up in front of him. He is mesmerized, feeling an almost irresistible urge to lick her pussy. His head starts moving forward and down. I intervene, letting a wall come down between them. The others are all mad at Big Honey. It is so inappropriate. The mood of reunion and graduation is spoiled. The new man goes to bed, and the others gather around to guard him.

I was irritated. I had the same thoughts I always did whenever strong, female sexual energy emerged in trance. Was there a female abuser? Was it Mom? Was it my own unintegrated, female sexual energy? I didn't know.

What had happened? I worked hard the next week trying to understand the trance. It was like trying to understand a dream. The reunion with the new man had seemed so positive, like the completion of something important, but it was interrupted in a deflating, trickster-like way. Big Honey's sexuality had been so sultry, so compelling. Was it a message about my incomplete sexuality, my passive longings? Did it mean I was vulnerable to a certain kind of sexual attraction and might do something stupid?

Who was the new man? I wrote him a letter telling him I wanted to know whatever he had to tell me, no matter how painful or upsetting it might be. I didn't want him to have to keep secrets or carry pain or shame alone. I acknowledged my fear of the possibilities that I was an offender or that Mom was involved in the abuse.

Early Thanksgiving day I saw Mom sitting on her deck, playing with a neighbor's cat. She looked so lonely, feeble, and sad that I felt sympathy for her. When she came over for dinner, she was her usual self, walking with an exaggerated limp and talking about her pills. Fortunately, one of the other guests was very loquacious, and he carried the conversation. I ate and drank too much, but I felt none of the bleakness I usually experienced at holidays.

I was back at Nan's the following Tuesday.

The new man appears. He points to a pregnant woman. . . . Image-memory of my face down in a woman's crotch, eating her. She rolls over and I lick her asshole.

I ask the new man, "Was it Mom?" He nods. "How many times?" No clear answer. No emotion. Distinct memory of being grabbed by the back of the neck and having my face forcefully shoved down into her crotch. Another memory of being put on top of her and humping away. Another memory: lying next to her, rubbing against her, and feeling sexual. . . .

It seemed that Dad was there. Just like him to arrange this to shut her up and to shut me up. Was she drugged? Was I making excuses for her?

Q: Yes, it was Mom. He doesn't think it's a big deal; it was so much less vicious and sadistic than the other stuff. We ask Q if he resents Mom's not protecting him. "Would you expect a mouse to protect you from a mad dog?" I ask Grace. She is lying on her back raising her crotch. She nods yes: It was Mom. I ask Little Honey. She's thinking of the old spiritual, "Sometimes I feel like a motherless child." I have no mother, she tells me; I have the Bear. Bear nods yes: It was Mom. Robert nods yes, his eyes filled with tears. Frankie: Yes.

There was no big wave of emotion. I was numb. I didn't want to believe this stuff; it made my life harder. Anything but this. I'd had these memory fragments before but dismissed them. Somehow this time it wasn't dismissible. It felt conclusive.

I thanked the insiders for letting me know. It hurt, and I didn't like it, but it wasn't their fault at all.

That night I drank, smoked pot, and went to bed at seven so I wouldn't have to see Linda. I kept hoping that maybe Mom had been unconscious, that Dad had tricked me, making me think she was taking part. Even as I hoped, I knew this was a lame excuse. I didn't want to look at this, but I couldn't bury it again.

What a pathetic, blind jerk I'd been. A forty-three-year-old man, living next door to his mother who had participated in abusing him as a child.

I wished that Mom would die in the night.

Chapter 12

The Cost of Denial

December 1991-May 1992

As John Watkins puts it, insight is rarely an "Aha!" experience; it is much more often an "Oh, no!" experience.

Mom was no victim. She was an active perpetrator. The message was clear and unmistakable.

I was ashamed that I'd ever needed a mother. I wondered what she'd thought when I confronted her about Dad's abuse. I wanted to confront her all over again, but I told myself that it would be foolish to take any such action until things became clearer.

Little Honey feels isolated. Mom's betrayal has cut the last possible interpersonal bridge. Bear has patches of fur missing. . . . Dad grabs me by the neck and forces my face into Mom's crotch: "You've been bad. Lick this." She can't be completely unconscious. Her knees are up. She moves when I lick her. Dad laughs: gloating, triumphant. He tells me to roll over onto my hands and knees. After I lick her he fucks me in front of her, in the same bed. He's more gentle than usual. He makes it look nice.

Big Honey still has her crotch up in the air. Robert holds himself together with his arms across his chest. Q seems to feel that being sexual is the only possible path for relationships. Frankie is speaking so fast he is incoherent. Grace feels chastened. Nan asks about the new man. I don't know who she's talking about until she reminds me; I've forgotten him completely.

I wondered how many times it happened. It seemed like there were at least two or three separate incidents. I wondered if it ever happened when Dad wasn't there. I thanked the insiders for the clearness of the information. I told them I wanted all their secrets, pain, and shame, even if they confirmed my worst fears.

The struggles and deep depression of the preceding months now seemed perfectly clear. I'd looked at everything except what was right in front of my face. No wonder I'd felt stuck. No wonder I'd felt such irrational rage at Nan and Linda. No wonder the insiders had built fortifications and refused to appear. No wonder my confronting Mom had produced no movement—and what dark irony there had been in my asking her how the abuse had stopped, in my desperate attempt to give her some positive role! Instead of confronting her about Dad, I ought to have confronted what she had done.

Denial is an amazing thing. Months later, going back over my journal and reviewing my accounts of therapy, I was shocked to find that I'd had repeated, explicit memories of Mom's being an abuser. The insiders had confirmed them, but I'd resisted believing or even hearing them. I'd reburied them. Such re-repression is common among survivors, a testament to how hard it can be to assimilate hugely painful material into consciousness. It was why I had always made a point of writing up each session.

Accepting that Mom had been an abuser was painfully ego dystonic for me. I was filled with self-hate at the thought that I'd been taking care of her, that I'd taken money from her. The psychological payoff had been in believing her to be another of Dad's victims. That way I could still have a mother—weak, sometimes insane, but a mother nonetheless. The mountain of denial had been so huge that now that I'd accepted the truth, there was no back-and-forth struggle. Mom was an abuser. I hated the fact. It complicated my life; it made me feel like a fool; it humiliated me, but denial did not return.

Linda asked me what I wanted for Christmas. What I really wanted was a dead mother. I thought that if I could get away with it, I'd kill her.

Little Honey is dependent, needy. Bear is hurt, staggering. Q is horny. He feels that sex with women is now as contaminated and potentially reiterative as sex with men, so we might as well be gay. He sees sex and drugs as good ways to avoid pain. Grace feels ashamed, disgusted by her female sexuality. Robert is split: one part wants to reconcile with Mom, one part wants her dead. Frankie is tired from flying around. He falls to the ground, twitching and unconscious. The

new man picks him up and takes him over to Little Honey and Bear.
New Man is afraid he'll be hated for the message he brought. That
solemn, formal greeting may have been an attempt to establish bonds
before the news was released. Nan says that he also brought the op-
portunity to heal completely.

Linda and I talked with Charlotte about how hard it was for us to
stay close. We'd spiral away from each other into loneliness and isolation. One of us would withdraw a little, the other would take it as rejection, and a cycle of distancing would begin.

We continued to talk about sex. I was flabbergasted when Linda
said she thought she initiated sex sometimes. We talked about the upcoming Christmas holiday. Linda was guilt-tripping me about my
plans to go to Esalen. It pissed me off, but I refused to feel guilty about
taking care of myself, especially after her initial response to my plans.

As it turned out, Linda was wonderful the day I left. She initiated
sex in a loving, sensual, and nondemanding way. I loved her.

BEING OK SEXUALLY:
THERAPY FOR CHRISTMAS HATERS

The workshop was led by a man I'll call Henry. He'd been leading
gestalt encounter groups at Esalen for twenty years, but I'd never
been part of one before. A lot of the participants were there because
they hated the holidays, so I had company. There were eighteen of us,
twelve men and six women, average age forty to fifty. We met three
times a day for five days.

The first day someone asked jokingly, "What do I have to do to get
your attention, pull my pants down?" Another guy, a big, muscular
man in his forties, got up and pulled *his* pants down, exposing himself
to the group. There is a lot of nudity at Esalen in the baths and at the
swimming pool, but I'd never seen anything like this. I was shocked
and angry. One woman left immediately. One man, Glenn, said he'd
been abused as a child and now he felt reabused and hurt like a helpless eight-year old. The flasher came back with some bullshit about
"working on his issues of shame." I loudly called him a creep, said he
should be thrown out of the group, and asked him if he also molested
children.

There was a lot of talk. Most people seemed to want to let him stay, with restrictions. Henry told him to leave for the day; he would decide about his attending the rest of the workshop the next morning. I was angry and forceful in the group, but when we broke for lunch I walked away in tears. Underneath the anger I felt violated and powerless.

The woman who had fled, Susan, did return. She turned out to be a major focus of attention. She was in her early thirties and had just completed a PhD in psychology. Even though she was not outrageously beautiful, she radiated sexual attraction. Just about every man in the room was affected. Luckily she started calling me "big brother," so I could be close to her without getting caught in the powerful sexual undercurrents.

Next morning the creep was kicked out of the group. I was pleased and relieved. However, several people got on me about how aggressive and abusive I'd been in attacking him. Jock, a handsome sixtyish retired businessman, identified himself as a sexual-abuse survivor. He said he'd been sold into prostitution when he was five. He objected to my language, and I really listened to him. I tried to tell him that my anger was directed at abusers and was protective in intent.

That night I soaked in the hot tubs with Glenn and some others. Glenn was a lot like me. We were both survivors. He'd worked in construction and had been athletic until he hurt his back. Now he was an alcoholism counselor, working toward being a therapist. I was surprised and pleased that there were three male survivors in such a small group.

The next day another guy got on my case about calling the exposer a creep. I told him off in no uncertain terms. Henry asked what buttons were being pushed to make me so hostile. I'd told the group previously that I'd had an abusive childhood, but now I laid out some of the details. Henry said something about my not wanting to be helpless like I was as a child, and I broke down crying. My body became rigid; I flushed and sweated. We kept talking about the abuse for quite a while. When it was time to end, Henry asked if others could touch me, and I said, "No, no, no." The feedback from the group felt good. They were crying, angry, and supportive.

That year I actually enjoyed Christmas! I felt very close to several people in the group. There was a "movement" class in the afternoon, and I unselfconsciously enjoyed dancing. Dinner was festive and happy. Some people brought wine. We stayed up late, laughing and talking in the hot tubs.

I woke the next day feeling sad, and I got sadder as the day wore on. In group I asked to work again. I didn't know what was bothering me. Henry put a pillow down in front of me and asked me to imagine Dad on it, to talk to him. That wasn't it. It was Mom I needed to talk to. I saw her sitting at her desk and me, as a child, telling her, "Daddy's hurting me." She turned toward her typewriter. I staggered away, lost.

It was strange going into this regressed emotional state in a room full of people. I talked about how I was caretaking Mom, and how I wanted her to die. At the end Henry asked, "Can you let some of the women touch you?" This time I agreed. Two women, Susan (the sexpot) and Anne, held me as I cried. Even Susan's comforting touch felt sexual. I was relieved when she stopped. Anne's touch felt good; I soaked it up. No one criticized me for wanting Mom dead. Charlotte, a widow in her sixties, said that a friend of hers was in a similar position. Her friend had prayed, "Okay, God, I'll take care of her, but you have to love her because I can't." I thought this might be a healing attitude for me. Her friend had also said, "I can't wait to slam the coffin lid closed." Another man said he was struck by how strong and challenging I seemed in the group and how weak I seemed in front of Mom.

Long after the workshop was over, I realized that I hadn't said anything about Mom being a perpetrator. I couldn't deny it any longer; but I could still ignore it, and ignore it I did. For several months, until Linda and I moved away from Mom into our new home, my unconscious kept this issue almost completely submerged.

When I got home from Esalen, I felt emotionally wide open. It was great to be with Linda. We made love a lot. We talked a lot. She joked that I should go away more often because I came back so loving. This romantic feeling with Linda was wonderful. It felt like a beautiful, delicate young flower that I wanted to protect and nurture.

Within a week or two the glow faded, and I started facing my life again. It was clear to me that I was vulnerable to sexual manipulation. That woman, Susan, could have wrapped me around her finger and made a fool of me if she'd wanted to. I realized that when I entered a room full of people, I often evaluated the individuals as potential sex partners. This kind of attraction seemed almost like a drug. The message I needed to hear was, "You're desirable sexually, you're not con-taminated." I'd never get enough of this message if I continually turned to new partners for it. Unfortunately, Linda went to see her parents for a few days and returned with the flu. This interrupted the warm, loving, sexy connection we'd been having. I worried that we'd lose it.

LINDA AND I DEEP IN EACH OTHER'S STUFF

Most of the insiders are scared and upset. Q is very attracted to one of the women we met at Esalen. It's new for him to be heterosex-ual. He also enjoyed the lovemaking with Linda. Again I forget New Man until Nan asks for him. He still fears that the others hate him for the message he'd brought. He says there's more about Mom that he'll reveal in due time.

Nan talked about her views of hostile alters or ego states like the Dad introject that had metamorphosed into Frankie. She thought they concealed vulnerability. The greater their hostility and strength, the greater the vulnerability concealed underneath. This fit my experi-ence. She said that some of the problems I'd had after seeing the Watkinses might have resulted from our not providing enough safety and comfort for Frankie. Fear is what had driven his behavior as the Dad introject—fear of more abuse and that the world was filled with people like Dad and Hugh. Frankie was no longer taking the protec-tive measure of toughening me against further abuse, but his fear was still present.

Little Honey is angry in general and angry at Dad, in particular. Her anger melts into sadness and tears. This is the first time she's ever expressed anger, and I congratulate her. Nan is right about Frankie: He's hurting. He needs more support. He's exhausted and hungry and sick with a cold because of his constant, fearful flying about. He does land on Bear's shoulders, and we make a safe place for him in Bear's warm fur. Bear looks okay. Little Honey still does not like or trust Frankie. She remembers his role as the negative Dad. She resents sharing Bear's attention, but she tries to be nice to Frankie anyway. Q is sad, but okay. Grace is not communicative.

We go to New Man. He greets each insider in turn. We ask for more memories and open the internal doors. . . . A clear, strong memory: I'm on my back, and a woman is squatting over my face, rubbing her cunt into my mouth. My body twitches. I feel aroused. Vivid image of her crotch as it descends toward my face. She turns around and makes me lick her asshole. She sucks and licks my genitals. Dad is here. He fucks me when she is done. This happened on the floor of my parents' bedroom, at the foot of their bed. The woman was clearly an active perpetrator, but was she Mom? New Man nods, yes, but I couldn't see her face in the memory, and her body seemed too small. Could Dad have gotten another woman to abuse me and tried to confuse me so that I'd never trust Mom? Am I making excuses? In denial? The memory seemed vividly, undeniably real, but was it Mom? . . .

At Charlotte's, Linda unexpectedly started talking about my drinking and pot smoking. She admitted it was not currently a problem and hadn't been for a while, but she went at it anyway. She'd been carefully watching and judging me all along, even checking the bottles to see how much I drank. She compared me to her abusive, alcoholic father. That really hurt. She also admitted disclosing to her ACA group that I was a survivor of sexual abuse, even though she had agreed not to tell anyone without my prior approval. That felt like betrayal. She apologized, but that didn't make it all right. Just when I'd been wanting to focus on the sweet intimacy we'd achieved, she left me feeling trashed and shit on. I wanted to go out and drink twice as much.

That weekend I told her that my trust in her had gone to zero. I told her my fear that as I healed and wanted a mate more than a nurse, she'd sabotage me so that she could stay in the role of caretaker. I asked her if she ever wondered why she'd chosen me as a partner. I told her that distrust was a basic issue for me; I'd been dealing with Mom's betrayal, and any betrayal by a woman was emotionally loaded.

I said it all calmly and without rancor, but Linda was hurt. I got her a bouquet of flowers to mark her first day back at teaching after the long Christmas break.

"You're hip deep in her stuff, her unfinished business with her father," Nan told me. She said that I needed to clarify my own feelings about alcohol and pot so that I could clearly refuse Linda's projections.

I did think hard about my use of alcohol and pot. At times in my life I had clearly abused drugs. In high school and college I'd thought it was cool to see how high I could get. More recently I got high to self-medicate, to make pain go away. This wasn't wonderful, but it seemed better than taking Prozac. I usually smoked pot only once a week, when I played music with the guys. Sometimes if I had it around the house I'd smoke too much, but this hadn't been the case recently. I did like wine or brandy before dinner, but I rarely had more than two drinks. My major concern was that it was fattening. I usually drank more around Christmas, but at Esalen I'd only had a little wine at Christmas dinner, and I hadn't missed alcohol. I'd brought some pot with me but hadn't used it. All in all, my drug usage was okay with me.

Next time at Nan's we started talking about Linda, but I felt we'd already spent too much therapy time on her stuff.

Little Honey is upset and wants to suck her thumb. This sets off bad feelings: When Dad found me sucking my thumb, he'd pull it out of my mouth and stick his penis in. Bear protects Little Honey so she can suck her thumb in safety. . . . Very early memory of Dad shoving his thumb up my ass. It hurts, and I start to cry. Dad chokes and bangs me until I shut up. It takes a lot of violence to silence a baby. He leaves. When he returns and picks me up, I'm like a rabbit frozen with fear. I'm relieved to be put down. I can no longer take comfort or warmth from being held. Same reaction when Mom holds me. A huge, sad chasm.

More memories of bigger and bigger things being shoved up my ass. Finally, when I'm about a head taller than Dad's knees, he fucks me. . . . I'm crying for Little Honey. I try to get her as comfortable as possible, with Bear close by. Q is hiding, hurt, sad and confused. Frankie is convalescing. New Man is worried that he made a mistake releasing the information about Mom.

I went back to Esalen in February for a weekend workshop with Mariah Gladis. Several people had told me she was a wonderful leader, and I hoped I could recapture the openhearted feeling I'd had at Christmas. Mariah more than lived up to her reputation. She called herself a Gestalt therapist, but what she did seemed beyond labels. Without ever being aggressive or confrontational, she quickly got to powerful, core emotional issues with each person. She had ALS (amyolateralschlerosis), also known as Lou Gehrig's disease, a progressive and fatal condition. Perhaps her mortality gave her some of her power. I didn't work one-on-one with her, but I made plans to do so in August, when she was to return to Esalen.

Right after I got home, Linda and I had a session with Charlotte. Linda said she was looking for a therapist for herself. This made me feel optimistic. She also mentioned that she'd had bad gynecological problems for the last month. "Yes, ever since we started having good sex," I immediately thought, but I didn't say it. I did talk about my fear that if we became sexual again, she'd sabotage it. I said that each time that happened it was harder for me to come out of my shell and reach out to her again. Linda asked Charlotte whether she thought her bringing up the stuff about alcoholism had been an act of sabotage. Charlotte's reply was all right: "This *is* a place to express resentments, but it *really* hurt Bob, and I can see how he feels, especially since he warned you. I can't know your unconscious, but you do seem to have unfinished business with your dad."

PAIN, SCREAMS, AND OTHER UNFINISHED BUSINESS

Little Honey has split into two parts, Little Honey the Younger and Little Honey the Elder. Little Honey the Younger is curled up drinking from a baby bottle. Little Honey the Elder is proud that she prevented Dad from getting to Little Honey the Younger. I feel like celebrating and crying at the same time. Little Honey the Elder has more memories of Dad's abuse: being fucked, curling up afterward and trying to forget, my butt hurting; Dad slapping my face, telling me to "assume the position," and then fucking me. Little Honey the Elder has lots of fears about body contact, but she gives me a hug. Bear comes over to comfort them both.

Frankie is deeply fearful that the others hate him for having played the role of the Dad introject. He and I are crying, barely able to talk. He asks Little Honey. There is no violent anger toward him, but there's no warmth or love either. Q is proud of his big erection. He wanted me to try to seduce one of the women at Esalen. He's afraid there won't be any good sex with Linda for a long time. Nan: "This is a desire for 'normal' heterosexual sex." Q, jokingly: "Okay, I'll come up with a juicy homosexual S and M fantasy."

Grace is on her back, "cunt first," masturbating. She's been stuck there a long time. Robert feels good, but he's worried about helping Q find satisfaction without losing Linda. New Man is sympathetic to Frankie and his fears.

So I was back to memories of Dad's abuse, after the insiders had promised more information about Mom's. My "forgetting" to tell the members Henry's workshop that Mom was a perpetrator now felt like denial. Whoever New Man was, he seemed to be afraid that some part of me would "shoot the messenger." Or did my unconscious still have unfinished business with *my* dad, work that had to be completed before we could tackle what Mom had done? This was what Little Honey seemed to be telling me. I'd thought she was the part of me that split off before the abuse began, but now I realized things were more complex. Little Honey the Younger was kept safe, but Little Honey the Elder experienced the anal stretching, the first rapes, and the beginnings of the sadism and group sex.

Little Honey the Younger comes running up for hugs with tears in her eyes. Memory of Dad changing her diaper and pushing the dirty diaper in her face. He also repeatedly tormented her with the safety pins. She, too, had trauma. I'm sorry we didn't recognize that earlier. I apologize and comfort her and make sure she has a fresh, clean diaper fastened with Velcro, not pins.

Now a memory from Little Honey the Elder: being fucked. No sensation from her butt. She's aware of her face rubbing the floor and the rhythmic movement of her body. We ask: Is this numbness, or is another part taking the pain? Image of a boy skinned alive—raw, red, oozing, screaming. As he appears, I start crying and can't stop. No way to touch him without causing more pain. He is very lonely. He knows no one wants to know him; his pain is too intense, too ugly. Only infrequently did the pain get past him and hurt the others.

I try to imagine some way to soothe him. He can't rest; he's too raw to sit or lie down. He needs to cleanse himself, but water would hurt. I thank him for saving us all from the pain. Still crying, I tell him I do want to be with him and get to know him. Maybe he can rest in a bathtub full of tears. Maybe some ointment would help. I don't have a

*name for him, but I call him Little Brother Painholder. I don't want to
end the trance and leave him alone. I promise him I'll check in with
him. The other insiders are almost in shock with the intensity of his
loneliness, pain, and sadness. I realize that Painholder also holds
screams. . . .*

I was amazed to discover this whole new level. This was why it had
been so hard for me to remember the actual, physical pain of rape and
torture. Throughout the week I checked in frequently with Painholder. It seemed as though he was part of, or had been concealed behind, Red. He liked to drink or get high or go to sleep. I wondered if
he was the center of my desire to get high or if I wanted to get high because I couldn't tolerate his pain.

The other Red, whom I now called Red the Elder, was proud of his
ability to endure pain. He was contemptuous of my weakness. He was
proud and angry at being the one left holding the bag. He was very
protective of Red Painholder, concerned, tearful—almost motherly.
He was scared that Painholder would die. I tried to encourage him.
This was a side of him I'd never seen before.

It was my understanding that when an ego state splits in two, the
original, unified state will sometimes reappear. Trance logic can
work this way. The original Red, my ancient man-of-anger, was the
unified being, whom I now called Big Red. Red Painholder and Red
the Elder were parts of him, and yet he coexisted with them.

The processes of memory retrieval and emotional healing often re-
semble a spiral. With each turn, the same issue is touched upon at
greater depth. Newly recovered memories bring new, dissociated aspects—more knowledge, sensation, or emotion—until the memory is
psychologically complete and becomes a no-longer-dissociated part
of narrative history. Three different insiders, Young One, Q, and Red,
had at some point appeared as the boy who had endured the brunt of
the abuse, but their aspects and memories were not the same. Each
one brought me face to face with increasingly difficult layers as the
"easier" ones healed.

On a different scale, the spiral pattern also applies to the splits
within each insider. In some ways, Red and (especially) Q are more
like families than individuals. They replicate the splitting I experienced on a finer level. Likewise Little Honey: I'd had memories of
being stuck with diaper pins before, but her new memory was not

simply a repetition. This time Little Honey the Younger was there, and she brought all her emotions too.

As one therapist said half-jokingly to me about this spiral, "Your reward for solving a difficult internal problem is to be presented with the next bigger, more challenging problem."

At Charlotte's that week I couldn't do much but cry and choke back tears. Linda and I did agree to read some sex books together. At one point Charlotte mentioned the word "pain," and that started me crying again.

Next time at Nan's I was apprehensive about going into trance.

Little Honey the Younger, Little Honey the Elder, Bear, and Frankie all come up and hug me. Little Honey the Elder leads me over to the Reds. Painholder: memories of being kicked or hit in the stomach, of being raped. There are screams inside his head, but somehow they get cut off before they reach his mouth. They were walled off somewhere inside of me. The more they fucked me, the more it hurt. It was worse when they took turns, one after another. It was worse when I couldn't get away or move with them. It was worse when I was tied by the feet or pushed against a wall so that I couldn't move. Grease made it hurt less. There was even some pleasure. Sometimes I'd try to make them come quickly so that it wouldn't hurt so much. Deep shame about this. . . .

Big Red is agitated and upset. He was helpless then, and he's confused now. He doesn't think he can guard Red Painholder adequately. Big Honey agrees to help him.

My body, especially my lower back, hurt a lot during the session. As usual, I had a massage afterward. It worked out a lot of the pain and proved again that there were people I could trust to touch me. I don't think I could have done therapy without regular massage and deep-tissue bodywork.

Several times that week I became irritable and filled with hate. I'd take long walks and soak in the hot tub and hope that, when I was tired enough, the hate would turn to sadness. My asshole was swollen and sore. There was a big lump next to it that started bleeding. These were more memories coming out through my body. I had the idea that the tense knots of muscle in my back were like the Japanese soldiers of World War II who were isolated on Pacific islands and did not surrender until decades after the war ended.

Big Red's stomach is cut open. He is full of hate. He hates feeling weak and dependent and wounded. He hates Nan. He calls her a jerk, an idiot. We try to find a safe place for him, but he stands there raging with hate and pain until he collapses from exhaustion. Some of the others agree to take care of him and Red Painholder. Nan handles the hate and insults without getting defensive. She asks Big Red how she hurt him. He doesn't respond.

Nan left on a three-week vacation. While she was gone I checked inside often, bandaging and caring for the wounded Reds. I had a two-week stomachache that seemed to parallel Big Red's wound. Frankie had made a nest in my chest, and this felt good. I felt like I was on the edge of a big depression, but my birthday was approaching, and this was to be expected.

Linda and I decided to quit seeing Charlotte. We'd convinced ourselves that we'd done all we could with her for the time being. We saw her one last time and agreed to come back in the future if we felt we needed to. Seeing her had been worthwhile. We seemed to have stated all our issues. A lot of old resentments had been aired out and cleared away. I'd learned that my prosecutorial, bulldozer-like tactics didn't work, even if I was right in what I was saying. I was learning to phrase my observations more tactfully. I had come to believe that Linda did not find me sexually disgusting; this was something I'd projected onto her. She had fears about sex, but they weren't about me. She had come to accept a share of responsibility for our problems and was looking for a therapist of her own.

Our plans to move into the new house were finalized. We'd move in June 1. It would be good to get away from Mom. When I told Mom we were moving, she didn't respond directly. Instead she complained about her alleged medical problems.

I bought some pot and spent a lot of time high.

THE COST OF IGNORING MOM

I didn't sink into depression on my birthday, but I felt resistance about returning to therapy. When I did, the insiders were distant and hard to see. Nan called it a "major shutdown." I felt guilty because I didn't want to go back inside and face the pain. There was plenty of pain. At the next session the memories, sensations, and emotions tumbled out in a confused mass. Q and Grace, the parts of me that wanted passive sex, were deeply shamed. There were good parts to hold onto: Bear, Little Honey, and Frankie comforted me, and the Reds were not angry with me for wanting to run from their pain; but the following session I couldn't get into trance at all. Nan suggested I try to sense what my body was feeling. When I did this I was filled with revulsion, self-hate, and suicidal thoughts. None of the insiders came, not even Little Honey. I felt a tremendous desire to quit, to say "fuck you" to them all and slam the door. I knew there was sadness underneath, but all I could feel was anger, hate, frustration. It didn't get better after I left Nan's. I didn't understand it at the time, but it seems clear now that these difficulties were part of the cost of ignoring Mom's role in the abuse.

I did check in that week in spite of myself:

Little Honey still is angry. She seems to think I've failed or chickened out. I ask for her advice. She says I'll have to go back there and be open. . . . Memories of being tied and hung up by the feet. A little boy's ass, shiny with oil, writhing in that position. Some arousal and intense shame. Is this the key to what I have to do next? Is the return of feelings and sensations part of healing, or is it a shameful reiteration of the abuse?

I feel inadequate. I offer to let Little Honey take over, since she seems to know what to do. Then I realize I need to check with the others. Bear agrees to help. Frankie is scared, but he agrees too. Q does not like the idea of Little Honey being in control. He wants a turn, too. Q looks beautiful, in a sadomasochistic way—a thin boy in leather pants and no shirt. He wears heavy eye makeup, and his crotch bulges suggestively. His job is to take all the sexual arousal. He smirks about his "job," but he's quickly sobered by the amount of self-hate and shame he has to bear. Little Honey backs off; she doesn't want to take charge after all. Grace stops masturbating and starts crying. I try to comfort her. Robert and New Man are okay.

It seemed again that the best thing for me to do was to stop trying to impose my agenda and to just go inside and be open. The memories that emerged over the next several weeks were new only in their coherence. They were memories of rape, degradation, and torture by

Dad, Hugh, and others, but they were precise and detailed. The body positions and sensations were vivid. They were complete episodes that played themselves out from beginning to end without flashbacks or jumbled images. I experienced them from the point of view of the child-victim, not from a disassociated observer position.

In trance my body jerked and twitched. I felt some arousal, and I cried silently. When the memories ended, I imagined going in the room, picking up the boy, wrapping him in a blanket, and taking him to Bear. Nan asked if I wanted to do something to the perpetrators to express anger or get retribution. No, I didn't. I wanted to devote all my attention to caring for the boy. Sometimes, when I checked inside he seemed to be sleeping or convalescing. Sometimes he screamed over and over. Bear, Little Honey, Frankie, and I tried to comfort him. Once I saw him lying limply across Bear's lap, like Michelangelo's *Pietà*.

Nan commented that there must be strength in knowing I didn't want this. This remark pissed me off. A huge, continuing problem for me was that there was arousal in the memories. I hated my body for responding, but I wasn't going to deny the response. Even during the worst of the abuse, Dad and Hugh made sure to suck my dick or rub it with oil, and some of the abuse itself was sexually stimulating. There was also the child's natural need for attention and touch. I never wanted the beatings or humiliations, but I did want contact with Dad, and this was the only way I got it. Nan's comment seemed to sweep these difficult, shame-drenched issues under the rug of Dad and Hugh's brutality. Thanks largely to Q, I challenged what she said, and instead of my sinking into resentment we cleared the air between us.

The boy and Red Painholder were clearly the same being. I started calling him Little Red. We reminded him that Dad and Hugh were dead. We promised that we'd stay with him and listen to what he had to say, even though it was painful and difficult for us. We warned him that we weren't perfect and would make mistakes, but we would not abandon him. He didn't have to carry it alone any more.

I came across an article by Dr. Peter Barach on attachment disorders in abuse survivors. In therapyland, attachment behaviors refer to the way we bond emotionally to others. A child's first response to abuse or trauma is usually "anxious attachment behavior": clingy and needy with their parents; often, sadly, with the abuser. When repeated failures of parenting occur, the child abandons its attachment needs, usually by dissociating and walling them off. The diagnostic question here is, "Does the person seek comfort from others when distressed?"

For me the answer was clearly no. When I felt hurt I retreated inside and erected walls. It was news to me that other viable strategies existed. I had abandoned and hidden the parts of me that needed love and human contact. The article ended by stating that it is inappropriate to call dependent or clinging behavior in a recovering survivor "regressed" or any other pejorative term. Such anxious behavior is actually a big step toward healing compared with the abandonment of attachment needs.

One Saturday I was trying to be affectionate with Linda, and she wasn't responding. As I gave up and left the room, she asked for a kiss. I kissed her hard. She said, "That was a Mike Tyson kiss." Tyson, the boxer, had just been convicted of rape. She laughed, but her tone carried fear and revulsion. I left the room at once. She came out and said she was sorry. I told her how it hurt to be compared to a rapist, and I started crying. She sat across the room, staring at me. I was uncomfortable and full of shame. Having sexual desires was so painful for me. I started getting angry, thinking it would be a long time before I tried to be sexual with Linda again. She had stuck a knife deep in the most vulnerable spot. To be compared to a sexual abuser when I was trying to be sexual and loving was the worst insult I could imagine. When we talked about it later, I told her that I didn't trust her; I did not believe things like this were accidents. Once again, I'd gotten the message from her that my sexuality (or just sex) was repulsive.

Linda said she was trying to work on her issues in therapy.

Little Honey remembers Linda's sweetness. She's sad about losing her. Q, in the background, yells, "Get rid of the bitch!" Grace is hurt. She's curled up in a fetal ball, wanting to be unconscious or dead. Robert takes charge of caring for her. He tells me to go to Little Red. Little Red has memories of rapes, seemingly endless rapes. My body twitches. Tears. Bear, Big Honey, and Frankie are sad but okay. Big Red is lying on his side. He still has a big open wound in his stomach. He says it's from giving birth to Little Red. He regrets he was too wounded to be on guard when Linda hurt us. He would have had the shields up and attacked instantly. I tell him I hope he'll concentrate on healing and not try to fight too soon.

Linda and I talked again. I clearly owned that it was my stuff that had been triggered. Still, I also reminded her that I'd warned her repeatedly about my vulnerability in this area, and she stuck her knife in anyway. Crying, I told her I didn't even want to hug her anymore. That got through to her. She said she was working on this stuff in therapy. I told her that if she needed to stop sexual interaction she should do it with a clear "I" statement ("I'm afraid"), not a blaming "you" statement ("That was a Mike Tyson kiss"). I also told her I felt there was a part of her that hated sex with men and in unconscious ways sabotaged our intimacy. I said that she needed to locate that part, talk to it, and find out what it needed. Linda stated her dislike of being told what to do, and I tried to phrase my ideas as questions. We lay down next to each other, but I was uncomfortable and tense. My body didn't trust her.

MEMOIRS OF A CHILD PROSTITUTE

Little Honey comes up and holds my hand. Frankie, nesting inside my chest, sticks his head out and greets me. It's hard to find the others. Finally, I see Q waving in the distance. He makes some hate-filled remarks about Linda and then turns toward Grace. There are big cuts all over and around her crotch. They look like ax-blade cuts. Each gash looks like a cunt. She's cut herself. The reward for all the pain of therapy is more pain. She wants relief at any price. She wants to die. She can get me to jerk my arms while driving and it will be all over. I ask her, "Don't you want to kill Mom first, or at least write her a note so that she'll know?" Grace said, "No, I haven't any strength to waste. It'll take all I have to jerk the steering wheel at the right moment."

Grace becomes unconscious. I'm crying hard. Several of us sew up her wounds and gently cover her. Dream Woman agrees to care for her. Some of the others are also attracted by the idea of dying. They are very tired, and it just keeps hurting.

Little Red: More memories of rape and torture. Nan asks if the memories are reiterative and gets no answer. She asks if Little Red knows that they're over. Image of a pitcher pouring out fluid. He believed there wasn't any more, but here is liquid coming out, and there's still more inside. Nan: "We'll find a way to contain the memo-

ries." I feel a strong wave of fear and sadness. Little Red: "Don't hide me away again. Don't lock me up." Nan: "No, no, we won't do that." Little Red tries to imagine himself without memories of rape. The only peace he can envision is passing out and sleeping. We put a metal plate under him so that no one can get to him. He twitches in his sleep, and I know he's dreaming about being raped. In spite of his bad stomach, Big Red is going to try to take care of Little Red.

During this trance I felt waves of face-twisting grief and pain. I had to restrain myself from yelling, "I can't take it any more." As I reoriented I felt dazed and somewhat ashamed.

Nan told me she considered me an active suicide risk. For the first time she insisted we schedule an extra session. I agreed to call her if I got in trouble. She asked me to check inside every day. She said that if I got no response from the insiders, I should not drive. She advised me not to get high because I couldn't afford to lose contact inside.

In hindsight, being suicidal was another price I was paying for continuing to ignore what the insiders had told me about Mom.

The next day wasn't as bad as I had feared. When I checked inside Grace was a raving, dangerous madwoman. I feared she was going to rip her wounds open. She agreed to leave them alone if I'd take out the stitches and put on butterfly bandages instead. Little Red was somewhat protected from the rape memories by the metal plate we'd put under him.

Linda and I managed to talk and hug and have some feeling of warmth between us. I checked inside again in the evening, and things seemed stable. I had trouble getting to sleep. My body twitched and cramped. I was awakened repeatedly by nightmares. In the morning I was tired and depressed, but Linda and I made love, and that comforted me.

The extra session with Nan was Monday morning, May 25.

Little Red agrees to let Grace go first if we split the time evenly between them. Nan says she'll watch the time carefully. Grace appears semiconscious. Her wounds look partially healed. . . . Dad and Hugh are making small cuts on my body. They fingerfuck the cuts. "You don't like it up the ass, so we'll cut you a new asshole." They did this more than once. One time the cut was on my ass, another time just under my navel. Sometimes I was gagged, sometimes free to scream. Afterward, I'd do anything they told me without resistance or restraints.

. . . Threats with a meat cleaver. They hold me down and tell me they're going to cut me in half. At the last instant of the downswing they turn the blade sideways and smack me with the flat side. I piss on myself in fear. They laugh. They threaten to chop off my penis and pull the same trick of turning the blade sideways at the last instant. . . .

I'm shaking and twitching with waves of emotion and terror. I offer Grace a blanket, but she refuses to cover her wounds. She wants to display them. There's more, about the needle and thread: It was one of Hugh's ideas. Training me to ask for sex acts and say please. They put the thread through the skin under my penis and lead me around the room by it. Once Hugh sucked me while the thread was in my penis and slowly pulled it out with the head of my hard-on in his mouth. Sometimes they put threads in my arms and nipples. Sometimes they'd leave several threads hanging from my body. I was terrified when the threads were in. If I made the slightest wrong move, they could hurt me very badly. . . . In trance I'm crying, twitching and aroused. Grace purposefully numbed it out because she didn't think I could take it. I apologize to her for having used needle and thread to close her wounds.

We go to little Red. . . . I've been left alone in a room with a few little toys; some plastic soldiers and a truck. Men come in and fuck me, one after another. I try to suck them because it hurts less, but many of them fuck me anyway. I try to hum softly to myself and think about my toys, but if it hurts too much, I can't do it. These men think I'm eager. I seem happy to see them. I try to give them blow jobs and don't cry when they fuck me. If I cry and Dad and Hugh find out, they'll really get me. Each time the door opens, I hope it's another stranger and not Dad or Hugh. The slow, gentle ones are best. If they're kind to me at all, I cling to them and really try to please them. . . . Many of the kinder men reacted with rejection and shaming when I did this. One man was nice, and I tried to suck him clean after he fucked me. He rejected me. Disgusting little queen, slut, whore, repulsive creep. . . .

Intense emotions; stronger then any I've felt in trance before. I'm sobbing so hard I have difficulty breathing. I'm dimly aware that I'm getting both these memories at the same time so that the immediate impact of Grace's stuff (being trained to respond) keeps me from dying of the shame of Little Red's (the feeling of being sexually disgusting, the self-hate). . . . My body keeps twitching and jerking. I remind Little Red that they're dead and they'll never get him again.

That night I felt sick to my stomach, woozy and dazed. My body twitched and cramped in bed, as it had in trance. Nevertheless, the new level of emotional intensity seemed positive. It felt cleaner—like a fire burning brightly, like taking a big shit, like being tired after working hard.

I told Linda some of the new memories. It was very emotional for me, but she seemed a little distant. I wondered if, from her point of view, it just seemed like more of the same. To me, the recent memories seemed huge, like a whole new realm. The words, "I was a prostitute. I was a child prostitute. I was a whore." echoed through my mind. It was like trying on a new-old identity.

Grace and Little Red are doing better. Big Red is recovering from his stomach wound. He's surprised that an effort has been made to save him. He'd assumed that if he showed any weakness, he'd be done away with. Everyone seems to be healing.

Chapter 13

Disintegration

June-September 1992

During the first week of June, Linda and I moved to the new house in the olive grove. It was gorgeous—a major step upward in lifestyle. It was important for me to feel that I wasn't fleeing my home to escape Mom. Nobody would think that.

It was a busy and chaotic week. The insiders cooperated by letting me work without the intrusion of emotions or memories. I thanked them later that week at Nan's.

Grace holds a rope out in front of her, as if she were waterskiing. She acknowledges that a near-fatal waterskiing accident I had when I was nineteen was her attempt at suicide. It was the summer after my first year at college, same as when Eddie had his fatal accident. Grace is angry at Dad and Hugh, and angry at us for restraining her. We encourage her to express her anger at the perpetrators. In a berserk rage, she attacks them with an ax, obliterating their faces and genitals, smashing them to bloody mush. She pours gasoline on the mush and burns it, dancing around the flames. She washes herself and stands naked in a pleasant breeze. She feels better, but she's still angry about being locked up all these years. Big Red and I reply, "I'm sorry. You tried to kill us, and you had to be stopped. I didn't know any better way to do it." She seems somewhat mollified.

Little Red rushes into my arms. Memories of being fucked, including a complete narrative from the first sight of the man until he leaves and closes the door behind him. Memories of waiting, with my ass in the air, of the first touch of penis to ass, of wondering fearfully, "How bad will it hurt this time?" Memories of the pain when they shoved their dicks in. . . .

Despite his sadness and loneliness, Little Red was cooperating and making mature, calm choices on how best to heal. I felt a strong desire to protect and care for him, to be with him as much as possible. I was afraid of Grace, her suicidal tendencies, her anger, and her sexuality, but I also admired her.

. . . She's whispering privately with Dream Woman. I feel threatened by her secrecy. I ask her to let me know what she needs and wants. She wants sex with a man. She has someone in mind. I ask Little Red if he's willing to comply. He starts rolling over and putting his ass up, but there's a big tear in his eye. He hoped that the sex was over. He feels a lot of self-hate because of his childhood compliance. I thank him for containing all the pain and shame. I tell him he saved our life. Grace is upset. She feels sorry for Little Red and doesn't want to hurt him, but she wants to be penetrated. If she can't have the kind of sex she wants, she wants the desire to go away.

This was the old dilemma on a new level. The imprinting of pain and terror onto stimulation had split my sexuality into opposing camps. They had struggled to a standstill that satisfied no one and left everyone shamed.

Nan said that the fire between Grace's legs must be the aftereffect of abuse. Normal sexual desire waxes and wanes, but Grace's was always high. Nan also said that some kind of sexual deconditioning might be needed. This sounded horribly unpleasant. Grace hated the idea. Neither Nan nor the Watkinses nor any of the books I'd read had any clear idea of how to cleanse and heal sexuality after childhood abuse.

BOBBY AND RED: THE INSIDERS PREPARE FOR WAR

Big Red is boiling with anger. He hates Grace and her desires. He shames and berates her viciously. Then he retreats into a fort he's building in preparation for war. I can't find Little Red; Big Red is hiding him. He no longer trusts Nan. She can't help him and Grace at the same time: "Either you get fucked or you don't; there is no halfway." He hurls insults at Nan. She responds by pointing out that he was doing his best to protect Little Red. Thinking of him as a protector lets

me have sympathy and respect for him, in spite of the pain his re-
marks cause.

Grace is very sad. I try to comfort her, but she wants to kill or muti-
late herself. . . .

I met again with Michael and Rick. I managed to tell them about
the recent memories. We talked about panic attacks. Until they
brought it up, I'd never thought I experienced them, but now I realized they were a regular part of my life. I often woke in the night
afraid my dog was sick, afraid someone was breaking into my home,
afraid of my nightmares, or just plain afraid. In a dissociated way I remembered that as a child I'd listened to every little nighttime noise,
wondering if Dad and Hugh were coming to get me.

Big Red is in his fort, but he's ready to surrender. He and Little Red
come out and talk. Little Red is willing to have sex, but there is still a
tear in his eye. Nan protests that he's a child who's sacrificing him-
self. We try to arrange for Little Red to leave if Grace has sex. Big Red
is crying. I reassure him how valuable he's been all these years.

Robert watches from the sidelines as the synthesis he put together
as an adolescent comes apart.

Little Honey takes Little Red by the hand. She tries to lead him
away from his ready-to-be-fucked position so that Grace can have sex
without hurting him. As soon as he leaves the position, he feels the
terror instilled by torture and training. Beyond the terror, a pit of
pain. Continuous screaming in my head. Cramps in my throat, twitches
in my body. Tears. Waves of sadness and anguish. Little Red has to go
back to the sexual posture and hide his fear. Nan asks Little Honey to
sit by him and touch his face gently. Bear helps too. I try to help but, at
the sight of an adult male, Little Red shuts down his emotions and
prepares to comply with sexual demands. I reassure him that the
abusers are dead, but he's not convinced. Grace is crying. She wants
to comfort Little Red but thinks he might hate her for her desires.

This was an intensely emotional session. The terror, the screaming, the trapped feeling, the helpless sadness, the isolated loneliness
were all lucidly real. That week I was bleeding from my anus again. I
had cramps in my groin and difficulty urinating.

I find Little Red in that room where he waits for the strange men to come have sex with him. He's friendly. He tells me that he wants to be called "Bobby," my name as a young child. He turns over and offers me his ass. Sex is the only contact he knows. Instead, I sit next to him and we look at his toys. He plays with them. He makes one of his plastic soldiers hump another one. He pushes the barrel of a rifle into a soldier's ass. We offer him crayons and paper. He fills a page with black and blue circles. He draws a big erect penis covered in blood. I offer him food. He eagerly expects drugs or alcohol. He lies down to sleep.

Grace is fantasizing about being fucked. She doesn't want to stop. When she does, she's anxious and uncomfortable from the confusion of living in the same body as Bobby. Q is sad and anxious too. His sexual desires have turned to ashes in the heat of Bobby's pain and terror. I ask Bobby if he needs anything. . . . Dad comes through the door with pliers in his hand. My heartbeat accelerates; I have a sick feeling in my stomach. I tell Bobby, "You don't have to do this now." It's really my desire to shut down. I can't handle it.

That day it was a struggle to get calm enough to leave Nan's office. I had three massages over the next two days, but my body wouldn't relax. My anus stopped bleeding, but my groin was so cramped up I could barely pee. My back hurt. My neck hurt. My head hurt.

At Nan's suggestion, we had been meeting twice a week on a regular basis. It was proving to be a good change. It provided enough time for the abuse memories to come out so that they didn't intrude quite so much on my daily life.

Bobby lets me hold him. He's reluctant to go back to the memories. Nan and I suggest that he can dissociate safely by seeing them like a movie. . . . Memories of torture flash by: The pliers. Hugh burning me with a cigarette, rubbing the burnt flesh off and poking at the sore. Rapes and bondage. Suffocation and choking. Beating and kicking. Dad making me beg for mercy. I cry, but the fear is dissociated away. Bobby lets me hold and comfort him. Only at the end does he assume the position. As I reorient, Little Honey and Bear come to take care of him. I thank Bobby for trusting me. I remind him again that his abusers are dead. I tell him that I want to help him carry the feelings; that even though fear is difficult, together we can handle it.

Big Red liked getting angry and being tough. He enjoyed the problems I was having with some sleazebags who owned a share of a small, private water company I ran.

Big Red tries to distract us with thoughts about business. When we're able to focus on him, it's clear that he feels ashamed and guilty. He hid himself away and left Bobby to absorb the torture. He failed in his most important, protective function. He thinks of himself as tough and strong, but he chickened out, and now he hates himself for it. Very sad memories of seeing Bobby hurt, exhausted and semiconscious after a session of abuse. Like a mother helplessly watching her child sicken and die. Nan: "Big Red has the strength of oak, and Bobby has the strength of willow. Bobby could bend; Big Red might have broken, gone insane."

Bobby is with Little Honey, but he's too tired to do anything. Bear and Frankie look hurt. We cry together. Grace is filled with self-hate and sexual disgust. She feels contaminated, diseased, gangrened. Q is defiantly proud of his sexuality: "I want to be fucked. I want to be attractive." Robert gives a detached, intellectual commentary. He says we're taking apart the synthesis he put together as a teenager to keep us from dying or going crazy. He points out how the parts all balance one another. He says that integrating fear and terror is the big task now.

It was more than a month after the move that Linda and I invited Mom over to the new house for lunch. The event itself was emotionless and trivial, but the next day I felt like I was losing my bearings. I had a desire to run away. I was surprised by the strength of the emotions, but after therapy that day I was more surprised by how numb I'd been at the lunch with Mom.

Bobby's face is bashed in. He can't talk. I ask Little Honey what's wrong. She shows me a child's crayon drawing of Mom looking like a monster. Behind it is an image of a much younger Mom, floating and drifting. Now memories I'd had before: Dad pushing my face into Mom's crotch, his glee when I lick her cunt. . . .

Big Red is violently angry, planning to hurt me for letting Mom into the house. It violated Bobby's sense of sanctuary. Bobby had thought my reassurances that "the abusers are dead" included Mom.

Grace and Q are hurt and withdrawn. Little Honey blames me and Nan, but Little Honey never warned us how bad it would be.

The emotional deluge of the days that followed may have been a good thing. Dissociating and numbing out when Mom was in the house had caused me to hurt Bobby. Big Red was pissed off at both me and Nan. He had fortified his position and was determined to stop the therapy process. He called me a jerk, a feeble fool who belonged in a nuthouse. When asked questions he didn't want to answer, he flooded me with tension and anger. He was spoiling for a fight. He tried to pick one with Nan by insulting her, but she wouldn't be baited. He feared loneliness and recognized the need for healing, but these concerns seemed unimportant compared to the clear and present danger he perceived.

I was depressed. This was a big step backward toward internal civil war. My body hurt and I couldn't sleep. I felt absolutely no sexual urges. When I checked inside, Big Red tried to block off communication with Bobby.

OEDIPUS AND I

I was boiling with hate the morning of the next session with Nan. My body was tense with the effort of containing the feeling. I started to panic, wondering how I'd get through the day without attacking someone. My hate turned on Nan and what a jerk she was. I planned to attack and scare her enough that she'd refuse to see me again. Big Red loved this. My neck was so tense that my shoulders were hunched up and my head pulled backward.

I told Nan how pissed off I was at her and at the world in general. She said she wasn't leaving; my anger was at Mom and her repeated betrayals. My rage dissolved into tears.

Nan asks Red what he wants to do about Dad forcing me to be sexual with Mom. Gleefully he says he wants to hit Mom in the head with a hammer to get her attention, to make her see what she's doing. He wants to rip her cunt apart with his teeth and then hammer Dad's teeth down his throat to stop his grin. He starts fantasizing about torturing her, but this feels like something Dad would do, and he turns away from it quickly. Despair and helplessness. . . .

*Bobby lets me hold him. He's hungry for food and contact. . . .
Bobby taps at Mom's chest, trying to get her attention, but she just
floats away. Big Red comes and takes him back. He defends against
the loneliness and hurt with angry attacks. He's weak and tired. Being entrusted with Bobby's care feels good.*

Linda complained about our lack of sex. I felt like a resentful failure. I told her a civil war was raging inside me, bringing on some of
the worst feelings I'd had to deal with in therapy. I didn't go into details. Linda tried to comfort me, but her touch felt repulsive. After she
left I lay in bed, filled with fantasies of killing women and mutilating
their genitals. Finally, I managed to dissociate and escape into reading.

Nan's references to "anger at Mom" shamed me. My anger wasn't
focused on Mom. It was aimed, scattershot, at the world in general, at
women and their genitals in particular. I felt like an idiot because I
didn't get it.

*Little Honey is fearful. Image of a big splinter stuck in flesh. We've
been hitting the end of the splinter, making the flesh more swollen and
irritated. Little Honey says we need to cover it over or pull it out completely. I ask her to help me remove it. We turn to Bobby. . . . Long
memory sequence of sex with Mom: Me licking her ass. Dad holding
me on top of her and getting me to hump her. Sucking her tits. Mom
sucking my dick and licking my ass. I feel suffocated and disgusted as
Dad pushes my face down in her crotch. It's undeniable that she is consciously taking part.*

*I reassure Bobby that I do not hate him and will not repudiate him.
Big Red is angry, filled with shame. He sits with his back to us but
does not try to stop the process. He's made his painful last-ditch effort
to reassert his old protective position of anger, but now he's resigned
to letting the stuff come out.*

I predicted that this would be hard to integrate.

Ironically, I had to go to Mom's that weekend to make some repairs. I warned the insiders to protect themselves. Talking to Mom
was a repulsive experience. I felt a little hate and a large desire to run
away. My tools and supplies were stored in a garage near her house,

and I needed to go there about once a week. I didn't want to move the stuff out just to avoid her. I didn't want to give her that power.

As I drove to Nan's the next time, I was feeling much better than when Big Red's hate and anger were flooding me.

I focus on the image of the splinter and ask all the insiders to help me remove it. Frankie is upset. We soothe him before we go to Bobby. . . . Mom is sitting on my face, grinding her cunt into my mouth. My face is wet and slimy, and I struggle to breathe. I comfort Bobby, telling him I don't want him to have to face anything alone. I thank him for trusting me enough to tell me.

So they were loose, the memories I'd been shoving back in a corner since Thanksgiving. I could ignore them no longer. My mother was no victim. She was an active, conscious abuser. She was a perpetrator, a sex offender. She had used me for her sexual gratification. And Bobby had indicated that there was more.

Frankie comes up first. He feels ashamed for wanting to hide Bobby away. He apologizes to Bobby and promises to help him. Bobby reaffirms: Yes, it was Mom. Nan asks if there's something else he wants to tell. . . . I'm in a bathtub. Mom is bathing me. She rubs my genitals and asshole with soapy fingers. I get an erection and stand up in the tub. I'm very excited. She sucks my dick for a while. Then she stands with her back against the door while I lick her cunt, frightened and hurriedly. Dad is not here. . . .

Mom lies in her bed. Excited, scared, I approach her and put my head between her legs. I crawl up and start humping her. She pushes me down and gets me to lick her cunt. Extreme arousal. Extreme shame and guilt. I reached out for her. I started it. . . .

I can't take it. More memories are coming, but I ask for them to stop. With effort, I put aside my worry about how I'm going to integrate them and focus instead on the insiders. They confirm the memories: Dream Woman, Frankie, Big Honey, Little Honey, and Robert. I thank Bobby for telling and showing me. "They did wrong. Mom did wrong. Please let me know if you need anything. The shame is theirs. I am proud of you. . . ."

The memory of my hand reaching out, scared and trembling and excited, to touch Mom's cunt, kept coming back to me. I could feel her pubic hair between my small child's fingers.

I couldn't tell Linda or anyone else about this.

I focused on taking care of the insiders. The important thing was to make sure Bobby was safe. Dealing with Mom and integrating this stuff into my adult personality could wait. Bobby felt like a perpetrator, a sinner. I tried to tell him that he was powerless, but this only left him feeling belittled and invalidated.

Nan and I talked about the issue of responsibility and powerlessness. I'd heard it all before. Almost all authorities on child abuse assert that the adult is always the responsible party, even when the child initiates sex or bargains for bribes or rewards. A child doesn't have the power to give informed consent. Intellectually, I accepted this truth, but it didn't penetrate the guilt and shame I felt. *Motherfucker.* A classic major sin. Oedipus gouged out his eyes; what would I need to do? *A real motherfucker.* I didn't think I'd kill myself, but I feared that some day, when it was just too much, my hands would jerk on the steering wheel, and I would die as Eddie had.

Bobby comes up looking larger, tough. It's almost as if he's taken on some of Big Red's swagger. I can take seeing Mom, his appearance says; I can tolerate almost anything. More memories: a confused jumble of being "caught" by Dad in bed with Mom. Dad is self-righteous and irate. He gets her to help hold me down while he whips me with a belt. His sadistic pleasure shows through his pseudo-righteous anger. Bobby is angry at Mom's abject cowardice, her total failure to protect me or take any responsibility.

I was beginning to understand that some of Bobby's sense of power came from making adults have orgasms. The crescendo of their breathing, their bodies convulsing made him feel strong. He felt most in control when he could do this by sucking them. This had carried over unconsciously into my adult life in my attitude toward oral sex. I'd suck and lick a woman until she had multiple orgasms. I did this almost compulsively. With the focus exclusively on her orgasms, sex would become boring for me. I'd counter the boredom by looking for new partners.

Bobby is rebuilding his defenses. He realizes that this will lead to loneliness and sadness, but he doesn't care. The raging anger feels clean: no more terror; no more nervous pussyfooting around. It's al-

most intoxicating. We try to focus the anger at Mom. We can do it somewhat as an adult, but as a child we couldn't do it at all. Mom was our only hope.

Bobby as a younger version of Red had been hard for me to grasp. Bobby, terrorized and compliant, seemed the opposite of Big Red, who was tough and cynical. The clear, clean attacks of rage Bobby was feeling provided the connecting link. They reminded me of the seizure-like tantrums I'd experienced as a child. Uncontrollable rage was the flip side of terrorized compliance.

"MOMENTS OF HEALING": WORKING WITH MARIAH GLADIS

In August, despite the emotional instability brought on by Bobby's memories, I returned to Esalen. Mariah Gladis, the woman I'd been so impressed with that winter, was leading a workshop called, "Creating Exact Moments of Healing."

Most of the workshop consisted of Mariah working with individuals, one after another. Everyone got to work with her once, for an hour or so. She was amazing. Without ever being pushy, confrontational, or critical, she quickly got to people's core issues. I cried a great deal while other people worked, but I didn't feel embarrassed because most of the group cried too.

Much of what Mariah did was classically Gestalt. She put out pillows and had people address them as their parents or other significant others. She had people play roles in other people's work. I'd seen other therapists use these techniques with poor results, but Mariah's gentle intensity opened people's hearts. My trust in her grew as I watched her work, yet I feared that when people heard my story they would think I was a monster.

During a "moving meditation," one of Mariah's assistants asked us to put on blindfolds. I started to put one on, but I panicked and left. This depressed me. I thought about the things I unconsciously avoided because of the abuse. I wouldn't wear a tie, walk a dog on a leash, sleep in a bed with bedposts, have a boss, or learn from an older man.

I was feeling like an outsider. I needed friends badly, but my reaction to this neediness was wanting to strike out and attack. Working with one sexual-abuse survivor, Mariah had her attack pillows held up by the men. I helped hold the pillows, wanting to be part of the group, but even playing the abuser in this minor way left me feeling dirtied and bad.

The next morning I was thinking of leaving. I was too upset to eat breakfast. Instead I went to the meeting room early and volunteered to be the first person to work.

I told Mariah and the group of my fear that they'd find me disgusting when they heard my story. I told them I'd been sadistically sexually abused by my father, his friends, and my older brother, and that recently I'd realized my mother was also an abuser. Mariah stopped me and told me to look into the eyes of the people in the room. Nobody turned away in disgust. Some were crying. Several of them said, "No, Bob, you are not disgusting." I told Mariah that my father and brother were long dead, but my mother was still alive and I was deeply ashamed of the caretaking I'd done for her. Mariah said, "Oh, no, Bob, that's very good. They couldn't kill your compassion."

Mariah had a woman from the group role-play my mother, but I couldn't put my hate on her. Mariah put a big pillow on the floor and asked me to push down on it and tell Mom how much I hated her. Soon I was screaming in pain: "You bitch, you cunt, you bitch! You couldn't keep your goddamn itchy cunt to yourself. How could you? How could you?" Mariah kept encouraging me to vomit it all up. Several times I subsided, exhausted, and she'd ask, "Is it all out?" Then more emotion would come up. I was semicoherent, crying and screaming and choking. These were my first adult screams, and I'd held them in for thirty-five years.

When I could do no more, Mariah had me curl up in fetal position in her lap. She held and rocked me. Then she had the whole group gather around and touch me as I lay on the floor. Many of them were crying or sobbing. I was crying intermittently and feeling dazed. Several people hugged me. I lay down with my head in a woman's lap, and someone covered me with a blanket.

A man named Charlie went next. He was a survivor, too. He dealt with fresh, vague memories of his grandfather abusing him. I cried a lot as Charlie worked. My heart was wide open.

That night Charlie and I soaked in the hot tubs and talked. I told him that I'd repeatedly denied my memories and that, when in denial, I always looked for secondary gain. One reason I believed my memories was that I could find none. Charlie pointed out that in the group there was secondary gain: I'd expected my history to arouse revulsion and make me an outsider, but the group had been sympathetic. Because he pointed out this sympathy as a criticism of my idea about secondary gain and not as a reassurance, I believed Charlie. It really got through to me that my story aroused compassion and not disgust. I started crying. Charlie tried to put his arm around my shoulders to comfort me. Being naked and being touched by another naked man was more than I could take. I panicked and pushed him away. There were some hurt feelings over this incident, but we talked it out.

The next day I was hoarse from screaming, and I still felt wide open and vulnerable. Mariah had said that safe, nonsexual touch was very important for me. Some of the women held and comforted me during the group sessions. I soaked it up. Once, when we were standing in a circle, Mariah asked us to look around at the other people and see the beauty in each of them. This was the opposite of the way I normally viewed others, using all my powers to see their vicious, unconscious motivations and ugly faults. At Mariah's suggestion, I was able to see beauty in almost everyone.

One night at dinner I asked Mariah how she avoided burnout. She said she enjoyed her work; that it made her stronger because she followed the thread of healing instead of focusing on wounds.

Before the close of the workshop, I arranged to have a group reunion at my house that fall, and I signed up for another week with Mariah in January. I didn't want to lose the close connection I had with the people. It was the first time I really felt like I belonged in a group.

But I was fearing the end. I was starting to close up and hate some of the people. I was slipping back into the familiar, lonely role of outsider. My return home was darkened by the prospect of having to struggle with fear and dysfunction. I felt like a bottomless pit of neediness and was afraid that I'd come crashing down into a suicidal depression.

Reuniting with Linda was wonderful. Before the workshop we'd had a bad time over the usual issues, but now I found I could share my openness and lovingness with her. We made love frequently and listened to each other without excuses or defensiveness.

DIE SOON, MOMMY

I talked over the workshop with Nan. She saw my neediness as the layer underlying all the horrendous abuse stuff. I was worried that it would repel people. Nan didn't think this was a problem because I was usually extremely careful to appear self-sufficient. It was the clingy, vacuum cleaner-like people who were repellent.

Little Honey appears bigger and older. She's entering adolescence. The fact that she and Bobby are maturing seems to indicate healing. She's shy and conflicted about beginning to be sexual. We tell her that being erotic can be beautiful, but it is private. I reassure her that I'll never be sexual with her. I tell her that it was Mom's behavior that was disgusting and hateful, not her genitals.

Now Q jumps in. There's a faint image of him with his butt in the air, being fucked and liking it. A Cheshire Cat grin on a very sad face. He's almost ready to deny his longings. His passive homosexual stimulation is painful and awkward for the others, but I'm glad he stuck with his desires. He's mad at me for the way I dress. He thinks I'm a slob. I look like an old pickup truck; I get fat to avoid being sexy. He won't shake hands or hug me.

Grace is half asleep. Bobby is hard to find. He feels that I didn't protect him adequately at Esalen. He doesn't want any confrontation with Mom. He doesn't want her to see my neediness or vulnerability. He feels responsible for the sex with Mom. When hate and anger are expressed at her, he feels they are directed, in part, at him. He has more memories, but he's afraid he's already released too much information and thereby lost control. I promise him we won't confront Mom again until he gives his okay.

Often I found myself wishing and thinking that Mom was dead. When reality burst these fantasies, I'd be depressed. I tried to avoid them, not because hoping for Mom's death was an evil thing, but because it put me on an emotional roller coaster. Twenty years earlier, when I was in college, I'd been jailed on drug charges and held overnight. I knew people were working to bail me out. Every time someone walked down the corridor, I'd jump up, expecting to be freed. An old black man in the cell with me told me I'd drive myself crazy if I kept it up. He said I'd feel much better if I pretended I wasn't ever going to be freed. He was right.

Nan suggested that I write letters to Mom (and not send them) as a way of releasing emotions. I wrote several, but their content was all rather similar.

Dear Mom:
You sleazy, dishonest bitch. You didn't protect me from that psychopathic sadist and his live-in lovers. You pretended to be ill, out of cowardice, while they tortured and sexually abused me. You played on my need for a real mother and got me to take care of you. You sniveling shit. But that wasn't enough. Living a cowardly lie and sacrificing your children to a monster wasn't enough. You got me to be sexual with you. You couldn't keep your goddamn filthy itchy twat to yourself. You repulsive, degenerate hog. You used the power of your position as mother and took advantage of my abject, lonely neediness. You exploited and betrayed me. And you tried to hide your piggishness and foulness and cowardice behind the mask of a victim. You are no victim. You are a perpetrator, a child abuser. You committed one of the greatest betrayals possible for a mother. What you and Dad did killed Eddie and it damn near killed me. I don't want you to see my neediness, vulnerability, and pain, but my life has been a tormented and miserable struggle and I have been unable to enjoy the good moments. I hope you get cancer of the cunt and that it rots away painfully, stinking of corruption. You shit. You bitch. You demented pig. I hope every part of your body that you got me to touch sexually rots and burns and festers and bloats and gives off horrid puslike foulness.

Die soon, Mommy,
Bob

What came out in my unmailed letters was how ashamed I was of having needed a mother's love.

Bobby comes running up to me, scared. I'm gratified that he's here. I hold him and cry. Bear, wounded, comforts him too. Frankie is scared. He remembers how Mom was the only warm human contact in childhood. He fears absolute isolation without her.

Sinking deeper into trance. . . . I'm standing at the doorway of my parents' bedroom in New York City. I'm as tall as Mom, maybe a little taller. She gets down on her knees and sucks my dick a little. Vivid image of the glistening head of my erection. She leads me to the bed. I fuck her from behind. The wet, slippery sensation is unmistakable. A feeling of power. . . . I'm much older than in any memories I've had before. I could be thirteen.

Bobby curls into a ball, hiding his face in Bear's furry chest and shaking. The memories stop. Bear and I comfort him. Big Red makes some cynical remarks, but he quickly agrees to be gentle. I'm numb, but I'm afraid of what I'll feel later. Nan says she's scared too. She insists on making a contract with me that I'll talk to her before I hurt myself. She's afraid I'll take way too much responsibility, that I might see myself as a perpetrator: "Your Mom molested you and created the illusion that you were being sexual together." She asks me to shed my numbness right now. I try to let it go. I became shaky, crying and gasping for air. I feel ashamed of the feeling of power, of the arousal, of stuffing it and hiding it for thirty-plus years. Big Red: "You, you did fuck the bitch." Nan objects: "No, she molested you." But my dick got hard and I put it in her cunt, and I moved it in and out, and I came inside of her.

A real motherfucker.

Eighth grade, not age eight. Another five years of memories to assimilate.

I checked inside a lot. I felt certain that if Bobby and I didn't let the shame separate us again, things would be okay. I tried to comfort and care for him. I thanked him for vetoing my plans to confront Mom. I warned him that I was likely to make mistakes that might hurt him; I asked him not to run from me. "I love you, Bobby. I want to provide you with safety. I want to hear and see your truth, no matter how painful and devastating it is. Together we can carry it."

Needing support badly, I worked up my courage and told Linda what I'd remembered. For the first time in my life, I prayed before I talked to her. I just said, "Lord, help me," over and over.

Linda was wonderful. She cried with me. She told me I was blameless; they weren't human. She said she loved me. I told her this was harder for me to handle than Dad and Hugh's abuse, that it was a struggle not to feel responsible. I did not tell her my fear that if I failed to keep the hate and shame away, they'd be too much, and I would die. I was relieved that I'd managed to tell her and not to isolate myself in pain. I knew I'd be watching her like a hawk for any signs of distrust, of anything less than love.

Bobby is larger, less boyish. I think he might prefer to be called Bob now. He looks down, reluctant to talk, but once he opens up there's a flood of memory. Their bedroom at Lake George: I'm fucking her from behind. Hard, wanting to hurt her. Angrily squeezing her tits and ass to cause pain. Sucking her cunt, wanting it to hurt. Whipping her naked ass with Dad's belt. Wanting to cram my dick down her throat. She has a hairbrush with a penis-shaped handle. I shove it up her cunt, up her ass. I fuck her asshole. I tie her spread-eagled to her bedposts. She doesn't resist. Anger. I want to hurt her, but there's also sadness deep inside. She seems to like the roughness. I feel defeated by her cunt. What a horrible way to exploit my healthy anger. Many levels of emotion and sensation, clear and powerful.

Nan: "What a trap. She used your healthy anger to get you into sadomasochistic incest." I tell Bob again and again that we'll be okay if he doesn't leave; together we can handle it. I want to hug him, but he has a big erection, and there's no way to do it without feeling sexual. He's ashamed of his erection. Arousal is a soul-destroying addiction that brings pain and lonely, abject shame. . . .

She'd stayed with Dad because she was getting her masochistic desires met. They played a classic good cop/bad cop routine—a tried-and-true way to break someone's spirit and resistance.

I was shaking as I left Nan's. How could I keep self-blame and self-hate away with memories like that? What outsider would believe I was the victim?

NIGHT OF HORRORS

I told Bob I wanted all the memories and feelings about Mom. I promised him I'd take the time to process them. "It may not be possible to do it all at once, but what Mom did was poisonous, and I want to get as much poison out now as we can." He and I were nearly hysterical, trapped between incompatible emotions—grief and arousal. My mouth opened to scream but no sound came out. The other insiders gathered around Bob as he writhed in pain and they tried to comfort him. Someone prayed, "Lord, help him heal."

I jacked off compulsively so I wouldn't feel any arousal. I told myself my genitals were good, but I didn't believe it. Bob hated his erection. It was a visible symbol of the "adult" active sexual role. I told him that with the right person, at the right time, it could be a beautiful thing. I tried to direct the shame and hate at Mom and Dad and away from my body. Bob was disgusted by his masochistic cravings and angry at me because I didn't experience them as totally devastating. I told him that I took his grief and pain seriously and meant no disrespect, but, for me, being stimulated masochistically helped me avoid becoming a perpetrator, and this brought relief. Because both Grace and Q held similar desires, I'd already worked at redirecting the shame.

Bob wanted to discipline his body, to diet and exercise and be Spartan. Part of this desire was healthy, and part was our expression of his self-hate. His hatred of his erection made him want to "whip his body into shape." He wanted me to be tough and self-sufficient; he hated it when I let my vulnerability show.

Bob's image of Big Red became clearer and harsher. He saw him as a jailer who kept him imprisoned for his crimes, symbolized by his erection. Pot was one of the bars on the prison door. It seemed to stop the internal processing, particularly when I used it after therapy. "You have a drug problem," Bob said accusingly. This made me feel very bad, but not bad enough to give up getting high. Other insiders liked to smoke pot. *I* liked to smoke pot, especially when I played the piano. I was willing to promise Bob I wouldn't use any on therapy days for the rest of the year, at the end of which we could discuss it again. This seemed to be okay.

There were more trance memories of sex with Mom. There was a long, coherent scene in which she tied me to the bed and worked me over sadomasochistically. I could feel my body arching, straining against the ropes. I had a huge orgasm. She seemed happy. I liked it; I wanted it again. She used the promise of it to get me to do stuff. It was tremendously intense—the genital and anal feelings, the pain and pleasure melting into one huge ball that exploded into orgasm.

Between therapy sessions I was living for Bob. I found myself getting up at 4:00 a.m.; it seemed to be the time of day he preferred. I told him that feelings he brought up were both very painful and very valuable. I told him that I wouldn't be a whole man until I listened to all of his truth.

A huge portion of Bob's truth emerged at Nan's on September 17.

Lake George: I'm fucking Mom. She's spread-eagled on her bed, tied to the bedposts. Dad and Hugh burst into the room. They drag me off her. Image of my red, erect dick, cunt juices dripping off it; very vivid. Intense, mortal shame. . . . Dad and Hugh are angry, raving: "You disgusting shit, you creep. . . ." They have a knife. ". . . I'll cut your cock and balls to shreds. . . . I'll kill you. . . ." They choke me and pull me back by my hair and quickly tie me up. When I'm tied they kick and punch and slap me around the room. They yell at Mom and whip her with a belt. They whip me too. One of them fucks her and makes me lick her cunt.

They tie my legs far apart and push me face down over the bed. They burn my penis with a cigarette and put it out in my asshole. Now Dad fucks me. I'm screaming, begging him to stop. "I'll kill you," he snarls again and again and again. "We could kill you and get away with it after what you did. You little shit. You little motherfucker; I'll cut your balls off." He stops raping me to listen to me beg. He burns my asshole with his cigarette and fucks me again. He comes, punching the back of my head and screaming threats. . . .

I'm returning to consciousness. I guess I passed out. Now they make me suck them clean. They poke my genitals with a knife, snarling threats. They untie my legs and throw me on the floor in a corner. I see Mom still tied to the bed. They rape and beat me again; I don't know how many times. They tie me up again, my feet together and my hands behind me. They throw me in a closet, on a pile of old shoes. They pull my arms up sharply behind me and close the door, leaving me face down, half-suspended in darkness.

Terror. When will they come back? Will they kill me, castrate me, blind me, or just start torturing me again? . . .

I don't know how long I'm there. When they bring me out, Mom is gone. They've decided my punishment. They should kill me, but they're going to be nice because they don't want to hurt Mom. If word ever got out, it would kill her. I deserve to die; I deserve to have my genitals sliced up. Instead, they're going to whip me and then both fuck me again. My asshole hurts so badly from the burnings and rapes that I beg them not to fuck me. Hugh: "Maybe, kiss my feet." I do. I give him a blow job. He holds me bent over the bed while Dad whips me. Then Dad fucks me. More threats. They cut me free of the ropes and leave me huddled naked on the floor.

I go up to my room, clean myself, and sleep a little. I want to stay in my room forever. When I finally come down, hungry, nobody says anything; it's as if nothing happened. . . .

My heart is racing as the memories come out. I feel nauseous. The pain of Dad fucking my burned asshole is very vivid. I can't tell how long it went on. As I reorient, there's a sudden, short wave of tears and sadness, but mostly I feel numb. As I look at Nan, I repress a hysterical giggle.

That night I slept nearly eleven hours. In the morning, half asleep, I checked in with Bob. He was pacing and angry. Frankie and Bear comforted him.

Bob was boiling with conflicting emotions. I tried to stay with him. I told him that I really needed him, that I hoped he'd let me know the truth no matter how horrible, and that I wouldn't be whole until he did.

I knew Bob would be offended by positive feelings, but I felt relieved, almost celebratory. Beneath the cautious hope that the night of horrors might really, finally, be the last big chunk of memory was the realization that there was nothing in it about my ever having been an abuser. They had inflicted their worst on me, but they had failed to turn me into one of them.

Chapter 14

Healing

September-December 1992

Bob has reisolated himself in anger. He resents my relief and hope. I apologize to him and try to let him know how scared and revolted I was by the thought that I might have become an abuser. After all the amnesia, it's hard to be certain of anything. My pride of intellect has been humbled.

Nan asks Bob, "Did you ever want to hurt others the way you were hurt?" No, he didn't, but the other insiders kept his masochistic longing hidden and disowned for over thirty years. No one knows how to remove it; he's not even sure he wants it removed. The best solution he can envision is asexuality.

I was beginning to understand that Bob's masochistic longing was a symbol of more complex needs: the yearning for human contact, for warmth, for someone to help deal with the aftereffects of the night of horrors.

I wondered whether that night had been a set-up that Mom had been part of. The timing couldn't have been more perfect. They'd pinned all their shame and guilt on me. They'd succeeded in isolating me when I most needed human contact. The mortally fearful neediness and loneliness shut my mouth. Bob had wanted to die, so a psychological death was arranged.

This was the matrix out of which Robert was born. Robert was the synthesis that put a lid on the cauldron and gave me a mask to present to the world. When I first met Robert at the start of therapy, he was sitting on the porch swing of that same house, singing, "Swing Low, Sweet Chariot" to himself. It was his birth song and Bob's funeral dirge.

Frankie says he was born that night too. One reason he'd sounded like Dad all these years was to keep everyone ready for Dad's worst and try to prevent another night of horrors. It was painful for him to take on the role of the mocking, sarcastic father, but it seemed the best way to be sure my defenses were always up.

Little Honey looks strong. She reassures me that I've never been a perpetrator. She and Bear take care of Bob.

At night I comforted Bob. He was reliving the horrors while I was asleep or half asleep. Despite his pain, he seemed to be getting closer to the other insiders.

More details of that night—or was it several nights?—kept surfacing in trance. I remembered being beaten repeatedly. I remembered Dad and Hugh threatening to poke out my eyes. I remembered them sticking pins through my nipples and flicking and twisting them. I remembered them peeing on me while I was tied up. I remembered Dad sucking my dick until it got hard, then cursing me for my erection and punching me in the stomach until I puked into a wastebasket. I remembered splinters shoved under my fingernails. Being tortured with cuticle scissors. Shitting from fear and having my face pushed into it. Being held under an ice-cold shower. I remembered them putting my penis in a door jamb and threatening to close the door. I remembered screaming and screaming and screaming.

I wanted to scream in trance, but my throat and jaw muscles went crazy, and I could do no more than whisper. We kept reassuring Bob that these were old memories, that Dad and Hugh were dead. He knew that, but he still feared that they were lurking just around the corner, waiting to get him. There were several heart-pounding startle-response jolts when he thought they might be coming.

In one session Nan started pushing Bob to express anger at Dad. She wanted it to come out so it wouldn't be directed onto others or come out through my body. I got uncomfortable and told her to stop. Bob felt blamed. Perhaps he didn't feel anger. Perhaps the only emotions he had were those which had overwhelmed him before his isolation: shame, terror, loneliness, neediness.

I dreamed I owned rural land with several homes on it. A utility crew came and bulldozed out an old, complex water-distribution system. I was suspicious, but I talked to a foreman who showed me the spot where they'd place new water tanks for a gravity-feed system.

Replacing an old, complex system with a new, simple, and natural one seemed like a positive picture of therapy.

Frankie feels cut off and lonely. He feels that the others hate him and will attack him, but he agrees to go meet Robert. They meet in a guarded but friendly way. Robert suggests that Bear join them. All three of them get together and, after some initial fearfulness, it's okay.

I need to see Bob. Frankie wants to come along. He agrees to stay back with Robert and Bear and let Bob be the center of attention. Bob is in Little Honey's arms. He's emaciated and semiconscious, but he nods that there is more memory. . . . My burnt ass hurts terribly. I'm lying in my room after the assault, terrified they're coming back for me. Powerful startle responses jar me from sleep at every little noise. . . . My ass is too sore to wipe. I splash water on it and try to pat it with damp paper. . . . I stay in my room, unwilling to go downstairs. I'm hungry. I don't know how long it's been since I had food. I come downstairs shaking and trying not to look at anyone. I eat alone at the kitchen table. I need to use two hands to drink milk without spilling it. Mom is working in the kitchen. No talk. I go out and sit in the porch swing. My tremendous urge to run away wars with my fear of what would happen if I were caught. Bob, with great relief, disappears inside and Robert emerges.

Frankie wants desperately to get close to Bob, but I remind him of his promise to stay back. Finally Bob says to let him come. It's an emotional reunion. Frankie really needs to feel the forgiveness that Bob offers. The old platitude that bullies operate from a basis of fear seems to be true for Frankie. He was a bully, and now that this mask is off his fears are running loose. I expected Frankie to protect Bob, but now Bob is comforting Frankie.

"The mother wound is always deepest." This old saying clearly applied to me, even though what Mom had done to me physically was nothing like Dad's vicious sadism. The mother-child bond is biologically the strongest; violating it is the greatest betrayal. Our culture doesn't think of women as sexual abusers. She was seductive and manipulative, yet it was even harder with her to escape the toxic feeling that it was all my fault.

Pia Mellody talks about two kinds of abuse—disempowering and empowering. I prefer the terms deflating and inflating. What Dad did to me was deflating abuse; he degraded me and destroyed what little power I had as a child. What Mom did to me was inflating abuse. She gave me poisonous narcissistic strokes. It made me feel like something more than I was; her lover, a powerful adult, her equal or superior. Mellody makes the point that inflating abuse is often more difficult to heal than deflating abuse. The child not only must face the pain of abuse and betrayal but must also give up the false self-esteem that rested on those early, toxic lies.

AA members refer to themselves as "just ordinary drunks." This may seem like adding insult to injury, but I think it's a crucial point that also applies to inflating abuse. People who have been hurt and shamed have a tremendous need for compensatory grandiosity, a need to believe they're special. The greater the underlying self-hate, the greater the conscious craving for grandiosity. People have killed because of this pathological feeling of uniqueness. Feeding it can be a very effective way to manipulate others. It is also a huge pitfall in therapy. It provides temporary, self-righteous euphoria but blocks long-term recovery. If you are feeding the grandiosity, you cannot confront, and thereby heal, the underlying shame and wounding. Any message from a therapist such as "you're a special client" or "you've suffered more than anyone" is sugarcoated poison.

Frankie remembers being turned on by some of the abuse. This fills him with shame, but it's old hat to the rest of us. Red feels he has completed his task of keeping Bob hidden and giving birth to him when it was safe. Grace is unhappy, shamed: We've all now seen how poisonous female sexuality can be.

Bob is withdrawn. He wants to go back to sleep, permanently. Being awake hurts too much. Everything is confusing and conflicted. He feels he is a weakness, like the places on my body where Dad would burn and then rub to control me. Nan suggests that maybe Bob can just watch the sunrise or soak in the hot tub. She suggests that we might make a safe room for him. Bob feels that this is like a family locking away an insane relative. He's very sad, but he agrees to stay where he is for now.

"THE MOTHER WOUND IS ALWAYS DEEPEST"

The next time I was at Mom's, I noticed that her extensive collection of old tools was gone. When I asked about it, she said she had sold it because she was planning to move to a retirement home. She was on a waiting list and would probably move in about a year. The home was a couple hours' drive away. Mom had relatives there: her great-niece Susan, Susan's husband Don, and their children. They had helped her find the home and planned to help move her in. Ever since Mom had let them know she had money, they been assiduously kissing her ass.

I was surprised and confused by Mom's announcement. Rationally I thought it was a good move for her to make, but I was worried about the money. I had been managing her investments for years; I knew exactly what she was worth. I'd always been told that I would inherit it all. I was sad, too, that she'd sold off the tools. I'd wanted some of them, and I was sure she knew this. I suspected that selling them was her typically indirect response to the distance I'd put between us.

I felt a lot of conflict about wanting the money and the family heirlooms. Part of me felt it was all toxic and I should reject it all. Yet if I carried this line of thinking to its logical conclusion, my own body was a legitimate object for hate. Besides, at times I felt more entitled to the inheritance than ever. After all they'd done to me, they owed me.

The next night I woke at 3:00 a.m. wondering if I was hurting myself by putting too much emphasis on the money. I didn't really need the money, but Mom's moving was tough for Bob. I felt it wasn't okay for me, at age forty-four, to still be longing for the mothering I never got as a child.

Although I knew I was not emotionally ready for it, the idea of confronting Mom again was in the back of my mind. I regretted having confronted her about Dad before my memories of her role were clear. I would not make a decision until my feelings were more stable, but her plan to move seemed to accelerate the timetable.

Frankie blows up in my face, blocking my view of the others. He's angry. He doesn't want me to see Bob. He fears that Bob is a liability, especially in dealing with Mom's money. "Somebody has to say the unpopular things," he says. We go to see Bob. He is not immediately visible. . . . Dad and Hugh have pins or hooks stuck in my flesh. I'll do anything to keep them from pulling or twisting them. This fragment symbolically confirms Frankie's fears. Having hooks in you makes you vulnerable.

Frankie thanks Bob for revealing this. I remind Frankie that the cure is to remove the hooks, not to hide them.

Over the next few days Frankie and I brainstormed the money issue. Mom had her assets in a revocable living trust, a legal arrangement that keeps an estate out of probate when the owner dies. The best solution seemed to be to get her to change it to an irrevocable trust, to give up her power to alter how the estate was to be distributed after her death. I would argue for this for two reasons: One, Susan and Don were members of a small religious group with a reputation for manipulating seniors. Two, if she did it before the end of the year, it would avoid a proposed tax increase. This deadline allowed me to push for a quick resolution.

If she refused, I could sue her for damages resulting from the abuse.

At Nan's we talked a lot about Mom and her money. Nan suggested separating the emotional issues from the financial issues and dealing with the financial ones first. This seemed like a wise strategy.

Frankie smokes a cigarette while counting money and making notes on a pad. He looks like a bookie. Bob is lying in Big Honey's lap. His eyes are intelligent and calm. He gets up, takes a few uncertain steps, and lies back down. There's a great longing for contact with Mom. It goes back much earlier than the abuse, back to something I didn't get when I was very young—being safely held close. I start crying. Bob still hopes I might get that tenderness from Mom. He wants it so badly, he's willing to ignore or minimize or forget the incest. If he can pretend that didn't happen, maybe he can get the contact he longs for. Nan: "That's understandable, but it's not a healthy desire."

Grace: shame about her genitals. She wants clothes; we get them for her at once. Q: typical homosexual fantasies, but he's also attracted to the warm, tender, nonsexual contact Bob longs for. As I reorient I ask Bob, "Please don't lose that longing, even though it has hurt you. It's important." Nan: "It's that hope and desire that lets you grow. It's what let you be with Mariah."

Mom asked me to come to her house to pick up some mementos she'd been sorting through. Most of the stuff was innocuous, but some of it was toxic: a pair of large framed photos of Dad and Hugh and blankets that had been on their bed in New York, the very blankets I'd been molested on. Most offensive: a matched pair of full-body reclining nudes of herself and Dad, painted in oil by one of his male lovers. It astounded me that she would give me those nudes. I felt glad that we never touched or hugged. I had to use all my dissociative skills to be able to be with her at all, and I still felt a vague revulsion.

The toxic stuff never came into my home. I isolated it in a corner of the garage. The boxes I did bring inside I smudged first. Smudging is the Native American practice of purifying with smoke from burning herbs, usually sage; a cleansing ritual that can have emotional value if you put your heart in it.

BREAKING THE FANTASY BONDS

Frankie is full of plans. He doesn't want to feel any emotions until the money issue is resolved. Little Honey comes running up, happy to see me but upset by the stuff Mom gave me. Bob has gone far, far away to get through the week. It takes him a while to come back. We arrange for Big Honey, Little Honey, and Q to go with him so he won't be alone. Bear and Grace will form a barrier so that he won't need to retreat so far. Frankie and Robert will be out front to deal with Mom.

In Renee Frederickson's *Repressed Memories,* she introduces the concept of "fantasy bonds": a love bond to a parent that denies reality. These bonds are often found in abused children. Children need someone to love, even if that love is an illusion. This sounded painfully accurate. H. F. Harlow and C. Mehrs (1979), and many researchers after them, have studied the effects of isolation and trauma in young monkeys. If a baby monkey is isolated for crucial portions of its infancy, it will develop lifelong behavioral problems and neurochemical changes. If these isolated baby monkeys are given a fake mother—a basket of wire mesh covered with fur—they will cling to it and suffer less damage. The ability to create a fantasy bond can help preserve sanity and emotional health.

I identified with the baby monkeys. I had endured by creating fantasy bonds to Mom. Patrick Carnes, the author of *The Betrayal Bond,* calls them trauma bonds—fantasy bonds driven by the desperation of a traumatized child. (One distressing finding in the monkey studies was that the more a mother would abuse its infant, the more the infant would cling to her.) Carnes focuses on how these patterns, which can be lifesaving for a child, are highly destructive to an adult. They are found in such situations as battered women who stay with the batterer, people who are loyal to abusive cults, and codependents who repeatedly form relationships with addicts.

Little Honey is sad, but she's okay. She wants nothing to do with Mom. To her, Mom is a gory accident that she's drawn to look at and repelled by at the same time. Robert and Grace are side by side, guarding access to Bob. Grace is wearing clothes. We put a pillow between our lower bodies so we can hug asexually. Robert is used to guard duty. Behind them, Bob is lying across Big Honey's lap. The night of horrors broke the sick, loving connection he felt for Mom. He has no desire to reestablish it; he just wants to tell Mom he remembers. He knows.

Big Honey is crying, but she's okay too. Red is running around, agitated and frantic, tearing his hair out. He wants to attack Mom but fears she's his only buffer against Dad. Nan suggests that he get mad at Mom. He attacks her with a baseball bat. He starts hitting her genitals, but he realizes they aren't evil. It's her head he needs to attack, and he does. His release of anger arouses the shame I feel over the amnesia, over having lived next door to Mom as an adult for years. I start getting down on myself for being phony in my current dealings with her. Nan: "Yes, it's phony, but is it worth it?" No course of action would be pain free. I reaffirm my decision to separate the financial and emotional issues.

Nan commented that all my process, including Frankie's wily scheming, was about separation from Mom. I hung on to that idea. It hurt to deal with her. A part of me could hardly wait until she was gone, but another part still wanted and needed a mother. Bob's neediness was raw, but it was a treasure that let me connect with good people and let me heal. I wanted to protect the neediness without isolating it.

Little Honey runs up and hugs me happily. She leads me to Bob, who's still lying in Big Honey's arms. He's bigger. He gets up and walks a little. He seems happy, out-of-it, almost blissful. Nan: "Healing from where he was must be an extraordinary feeling." Q is watching intently. There's something he wants from Bob. He seems to feel that Bob might hold a resolution for his own dilemma of having sado-masochistic homosexual urges that he can't act on. He knows his erection might upset Bob, so he keeps his distance. He's enjoying our revulsion to female genitals, but when he sees how much this hurts Grace he tries to reassure her. . . .

My disgust with female genitals and lack of sexual desire was a big issue. I'd pushed it into the background to deal with the separation issues, but I knew I'd have to face it sooner or later. I was frequently invaded by the image of Mom's cunt coming down towards my face, by the memory of her getting me to lick her while Dad fucked me. She was "one of them." She had raped me.

She had also fed and clothed me and put me through college.

Whatever she'd been years ago, she'd become a foul old bitch. God, I hated her and wished she'd die.

I talked to a lawyer and an accountant and went ahead with my plan to get Mom to make her trust irrevocable. When I explained my reasons—the religious sect and the tax advantages—Mom seemed to agree. I promptly set up the necessary appointments. I wanted to celebrate, but I didn't. A voice inside (Frankie, I thought) said, "You can't let up now. Don't celebrate until it's a done deal."

It was physically unpleasant for me to be with Mom. Nan suggested I do as much as I could by mail or phone. Unfortunately, I would need to bring her to meetings with the lawyer.

Frankie is pacing, worried. He doesn't feel supported by the insiders. He feels like an officer leading green troops who might desert or shoot him in the back. I try to reassure Frankie. I tell them that the reward of a clean separation from Mom will be worth all the effort, regardless of whether I get control of her money.

The first meeting was the Friday before Thanksgiving. Walking into the lawyer's office, Mom insisted she needed help. I let her hold my arm. It felt disgusting and hurt inside. The lawyer who was representing her raised several possible problems with irrevocable trusts, but I'd foreseen them and prepared Mom for them. At the end of the meeting the lawyer agreed to have the new trust papers ready in two weeks. Once again I had to stifle the urge to celebrate. It wasn't over.

I hoped to disrupt my usual seasonal depression by spending Thanksgiving week in a workshop at Esalen. Unfortunately, the leader, whom I'll call Mia, turned out to be a jerk. She was a brittle, condescending woman in late middle age who wore clothes appropriate to an adolescent and sported obvious plastic surgery. The first night she stated, "All people who were abused as children grow up to become abusers." This was a stupid assertion, but I let it pass. I didn't want to start the week being disagreeable. When I awoke the next morning, my first conscious thought was about her remark, and I knew I had to say something.

At the first session that morning, Mia repeated her dictum. I spoke up and said that it was both wrong and highly offensive. I'd been abused as a child and had not become an abuser. She rejoined that if one didn't abuse others, one abused oneself. She asked me if I had ever done anything self-abusive. The conflict became loud and acrimonious. I pointed out how her statement would silence abuse survivors, and how convenient it was for therapists who couldn't handle the issue. Several people became angry at me for daring to disagree with our leader. One woman supported me by telling Mia how labeling, shaming, and blaming her statement was. Nothing was resolved.

I didn't go to the afternoon meeting. I soaked in the hot tubs and thought about leaving. Several people privately expressed support to me that they'd been unwilling to offer in the group. I decided to stay. I liked the people in the group, and I liked Esalen. I did most of the exercises and interacted with the other people, but I ignored Mia as much as possible. I felt accepted by the group and formed close connections with several people.

Mia had been giving workshops at Esalen since the 1960s and favored the sort of invasive encounter-group exercises that were de rigueur then. Toward the end of the workshop, she had us do an exercise she called "the sinking boat." She divided us into groups of ten. She told us we were on a sinking boat and the lifeboat had only room for six. We were to take turns playing the role of captain and tell the others who we'd take and who we'd leave to die. Mia encouraged us to base this decision on emotional connection. She insisted that the rejected people were actually being given a gift because they were being told why they weren't wanted.

I regretfully admit that I participated in this nasty exercise. I blunted my rejections of people by making it clear that they were based solely on their likelihood of survival, but I still felt bad about participating. Only one person had the courage to refuse to play.

The next day in group I told Mia that I thought the exercise was mean and unnecessary. I mentioned M. Scott Peck's description of evil—intentionally inflicting unnecessary pain—and said I regretted having been a part of it. Most of the group liked the exercise, but several felt the way I did.

As I drove home I felt good that I'd connected with the people and enjoyed Thanksgiving despite Mia. I also realized with a shudder how much damage she could have done to me at an earlier, more vulnerable time in my healing.

Little Honey comes up slowly with one arm bandaged and in a sling. The injury is from letting Mom touch me when we walked into the lawyer's office. Little Honey and I hug a lot. At her request, I smudge her arm. Bear is grinning: The tie between me and the insiders was tested at Esalen and proved strong. Bob is sitting in Big Honey's lap with both hands over his face. He feels like he is waking from a nightmare. He sees Mom as a slimy, poisonous monster and fears being contaminated by contact with her.

Q is tired and subdued, but he still has an erection. Images of Mom's cunt over his face fill him with disgust and anger. He still thinks passive homosexuality is best: it's like neither Mom nor Dad. Grace is wearing plain pants and a shirt. Frankie looks ill, dirty, tired, and busy. Dealing with Mom is hard, and he's doing most of it. Nan suggests that I hire someone to deliver the legal papers to her. Frankie and I feel shamed and angered by the implication that we're inappropriately being her gofer. Frankie is obsessed with finishing the task he set for himself.

It's hard to make a decision and reconcile all the parts without hurting anyone.

The lawyer didn't have the documents ready on the date he promised. This set off my fears. We'd have to get the paperwork, review and revise it, have him prepare final copies, and then go in and sign off. All of this had to be finished before New Year's Day, and all of it required that I interact with Mom.

Nan and I talked about whether or not I should get Mom a Christmas present. Would it be an act of self-betrayal? Does one owe self-revealing honesty to the dishonest? I checked with the insiders and confirmed that they wouldn't be hurt if I got her a token gift. I found the perfect present: a primitive Indonesian statue of a deformed, ugly woman grasping a child with oversized, clawlike hands.

ANOTHER CHRISTMAS WITH THE INSIDERS

Little Honey is damp, shivering, and wrapped in a blanket. We dry her and get her fresh clothes. Bob is feeling better, and Q approaches him. Q asks Bob what kind of sex he likes and if he can see Bob's genitals. Bob tells Q he doesn't know what his sexuality is and declines to show his genitals. Nan asks if they could have a nonsexual friendship. Q feels shamed; he doesn't know what he is when he's not sexual. Bob asks him if it hurts to have a constant erection. Q gives an odd answer: What hurts is not being able to act out his sexuality, but he's no longer sure he wants to.

Frankie is upset by the delays. He feels stuck, powerless. Bob dislikes dealing with Mom but realizes the necessity of separation work. It's like scraping shit off your shoe. Bob thinks of the future. He wants to be with new, loving people.

Grace is fully clothed. She lets loose a bunch of memories. Mom has a vibrator-dildo. She takes my cock in her mouth while she fucks me with the dildo until I come. Extreme arousal. I love it. It makes me feel like a woman, passive and receptive. Mom knew I liked it and would bargain for other sex acts. Sometimes she seemed like a different person, totally crazed with sex. . . .

The lawyer finally had the papers ready the Friday before Christmas. I photocopied the documents and delivered copies to Mom. We both reviewed them over the weekend and generated a list of revisions. On Monday I went over them with the lawyer and an accountant. I had the paranoid suspicion that the lawyer was putting loopholes in the agreement, but it did look as though we'd get it done on time.

For the first time in months, I was feeling sexual arousal in my conscious life. It was unpleasant, and I'd jack off to make it go away. The last session with Nan had set off a new round of shame. It made me realize how overwhelmingly stimulating Mom's dildo-blow jobs were. She was good at it and I liked it.

Little Honey says she's okay, but there are tears in her eyes. Grace: more memories of Mom's vibrating dildo. She rubs it under my balls and around my ass. She sucks and licks me and then sticks it in a little. When I'm really excited she shoves it all the way up my ass. Extreme arousal. Tremendous shame at the memory of waiting, cheeks spread wide, wanting her to stimulate my asshole. This hyperarousal is the message behind Grace's long-time posture of exposing her swollen genitals. She feels the desire and the shame with equal intensity. Unexpected and ironic that Mom's abuse made me feel female and receptive. She achieved a more subtle, more complete form of control than Dad did.

Grace crumbles in tears, overwhelmed by shame. Big Honey and Bear help her. Big Honey and Q feel anger at Mom, but we know we aren't going to express it to her until the legal arrangements are finalized. Frankie winces at Grace's pain, but he feels proud to be handling the legal hassles.

I talked to the lawyer again two days before Christmas. We'd gotten the revised copies, and they were okay. All that remained was to take Mom to his office on two successive days to have her signature notarized. It was almost unstoppable.

I dreamed that I was directing a construction clean-up crew at my boyhood home. The place was starting to look good.

Little Honey is afraid. She wants Christmas to be over. Vague memories of being awakened on Christmas Eve: "If you want presents tomorrow, you're going to earn them tonight." It seems this was a regular part of Christmas. Grace is sad, full of shame because she liked Mom's dildo-blow jobs so much. The pleasure and desire she experienced makes her feel disgusting, rotten to the core.

Bob is sad. Memories of young Bobby being tied by the feet and raped by Dad and Hugh on Christmas Eve. My face bangs into the bedposts. Very lonely afterward. Total isolation. I had a black eye Christmas morning. Mom ignored it. She must have known. The sad, eerie, timeless feeling comes up. . . .

Christmas morning I was awake before five o'clock. I lay in bed trancing out and checking with the insiders. I comforted Bobby. He no longer felt alone or isolated.

Linda and I had a pleasant breakfast and exchanged presents. Then for the first time in a long time we made love. It was warm and good.

The following Monday I took Mom to the lawyer's for the first round of signing. The bitch took my hand as she got out of the truck, but Frankie handled everything well. Mom signed the trust revisions. The revocation was to be signed and dated the next day.

On the way home Mom asked about one of our dogs. She was in heat, and we planned to breed her. I told Mom we planned to trade one of the pups for a male breeding mate, "because you can't let her breed with her son." Part of me clearly enjoyed making that remark, but I felt a flash of anger at Mom's response: "Yes," she said, "it's considered wrong." When I got home I smudged myself and my truck.

The next morning before therapy I took Mom back to the lawyer's to sign the document making the trust irrevocable. As we left the office she said, "Now I don't have any money." It was a victimish exaggeration, but she understood that she had no more significant financial power.

Little Honey is sad. She wants to hide. Frankie is strutting, smoking a cigar. He wants to celebrate. He calls Little Honey a party pooper, but deep down he's sad too. He tries clumsily to comfort her. Bobby appears: a succession of images of being raped and crying. Of all of the insiders, Bobby had to hide the deepest to deal with Mom. Bob, his older counterpart, is with him, and so is Big Honey. Her anger is tempered with joy: We've gotten Mom to give up her power, a good strategy in dealing with an enemy before you attack. Big Honey wants to destroy all emotional connections to Mom now as a prelude to confronting her. She wants to hammer Mom and burn her out of my heart. Her plans and anger scare Little Honey. Mom provided the closest thing to safety I knew as a child. Big Honey agrees to take no action.

I wanted to celebrate, but I didn't. New Year's Eve brought on its usual bad feelings. I had nightmares that reflected Little Honey's fears. Big Honey did not want to hurt or scare her, but she knew the separation was necessary. There might have been loving connections early, but Mom had turned them into ropes as cruel as the ones Dad tied me down with. They needed to be destroyed.

Lola was deteriorating. I loved that old dog so much. She was leaking pee and unable to straighten her hind legs. It was heartbreaking to see her struggling to walk. The vet gave me a supply of painkillers and hormones. He offered to come out to our home if she needed to be put down. On the way home I held Lola next to me and cried.

Big Honey dances in a circle, Native American fashion, swinging her hammer like a tomahawk. The ropes must be cut. The bloody mortal anger must be expressed. Little Honey is wrapped in a blanket that looks like a teepee. Many strands of yarn are attached to her. She's cutting them off with scissors. There's a long, thick umbilical cord attached to her stomach that she doesn't touch. Am I using my sadness about Lola's condition to process the emotions about Mom?

Big Honey wanted to chop free from Mom, Bobby felt threatened by the idea, and Little Honey was ambiguous. Grace longed for passive sex, Q longed for kinky, masochistic sex; Red blocked the kinds of sex that Q wanted, and Bob saw any arousal as reiterative and shameful. Red gratified himself through eating, drinking, and getting high, while Bob saw such self-indulgence as an obstacle to healing. Frankie was a great help in dealing with the world, but he had little sympathy or patience with the more vulnerable parts. They all wanted things their way, and Robert feared we'd fly apart if he didn't keep them all controlled.

Little Honey is in her teepee. She blinks back her tears so that she can see well enough to continue cutting the strands. Eventually she comes out and lets me hold her. We cry together.
Frankie wishes it was over. He is crying. He's afraid of being out of control emotionally. Q and Grace are sad, hiding their sexuality. It seems so out of place.
Little Honey starts sending out her cut-off strings to attach to the other insiders. Bob holds her for a while. Big Honey takes her out to the killing field.
Little Honey agrees that it's time. She holds out the umbilical cord attached to her stomach. Big Honey chops it off with her hatchet. She stays behind to burn the cut-off part, while Little Honey returns to the others.

In my Scottish way I calculated the cost of my therapy: Nan, the master's degree, my weekend with the Watkinses; books, tapes, and periodicals; workshops and seminars, bodywork and massage. A huge investment of money and time, and I still wasn't finished.

How many abuse survivors could afford to do this? Something more than my own healing must result from the experience.

Chapter 15

Burning Mom

January-May 1993

We need a new metaphor for positive relationships. Little Honey feels pulled and held by the strings she sent out to the other insiders, and she feels guilty about needing to be free. Nan asks her to look at how the strings are attached to her body. They're tied to rings in her flesh, like the ring in a bull's nose. These are places where I can be hooked: one ring is sex, another is the need for love—we don't know what all the rings are. There is a desire to cut each ring and gently remove it, but instead Little Honey puts on a quilted coat which covers the rings. She doesn't want to work on them; she wants to play.

Q comes up with Grace behind him. He doesn't want to be dismissed as a "ring." Nan gives a little speech about how sexual desire and behavior are separate, how many different behaviors may satisfy. Q feels patronized. He gives Nan the finger.

It was finally becoming clear to me how important it was to stop the civil wars. Confronting Mom could wait. I made an agreement with the insiders to postpone any decisions about her until mid-April. I needed to focus on repairing the inner splits.

I was pissed about Nan's sermonette. It made me feel misunderstood and shamed. I hated being lectured. It felt like Nan was playing one-up games. She did not get defensive when I expressed this to her. She apologized and explained that she was trying to widen Q's possibilities for satisfaction, but at one point she slipped and called him "Hugh."

Little Honey is unhappy wearing the quilted coat. It feels like a bulletproof vest, and she doesn't like needing it. Q is near despair. He's thinking of chopping off his genitals, of suicide. He says that Nan's calling him "Hugh" shows what she really thinks. He lies down and curls up under a blanket. Little Honey goes over to comfort him. He reaches up and rips a ring out of her left side. She retreats, crying. Bear gets between them. We bandage Little Honey's wound, and she throws the ring to Q. I tell Q how important he is and how much I want him to live. Frankie tells Q about his own transformation. He wonders if something like that might help Q and Grace.

Bobby is hard to find and to focus on. He's dazed. To him Mom was like half a cracker given a starving man—pitifully inadequate, but the only nourishment available. Her denial and the sexual stuff she got him to do wasn't as bad as what Hugh and Dad did. He expected to have to pay for it later. But he agrees that Big Honey can cut away as long as no one hurts him.

Lola made a miraculous recovery. She was walking almost normally and had largely regained control of her sphincter. I felt joyful for most of a day.

Q lies in Grace's lap. He looks ill and angry. He says, "I've still got the sex images that turn you on." Passive, masochistic images; I'm afraid I might get an erection. Nan reminds me that we've identified Red as the one who blocks the sex that Q wants. We try to call him up without success. From his hidden position, Red feels he's winning the war with Q and sees no reason to change.

I didn't want war at all. I wanted Red to be open to negotiation. His life didn't look so great. He kept himself hidden; he ate and drank and got high too much. I suggested that maybe his situation could be made better and more comfortable too.

Red appears, with Robert accompanying him. . . . Image of myself jacking off into a toilet, each stroke a punch at my genitals. This is what Red wants. He's not strong enough to cut them off, so he does what he can. If he jacks off and eats and drinks and gets high, he doesn't need sex with others. For Red, sex is dangerous, especially Q's kind of sex. His erection is a bridge that links him to Dad and Hugh. Desire equals vulnerability. Compulsively pleasing women with oral sex gives him control and makes him feel safe. Red admits he's worked to prevent me from having gay sex. He can tell by notic-

ing body language if a man is interested, and he can usually discourage him with his own body language without the transaction entering consciousness. Getting me to pick unavailable or impotent partners is his triumph. As an adult, when I did have sex with a man; he numbed my body below the waist and created partial amnesias. He tells me I'm too old and fat to be sexy, and soon I'll be old enough to give it up forever. He's pleased with having chosen Linda as a mate. She hates sex too. She likes being able to avoid it and blame me.

Red starts spiraling into panic and fear: "I'll drink and get high. I'll get you grossly fat. No one will want you. I'll pick people who'll reject and humiliate you . . . " He calms down a little when I tell him repeatedly that Dad and Hugh are dead. He wants Mom dead too.

Q offers to shake hands with him, even though nothing is settled. Red agrees. I'm pleased. Red is tied by a net of ropes to an image of myself as a young child, screaming in pain. Big Honey cuts him free. I thank Red for revealing so much, and I ask him not to do anything self-destructive.

GESTALT AT ESALEN

Late in January I returned to Esalen for another week-long workshop with Mariah Gladis. On the first day, when Mariah was working with a woman who had been sexually abused, she asked all the rape and abuse survivors to come forward and offer support. Out of a group of twenty-two, three women and I went up. At first I felt self-conscious and out of place, but then I felt good.

I wanted to work on my sexual conflict but was concerned that I might be inhibited by shame. I outlined what I wanted to say and checked it out with the insiders. I boiled it down to four issues. The first issue was the self-hate that arousal brought on, carried by the image of myself as a child screaming in pain. The second was control; I did okay as a sexual pleaser, but if I wasn't in control, sex was very upsetting. The third was the vulnerability, shame, and neediness that arousal set off in me, which again led to self-hate. The fourth issue was the split. Part of me was a horny adolescent who wanted to be promiscuous, bisexual, and wild; another part hated my genitals and would do almost anything to avoid being sexual. The part that hated sex seemed to be winning.

I went back and forth between wondering if this presentation was explicit enough to be honest and wondering whether it was safe enough not to overwhelm me with shame. I didn't want to "forget" it when I was talking in front of the group; but once it was clear in my mind, I wanted to act.

I took my turn just after dinner, on the third day of the workshop. I was able to go through my four points and a very brief description of my abuse without "forgetting" or skipping too much. I neglected to say "bisexual" or "kinky," but I did say "promiscuous" and "wild."

Mariah asked me if I could function sexually. When I told her I could, she said, "You know, Bob, that is a miracle." She had me look around the room, into people's eyes, and say, "I deserve good sex." She commented that early stimulation gets wired in.

Then she arranged an exact moment of healing. She had me choose people to play myself as a child, my parents, Hugh and other abusers, a "new, good Mom and Dad," and some support people. She had the person playing the child-me recline on a mattress and had me adjust his posture until it was the way I'd slept as a child. I'd told Mariah how terrified I'd been by the sound of them coming up the stairs. She asked me what words Dad and Hugh would say. Then she had the people playing the abusers leave the room. They were going to come after Bobby. My job was to keep them off him and get him over to the new parents who were waiting at the side of the room.

The lights were turned down. The man playing Bobby started sobbing. The abusers outside the door started stamping their feet and yelling, "You little shit, you're really going to get it this time." I snapped back to my childhood terror. Dad, Hugh, Mom, and the others came in, threatening and stamping their feet, coming for Bobby. I was shaking and screaming: "No, no, stay away from him! Stay away, I'll kill you!" I grabbed Bobby's arm and began pulling him over to the good, new parents. I told him, "I know it's Mommy and Daddy, but they're evil. We've got to get away." When I'd dragged Bobby to safety I collapsed, drenched with sweat and tears, into the arms of my new parents.

Mariah put her hand on my lower back and spoke into my ear. I was too emotional to remember consciously what she said. She got me to lie face down on a mat in the middle of the room. The others gathered around. She asked all of us to visualize a golden light connecting my genitals and my heart. This felt new and good to me.

Mariah said, "If you have fantasies of being forced sexually, they can become fantasies of being forced to be loving." Why hadn't I realized this before? If I could keep that strong, clear connection between genitals and heart, sex would be okay.

I rolled over and looked up into people's faces. Most of them had been crying. Many of them hugged me when I got up. As the next person started working, I held two of the women survivors. I told myself I didn't want to pick apart or criticize what had happened. I wanted to stay focused on what was good and useful and let go of the rest.

The next day I was radiating warmth and love for everyone, and people noticed. Two things about the exercise especially stood out. The first was that moving away from my parents was scary and hard to do. I'd hoped to find safety with them despite all the viciousness and pain. The second was the idea of connecting my genitals and my heart. I hoped that the connection would let me know what sex was okay and what wasn't. If a sex act strengthened the connection, it was good for me; if it weakened it, it was bad.

In the years since the workshop, this imagery has proved its value. When I make love, some part of me is usually aware of this connection. If a specific sex act weakens the connection, I stop. Sometimes the same act will affect the connection differently on different occasions. I follow the image. It has played a big role in letting me, finally, have a satisfying sex life.

One of the guys at the workshop told me he had molested two of his sisters as an adolescent. When one of them told their parents, he stopped, and the family never spoke of it again. As an adult he had contacted the two sisters, apologized, and offered to do whatever they wanted to deal with the issue. He answered my pointed questions. He took full responsibility. The pain and regret he expressed seemed very real. I hated sexual abusers more than anything in the world, but I didn't hate this man. He had confessed to a hanging judge, and I couldn't condemn him.

As the workshop ended I felt love for everyone in the group, largely because they had showed their woundedness, their humanity. It is so ironic that most of us struggle so hard to hide the very parts of ourselves that make us loveable. Several of the people were beginning to feel like real friends. Again, I scheduled a reunion at my house.

THE INSIDERS ARE HEALING ONE ANOTHER

As a child Bobby's need for parents was a horrible vulnerability, but now the other insiders can take care of him. Little Honey is very happy. Q seems sad. I ask him if I did something wrong at Esalen. He shakes his head. His defiant pride in his erection is what preserved my ability to function sexually. He's not sure about the idea of a connection between his genitals and his heart. He needs to try it out.

Red wants privacy from the others, so we hang a curtain. Red has split again. There's a tiny Red, about the size of an ant, and a frozen, catatonic one who stares at the ground. Tiny is good at hiding and distraction. If Dad and Hugh had ever found him, they would have enjoyed crushing him. He distracts people from seeing Frozen. It feels like an act of trust for Red to let me see this defenseless part.

For several sessions Nan and I focused on these new aspects of Red. If I was going to heal my splits, I'd have to acknowledge all of them. At first Frozen could only see and interact with Tiny; everything else was a foggy, gray blank to him, like being inside a cocoon. He was very lonely and looked to Tiny with sad, trusting, doglike love. He was sure that any show of love would bring pain to the loved one; that any show of tenderness would give "them" something to hurt. I got Tiny to tell him Dad and Hugh were dead and we were a middle-aged man now.

Grace was eventually able to communicate with Frozen. His need to retreat was mainly about Mom and sexual pleasure. He could fight against pain, but the penetrating pleasure of her blow jobs with the vibrating dildo was an irresistible seduction. The body's pleasure, its orgasmic response, was against him. It caused him to flee so far inside that he was blind to everything but Tiny. Tiny was scared that he had let Frozen be found. He'd distracted everyone for all these years and prevented certain kinds of sex that might have touched and disturbed Frozen.

Then Frozen's body began to ooze sludge—a disgusting mixture of shit, blood, mucus, and vomit that soiled the inner landscape. His mouth was full of the stuff. Little Honey was ankle deep in it. It was a symbol of Frozen's wish to die from the shame and pain of the abuse. Grace and Dream Woman led the cleanup crew. They scooped the gunk into barrels and burned it. They cleansed Frozen with warm cloths and gave him a wet towel to chew on. They burned their clothes and washed everything down with chlorine.

This process was manifested in my conscious life by a fever and sore throat. I saw a doctor and got antibiotics, but for a while I was coughing up blood.

In response to Frozen's screaming pain, Dream Woman was taking an active role for the first time. This made me cry a little. I sensed immense sadness in Frozen's memories, but I didn't feel much. I tried to list the experiences that Frozen contained: mouth trauma (from being forced to eat come, shit, vomit, lubricants), suicidal tendencies, hate for sex and the body, feeling betrayed by my body, seizure-like states, the love of getting high, and the desire to isolate and hide.

As I started getting better physically, I worked my way through more books. Bessel van der Kolk's *Psychological Trauma* was excellent. It clearly summarized the impact of trauma on human development, packing a great deal of information into a short volume. Van der Kolk makes the point that the child often bonds to the abuser because trauma causes extreme need for attachment. He compares this bonding to the "Stockholm Syndrome," the phenomenon often observed in hostage situations in which victims bond to their kidnappers, defending and helping them even after their release. (The case of Patty Hearst is a well-known example.) Nan had once commented that for me, traumatic bonding with Mom was inevitable.

"Traumatized people," Van der Kolk (1987, p. 64) writes, "have poor tolerance for psychological or physical arousal. . . . Because they respond with hyperarousal to stimuli[,] warding off anxiety. . . becomes a focal issue." This certainly sounded like my fear-or-boredom response.

Mic Hunter's two-volume work, *The Sexually Abused Male,* was at the other end of the spectrum. I contained a couple of good chapters, but most of it consisted of windy preaching about "the patriarchy." (Peg, the massage therapist, once remarked that any book on psychology or trauma that uses the word "patriarchy" more than twice is probably garbage.) Therapists ought to observe ideological as well as sexual and personal boundaries. Imposing one's cultural and political views on a client has nothing to do with healing and violates the client's independence and integrity. I was both annoyed that such stuff gets published, and disheartened at the low level of care most male survivors get.

Ken Graber's *Ghosts in the Bedroom* theorizes that two basic types of abusers exist, narcissistic and overidentified. The narcissistic abuser sees only his own needs and desires and justifies any means of satisfying them. The overidentified abuser enjoys stimulating and manipulating the victim, presenting the abuse as a gift. Sounds like Dad and Mom respectively. According to Graber, the two require different types of healing. Survivors of overidentified abuse are often overly attached to their abusers and find it difficult to individuate. In some cases they are able to separate only when the abuser dies.

I tried to check in with Frozen during my convalescence, but the curtains were drawn and Grace asked me not to disturb him. They weren't angry; they just needed quiet. When Frozen was ready he let me know three things: He and I were invalids now and needed time to recover; he hated his genitals, especially when they got hard; and he liked fresh, cool water and a clean mouth. I began taking a bottle of cold water to therapy for him.

Dream Woman goes to Frozen and gently touches him. . . . Memories of being forced to eat my own vomit, semiconscious, struggling to breathe. Dad bangs my face into the puke again and again. He holds my mouth and nose closed so that I have to swallow in order to breathe. Intense shame. Sucking their dicks clean wasn't nearly as shameful. I have a strong desire for water, but they won't give me any. The only way to clear my mouth is to swallow. . . . Nan tells me I'm doing a good job of processing this stuff, but I don't believe her.

I received a flyer announcing that the Watkinses would be doing an advanced workshop in Berkeley in May and seeing people privately afterward. When I looked at the calendar, I realized that the private sessions would fall on Mother's Day. It seemed a perfect opportunity to deal with Mom and her betrayal. I registered for the seminar and arranged with Helen and Jack for four hours of their time. They had done an excellent job of helping the Dad introject transform into Frankie. Maybe they could help resolve stuff about Mom too.

Little Honey is lonely. She gets together with Bear, Bob, and Bobby. Q is nauseous. What happened to Frozen was truly sickening; it has completely wiped out Q's sexuality, arousal, and pleasurable feelings. Robert and Big Honey are okay. Frozen looks thin and ashen, but he's able to get up and move around a little. . . . Memories of being choked unconscious with the dog collar while being fucked. The pain disappears, leaving only the panicked struggle for breath; then that too disappears into calm blackness. Coming back to consciousness brings first the awareness of movement, then pain: Dad is still fucking me. Memories of my eyes rolling up into my head or bugging out. I sort of liked being choked unconscious; it was better that way. My vision would black out and I'd lose control of my body. . . .

We leave Frozen with Dream Woman, Grace, Tiny, and (at Frozen's request) a dog: a safe object for his love. . . .

That week a friend sent me an article on how to recognize child abuse intended for emergency-room doctors. The article contained vivid photos of injuries, burns, and genital bruising. One photo showed a naked little boy with his legs spread, showing bruises around his anus from being raped. The insiders were deeply affected.

"Frozen" is no longer frozen. He comes up first and insists that his name is Bob. He's adamant. Thankfully the other Bob (who grew out of Bobby, formerly Little Red!) is willing to be called Rob instead. Bob (the ex-Frozen) has more to tell, but it's okay with him if we check with the others first. Q is still nauseous from Bob's memories, and the medical photos hurt him deeply. When Q thinks of his constant sexual arousal conjoined with the images of hurt children, he feels self-hate and despair. Nan reminds him that he preserved sexuality, but he can't deal with this or value it. Little Honey is especially hurt by the picture of the boy's bruised anus; it reminds her of her own rapes. Bobby is hiding behind Rob. The pictures are a threat to him: "This will happen to you next." We have to reassure and remind him that Dad and Hugh are dead. Robert is sad: The picture of the boy's anus was so exposed; but he feels that the world must see it, must know.

Tiny is exhausted and needs care, like a bird with a broken wing. Frankie and Big Honey seem okay.

PUTTING THE ANGER WHERE IT BELONGS

The next day when I checked inside, Bob (the ex-Frozen) was full of anger. I asked him to put his anger where it belonged. He stabbed Tiny with a knife. Dream Woman took Tiny and held him. Again I asked Bob to put the anger where it belonged. He swung his knife and this time cut Grace as she came up to try to comfort him. Luckily she wasn't badly hurt. For the third time I asked him to put his anger where it belonged—-on Dad, Hugh, and the others. Bob had only recently left his frozen state, and I told him as clearly as I could what the rules and boundaries were. I told him it was good to express emotions and okay to attack perpetrator images and memories as violently as he wished, but attacking other insiders was not okay. He appeared sad and ashamed.

That night I dreamed that I was a boxer sitting in my corner, between rounds. I'd lost the last round (the pictures and Bob's misplaced anger?). My trainers were telling me that I needed to "jab, jab, jab." I realized they were right, that I'd win that way. With consistent, undramatic, steady work, I'd win.

Meanwhile, I was worried and bothered by Bob's attacks. At Nan's, in trance, we went to him first.

Bob apologizes to Grace, with difficulty. Asking him to attack Dad and Hugh was too much. It was in effect asking him to return to where he'd been hurt. He gets a tree trunk and starts hacking and stabbing it, but it's too phallic, so he gets a flat board and attacks that. Now and then he becomes frenzied and goes into dream-like seizure states, satisfying but scary. We agree to avoid these states unless we're at Nan's. Grace accepts Bob's apology and feels safe with him again.

Tiny is on Dream Woman's breast, absorbing warmth. He needs to stay there. Q is still ill and vomiting. The sexual dilemma is gone. The part that prevented him from getting the kind of sex he wants is no longer functioning, but instead of feeling free, he's sick and in pain. Little Honey and Bear comfort him.

Bobby needs attention. He's still bothered and scared by the photos; sees them as a threat. We reassure him. . . .

Then things got scary. Little Honey came up with an image of her hand amputated at the wrist and covered with blood. Had Bob gotten more aggressive with his sword? Was it a memory? There were images of Dad and Hugh chopping babies' hands and holding babies legs in fire. There were images of them eating burned babies. Were these memories? Were they stories told to scare me? I was very scared. I didn't want a whole new level of memory, but I didn't want to abandon anyone or repress anything. There were also images of Little Honey's hand being held in a fire and on a very hot piece of metal. The message seemed to be from Dad: "If you won't touch my dick, you'll touch this."

I was shaken. I hadn't expected trauma from Little Honey, and I'd hoped, as I had so many times before, that the memory work was essentially over. I reminded myself that hiding from memories would bring on another big depression. I didn't know if I could handle more memories, but I knew they wouldn't be complete until the insiders said they were.

I checked with Little Honey between therapy sessions. I held her gently and told her I wanted to know her truth, no matter how horrible it was. Bear was there too, helping her. Her arm still looked like a bloody stump, and I was afraid.

Little Honey's arm is bandaged. Has it been amputated? Q is depressed and wants only to get high. Rob protects Bobby. Big Honey is depressed. Tiny clings to Dream Woman. He is conscious but responds only with grunts or shrugs. Robert is scared. Frankie flies high above the others. Bob cycles between chopping and stabbing angrily at the board and feeling horrible, queasy self-doubt: "Am I okay? Did I hurt Little Honey?" Grace assures him that he didn't, but Bob doesn't remember clearly. He knows that his rage is global and unfocused. Little Honey feels that she and Bob can't exist in the same universe, an innocent playful child and a survivor of rape and torture.

It took several sessions for Little Honey's memory to become coherent; she felt exposed. I encouraged myself and promised to try to stay with the memory no matter how scary it got. I had been through this before.

Little Honey cuddles in my arms in fetal position, hiding her face. I focus on Little Honey and her hand and ask Dream Woman to help. . . . An oil-burning furnace, a huge masonry thing with a metal door on the front. The basement in New York City. The furnace door is open. I see flames. Dad holds me in the air and pushes me headfirst toward the open door. Little Honey puts out her hands to save herself; one palm makes contact with the metal frame of the furnace door and is burned badly. . . . Now Dad is fucking me and I can't stay on my hands and knees because my hand hurts too much. A blister pops open, oozing goo. . . .

Overwhelmed by fear, Little Honey left the only way she could: by fleeing inside. She didn't even look back; didn't know whom she left behind. It was Bob. We comfort Little Honey and switch our attention to Bob. . . . A dark, limited vision of coming into consciousness with hand hurting, ass hurting, Dad fucking me. Pain, but no fear. The fear went with Little Honey. Bob struggles, and Dad hits him on the back of the head and holds him down. When the rape is over, Dad takes Bob upstairs and bandages his hand while scolding him for burning himself.

Little Honey feels terribly guilty for running away. She goes to the place where Bob keeps the board he chops at. She puts her hand on the board, hoping that Bob will chop it off. She wants to make amends. Bob pushes her hand away and tells her, "You can start by keeping your hand off my board." Bob is angry at Dad, not her, but the anger is terrifying.

We remind Little Honey of how much she has preserved—the child-like joy and ability to love. Nan: "Little Honey has often been the only positive thing sustaining you through healing." Her splitting off allowed me to live as a child. Looking back would have killed her. This was her birth as a separate being. Intense fear was her midwife. . . .

I felt much better after that session, and I continued to feel better as the week progressed. Much of the fearful uncertainty was resolved, and Bob had acted with unexpected wisdom and understanding. I thanked Little Honey. I validated her fear and reminded her where the guilt belonged: "I know it hurt you to run away and not look back. I know you feel bad because of it, but it may well have saved our life." I also thanked Bob for his mature understanding. Some fear still existed that major new memories could surface, but it wasn't as strong as before. These memories were new only because they were Bob's. They were memories of being raped and beaten, of cold, sullen anger that he couldn't express. Nan encouraged him to let it out now, and as the other parts had done, he attacked Dad. He used his sword to cut off Dad's genitals and chop them up. Then he pushed his sword through Dad's heart. He wanted to kill him quickly; being a torturer was too much like Dad.

I ask Dream Woman if there is more memory. She scoffs at my poorly worded question: only precise, concrete questions can have meaningful answers. I can't formulate precise, concrete questions. What I want is more memory, no matter how scary or hurtful it may be. I want the wound to be completely clean so that it can heal. I don't want to leave any insiders to suffer alone. . . .

I continued to feel stronger.

TRUSTING THE PROCESS

Little Honey's hand seems to be healing. Big Honey is with her, angry that Dad got to Little Honey, sad about Little Honey's guilt and self-hate. Bob: memories of being raped, feeling numb, dark, and cold. Limbless. I got so numb that I lost control of my extremities. Only the vaguest sensation of movement. This numbed-out state seems to be a separate part that's been hidden behind Bob, perhaps related to his frozen state. A lump that just stayed put. "Waxy" is his name. ("Waxy immobility" or "waxy catalepsy" are names given to the condition of certain mental patients who become immobile but whose bodies will remain in any position they are put into.) *Bob recognizes Waxy as part of himself. It was dark; he was almost blind. It was silent; he was almost deaf. Sometimes, when he thought they wouldn't notice, he'd shift a little to a less-painful position. Sometimes the numbness failed—when confronted by surprise, choking, the pliers, intense pain—and we'd descend into screaming and struggling.*

We put Waxy in a hot bath, but he's afraid that if he warms up, pain will come flooding in. We remind him, "That was then, now is now. Dad and Hugh are dead. . . ."

Although at the time I was just staying with the process, later I realized that these new insiders, Bob ("Frozen") and Waxy, represented yet another turn of the spiral of healing. Their memories had already been expressed through Young One, Q, Red, and Bobby; but now we were dealing with a level of experience that was somatic, preverbal, nonnarrative, and more fully associated.

Dream Woman tells me that my request was better than my vague question. She tells me I haven't yet learned to get out of the way: "All the major breakthroughs have been unexpected surprises. Haven't they?" She's right.

It was the week of my birthday; I was accordingly depressed and fearful.

In a month I'd be seeing the Watkinses again. I wrote them a letter summarizing the aftereffects of our last session and the course of my therapy since then. I described the changes in my internal landscape and the new insiders. I told them about my relationship with my mother. I gave hard thought to the chronology of the abuse. It now seemed that Dad and his friends tapered off abusing me around age eight, when Mom took over. Her abuse apparently ended after the sadistic orgy of the night of horrors. I described to Jack and Helen my emotions in facing the truth of her abuse and in effecting separation from her. I told them that what I needed from them was help in getting as much resolution as possible regarding Mom, especially the internal Mom. I asked about confronting her but emphasized that this was less important.

Waxy's face is bent, twisted in pain. Memories of being raped: He's afraid that if he regains sensation he'll try to hit Dad, and then he'll really be hurt. Dream Woman soothes him, putting her hand on his forehead. She bathes Waxy and wraps him in soft flannel sheets.

Bob looks like a samurai, swinging his sword so fast that it's invisible. He slices up an image of Dad with little emotion. Now he throws down his sword like Musashi, the great Japanese warrior who put down his swords at the height of his prowess and became a monk. Little Honey's hand is still bandaged. She hugs me and then goes to Waxy and hugs him. I have the idea that Waxy's suffering was not purposeless; it saved Little Honey.

Grace feels a little abandoned because Bob no longer needs her. Q is still depressed. . . .

My birthday came and went. Linda commented that instead of sinking into a month-long depression as I usually did, I'd been okay until the day came. Then I fell into depression suddenly. It felt worse, because the contrast was so great. I thanked Linda for leaving me alone and not taking it personally. I needed to isolate to prevent my taking it out on her.

Our sex life was still almost nonexistent. It seemed that Mariah's
effort to help me heal my sexuality had failed. Partly, I blamed myself
and Linda, but mostly I blamed Mom. It was mid-April, the deadline
I'd given myself for deciding what to do about emotional separation,
and I was no closer to a decision.

While sitting in Nan's waiting room before my next appointment, I
went into a light trance. Dream Woman appeared. She reminded me
that I shouldn't set an agenda for the upcoming session; I should just
let it happen.

*I start off with Little Honey, but then I ask Dream Woman to take
over. . . . Image of Mom's big, sloppy cunt descending toward my
face; then the sensation of Dad fucking me. Partners. . . . I have to
confront her; I'm chicken if I don't. Dream Woman: "Yes, you need
to." Dream Woman mocks me: Big, tough man; can't even talk to an
old woman. All those images of hacking up Dad, and I won't even
confront Mom.*

*I am afraid of confrontation. It might give Mom power. Little
Honey is afraid: She wants a good mother; this makes her vulnerable.
Bob: "Confront." Robert: "Yes." Bobby, panicked: "No." Contact
with Mom is his only alternative to isolation. Waxy: "A calm, mini-
mal confrontation won't satisfy the anger and pain." He doesn't want
to talk to Mom; he wants to beat her to death.*

Nan, as I knew she would, declined to advise me one way or the
other. Confrontation might be a useless exercise, she said, but it might
also stop me from feeling like a coward.

Shame was the emotion I was grappling with: shame about the amnesia, shame about the caretaking and the traumatic bonding; but at
the core of the shame were the things I'd let her do for me. I felt like
someone paid to keep quiet.

I thought again about Harlow's monkey experiments. The delusion
of parenting had helped me, just as it helped the monkeys. Mom was a
fur-covered wire mesh; she gave me just enough to let me pretend I
had a loving parent. If I, or the monkeys, had known what we were really clinging to, it would have been devastating.

I was forty-five years old now; I ought to be able to handle it.

Little Honey is preoccupied, playing with her hand. She's afraid of Waxy and his anger, and she's afraid of confronting Mom. She wants Mom to die so she won't have to deal with her. Waxy no longer wants to come out. He wants to stay numb; to eat, drink, and get high. No sex. No reason to change. . . . Memory of being fucked, so numb I could barely feel it. This brings a smile of triumph to Waxy. It seems that the other side of his immobility was frenetic hyperactivity and tantrums. Another memory: being impaled on Dad's cock and holding still, scared, alert to any movement. Very intimate in a horrible way: I was "at his mercy," but he had no mercy. He could rip my asshole apart, make it burst. . . . Waxy goes suddenly from hyperalert to numb. He feels shame at the horrible intimacy, the helplessness. The others could leave, but he was trapped.

Bob is chopping angrily with his sword. He quickly becomes dismayed with the uselessness of it all. We let him attack Dad and hack him to bits. This scares Waxy because it blurs the boundary between then and now: If Bob can attack Dad, then maybe Dad is somehow alive. We reassure Waxy. He wants a safe place to hide. We put him a box-like room with only one entry; a nest. Little Honey, Bob, and Grace guard the door. As I reorient, Dream Woman says, "The only thing of value your mom can give you is the truth."

I was avoiding Mom. Some relatives from out of town dropped in to visit her. She invited me over, but I didn't go. The next day she called me with some phony questions about yard work. She was really calling to find out why I didn't come down. At first I was annoyed to hear her voice, but then I surprised myself by feeling sorry for her. I had the wishful fantasy that she really wanted to talk but couldn't bring herself to do it.

Little Honey comes up lovingly and leads me to Waxy. He lets me know that when I masturbate and rub my ass it feels like rape to him, and he shows up and numbs out. The harder I masturbate to get sensation, the number he gets. When I scratch my ass I'm actually clawing for sensation, and he responds with increased numbness and sadness.

I promise Waxy I'll be gentle. He wants heat down in my crotch and ass—hot tubs, baths, hot compresses. There is soft, itchy, painful, needy tissue under a wooden veneer. It needs to be soothed and healed. I get him to imagine a white room with skylights, a bed, blankets, and stuffed animals. He fears that Dad will use his desire for cleanliness and softness to hurt him again, but he goes to sleep in the clean room.

Little Honey is crying from happiness, and so am I. Nan asks me how I'm doing, and I almost make a joke. So often I've used humor to distract myself from difficult emotions. I tell her, "I don't want to discount my feelings, this is a hard-won moment."

It was a moment of healing—the sweetness, the clearness, and the light. I (Waxy) had the courage to come out of hiding and enjoy warmth and safety. Nan and I both cried softly, tears of joy and sorrow. This was the product of years of work.

Sensation returned to my ass and groin. It felt good to Little Honey, even though she felt threatened by it. She danced around, giggling and shaking her butt. For Waxy, the sensation was scary; the rapes happened only yesterday. Stretching the chronically cramped muscles around my anus triggered fear and terror, yet the relaxation felt so good. Grace was able to be with Waxy and turn his fear to tears and sadness. Until then my fear had always turned to anger. Nan said that because I was aware of my fears now, I could let new experiences interact with them and temper them.

LETTING MOM DIE

My Mother's Day session with the Watkinses was coming up. Two days afterward was Mom's eightieth birthday. I wrote her more unsent letters in which I expressed my rage and hate and my conflicting need and dependency. She was like a pebble in a wound. It was painful dealing with her and painful avoiding her.

In their workshop the Watkinses restated their position that confronting abusive parents in the external world was unnecessary and often harmful. Confronting them inside and finishing the work inside was what was important. When I met with Jack and Helen privately that Sunday, I knew what their basic approach would be.

They did no induction. They talked to me very briefly, then asked me to lie back in my chair and go into trance.

They talk about the need to let the internal Mom die: "See her on her deathbed and tell her everything you need to before she dies." . . . She's in a hospital bed, intravenous needles in her arms. I fill with anger and smash at her with a stick and a hammer, but I'm crying as I do it. "Hold me, Mommy. Let me cling to you. Please, if not that, then just let me be in the same room with you. I'll even take care of you." It's need, not love. The alternative is terror—stark, unrelieved, crazy-making terror. Shame and guilt: I've compromised myself and lost honor just by being with her.

Now back to anger: "You bitch. You betrayed me. You used me to masturbate with." That's what it was, masturbation. She used the effects of Dad's torture training and the first flowering of my adolescent sexuality to pleasure herself. . . . She leads me into her bedroom at Lake George. I feel torn between needing a mother and not wanting to go in. When the sex starts, all conflict ends. This is how I became a sexual pleaser.

Jack pushes me: "Get out all the feelings. Tell her how you feel." Anger and hate boil up, then guilt. I should have left, but I would have been alone in terror, waiting for Dad's attacks. She complains about how mean Dad can be. With anger I realize that this is simultaneously a "poor me" victim stance and an implicit threat of more torture from Dad. Sometimes I got away from her, but I always came back because I couldn't find anyplace to go. It would have been cleaner and more honorable if I'd died.

Again Jack pushes me to empty out all the emotions in turn: hate, need, love, fear, sexuality, disgust, longing, shame, hope. "You bitch! You were disgusting, not me. Healthy penises get hard when sucked and rubbed. Healthy mothers don't do that to their sons. Vaginas aren't disgusting. You're disgusting. . . ."

Before we let Mom die, Helen asks if any insiders will take care of young Bobby. Rob and Grace come forward. We can't use the words "mother" or "mothering," but they care for him with love. Bobby's needs are healthy; trying to get Mom to fill them is not healthy. I will have to feel each of the conflicting emotions individually, sequentially, to the point of exhaustion before we let Mom die inside. They have been pulling against each other like a tangled knot and holding me immobile, but now I can move through them one at a time.

When it is done I smash and burn Mom, pushing her back into the fire. As the flames engulf her body she winks at me lasciviously and beckons like Ahab lashed to the whale.

We go back to her bedroom at Lake George. We clean the room, taking out all her stuff to burn in a bonfire. We paint the room white. It is still not okay to stay there. The insiders imagine getting ready to get in a car and drive to California. Bobby doesn't understand where we're going, but he trusts Rob and Grace and is happy to go. His innocent trust sets off an intense wave of emotion and tears from Rob: "By God, I'll take care of you." There is difficulty leaving, as there is so much stuff to be burned. . . .

The trance lasted over three hours. When I reoriented I was dizzy and had trouble remembering what day it was. Jack emphasized how the pull of conflicting emotions had kept me stuck, and how important it was to separate each emotion so that it could be fully felt and released. He said that if and when I needed to, I could go back and do it again.

We talked a little about how I should treat the external Mom. It occurred to me that I would have to deal with her with the same impartiality and responsibility I would need if I were taking care of a ward assigned to me by a court. Anything less and I would feel like an abuser.

A lot happened for me in that session. Bobby's trusting innocence caused Rob's wave of sadness and intense commitment. My disgust was more clearly focused on Mom and didn't spill over to my erection or to other women's vaginas. I had killed and buried Mom inside. I had separated the tangled emotions from one another and felt them all. I had ended all hope for getting anything emotional from Mom. I had acknowledged that all her gifts had hooks attached. I knew that I could now treat her like a ward of the court. The Watkinses had repeated a lot of the messages I had heard before from Nan and read in books: not my fault; healthy bodies respond; no real choice; okay to be angry at your mother, to hate your mother. It was good to hear these messages from people who were so different: older, traditional, and Midwestern.

The next day I was still somewhat disoriented. When I checked inside, Bobby wanted to go back and be sure all the garbage was burned. I reminded him that when he felt needy, Rob and Grace would be there. He could get real love from them and safely place his hopes with them. I also reminded him that his need for love and his desire to be held were entirely good. Mom and Dad had misused those needs, but Rob and Grace would do right.

May 11 was Mom's eightieth birthday. I felt some guilt about not calling her, but I didn't want to, and I didn't. At Nan's that day we honored Bobby's request and began preparing her pyre.

All the insiders start gathering around the pile of garbage that remains to be burned. We put Mom's ashes on the pile. There's a sense of loss and grief. I hope that each insider will find something to throw on the pyre before we burn it. I hope it will help cleanse and free me from connections to Mom and to the past.

Had I felt and expressed all my emotions about Mom to the point of exhaustion? Had each insider done this? I made a list of all the insiders—even the transient, ephemeral ones—to make sure none was forgotten. I invited them all, named and unnamed, to feel and express all their feelings about Mom and to throw something on the pyre. I told them we didn't need to complete the process in one session. We could take all the time we needed.

THE PYRE

The ceremony was played out over eight sessions at Nan's.

Big Honey is in charge. We're in the field where she burned Dad's remains. The garbage is piled high, and the insiders form a circle around it. There are feelings of getting ready to say good-bye, saying everything that needs to be said, accepting and facing the loss, abandoning all hope for Mom, abandoning care for her as something that gives purpose or meaning.

Little Honey goes first. She comes up dragging a doll. I hold her for a while before she starts. She has felt caught: Her need for comfort and contact, as when Mom would bandage the burns and cuts from Dad's abuse, stifled her expression of anger. I needed the care. Need for Mom. Hate for Mom. Mom masquerading as a victim. A pathetic disguise concealing a hidden, terrified, devious, greedy bitch without boundaries or scruples. Sex was a horrible parody of what Little Honey wanted and needed—closeness, touch, and intimacy. For Mom, it was just one more step down the ladder.

The hate makes Little Honey want to smack Mom with a hammer, but she is not willing to take any joy in another's pain; it would make me like an abuser. She holds a dagger over Mom's heart, ready to lean on it and drive it home. Fear: Attacking Mom will leave me alone to face Dad's next assault. We ask Little Honey if she can transfer her hopes from Mom to others—the insiders and people in the external world. She nods yes. She leans on the knife and sinks it all the way through Mom's heart into the ground below. She throws her doll onto the pyre. The doll had once meant a lot to her, but it was incapable of returning emotion. Like Mom.

Little Honey returns to the circle, and Bear comes out. He feels released. He's been angry at Mom for decades but has held his anger because Little Honey needed her. Now he can attack. He stalks her, intent and silent. He rakes her with his claws, disemboweling her. He shakes her like a dog shakes a rat. This is how a mother bear protects her young: with power and fervor, even driving off larger males. Bear rips off Mom's head to make sure she's dead. He begins washing his bloody paws and mouth. Little Honey comes out and helps groom her longtime protector, supporting his rage. They throw the dirty water on the pyre and return to the circle, where they smudge each other.

The dog runs out, lifts his leg, and pees on the garbage. No animal would torture its young. He puts back his head and howls. The sound is echoed by the surrounding hills. He returns to the circle and is smudged.

Now it's Robert's turn. His arms are crossed over his chest, and a knife is sticking in his heart. Mom's wound was deeper and more vital than Dad's. It caused Robert to cut himself off from his own heart, from the child inside who is reaching out for love. He pulls the knife from his chest. He will no longer cut himself off. He cries for the wound he inflicted on himself and for the needy, loving child. He yells and screams. The dog howls with him. When he's done he rejoins the circle and is smudged.

All the insiders join hands for a while and then break up, hugging and talking. Robert shows his wound. He's cold and implacable. Little Honey is bigger, more mature. Bear feels relief at having released his long-held anger.

Q wants to go next, but he doesn't know what to do. On the surface he feels Dad's scornful contempt for Mom, but underneath is a secretive connection that shames him. "Mommy's boy." I try to tell him that his need for contact is good. I try to get him to turn it toward one of the other insiders, but his constant state of sexual arousal makes this difficult. He spits at Mom. She reaches out pleadingly. She starts touching him, caressing his erection. She sucks him. It feels good. Conflict. Q pushes her away with sticks, poking them in her eyes. He smashes her face with a sledgehammer. He wants to cleanse himself of her; she is sticky poison. She's still twitching. He ties her to the pile. He washes his genitals, throws the water on the pyre, and returns to the circle to be smudged.

Take all the time you need, Q. Don't quit until you can safely and confidently turn your back on her. What you did in preserving my sexuality was a miraculous achievement. My erection isn't disgusting. Vaginas aren't disgusting. What Mom did was disgusting and a great betrayal.

Waxy is next. He senses the solemnity, but he doesn't know Mom. He asks, almost incredulously, "You mean someone could have helped and didn't?" The others nod. Waxy throws a rose onto the pile, symbolizing what should have been.

Grace: vivid close-up images of swollen female genitals. She feels that she's doing what Mom should have done—nurturing, protecting, caretaking. She washes her genitals and ass and throws the water on the pyre. "My genitals are fresh and clean. You were slimy and disgusting and repulsive. Take back what's yours." She smudges, dresses, and rejoins the circle.

Now Bob. He is angry, but he can't fight this battle as a warrior. Sniveling, whimpering cowards cannot be cleanly attacked. He walks around between the pile and the insiders' circle, cutting the insidious cords, the spider's web of sticky connections. He wipes his sword repeatedly. He's attached by a net to a ball of rotting putrescence. He cuts it free and puts it in the pile: It's not healthy to maintain a connection just because of what it should have been. He turns his back on them and faces the others for his new connection. No fear. He washes, smudges, and rejoins the circle.

Q still has more to do. He feels complicity, a guilty bond with Mom; attempts to kill her are also attempts to kill him. Q got guilty pleasure from fucking Mom roughly and enjoying the power. It made him feel like "one of them." Mom got her hooks into him and dragged him deeper into the slime than Dad and Hugh had. A very sad memory: looking down at my dick still wet and glistening from fucking her; sad that I was hooked into being active, angry, and abusive. Q wants to apologize, even though Mom wanted it. Big Honey consoles him.

Now Q is angry enough to chop at the rope of guilt binding him to Mom. He removes the fishhooks from his body, cuts himself loose, and angrily faces the pile of garbage, taunting Mom to try to get him again. Q acknowledges that his sexuality doesn't feel clean or proud, but this is a separate issue. He needs to be free of the bitch before he can start to heal. He smudges and rejoins the circle.

Rob comes forward next. He tells Q that Q's anger and hate are good and clean; the sad part is that they sexualized it. In cold anger, Rob addresses Mom, "When I think of the pain you caused . . . " She tries to play the victim, pleading, reaching out. Rob rejects her whimpering. She has neither truth nor dignity. She has no concern for others. She abandoned and betrayed everything for her selfish motives.

Now Bobby. Most of his stuff was taken care of with the Watkinses. He stands up to Mom alone, even though Rob wants to be with him. She starts coming at him, pleading. Some of the others want to push her back, but Bobby takes a hatchet and buries it in her forehead. He pushes her back into the garbage and ties her there. Standing near her, he turns his back to her to test his safety. He's fine. He washes, smudges, and returns to the circle.

Dream Woman comes forward. She points at the garbage pile; holds up her palm in a "stop" gesture. She throws some bits of garbage onto the heap. Then she holds a big mirror up to Mom, propping it up so that Mom will have to see herself. This seems almost too cruel. Making Mom see herself clearly is the most devastating thing that could be done to her. Dream Woman carries no emotion. She smudges and returns to the circle.

Big Honey is next. I've been assuming she would go last. She is angry: "Your life is a lie, Mom." She is sad: "It's not what it was supposed to be." She is revolted: "Just don't come to us, don't reach out for us. Quit putting out your hooks. Quit whimpering. It doesn't work anymore." She has no desire to hurt or punish. She washes, smudges, and rejoins the circle.

Frankie comes forward and shits on the pile. In his guise as a bird, he pecks at Mom's eyeballs. He stands with his back to the pyre. Nothing there can hurt him anymore. I ask him if any part of me is hidden in the pile the way he once hid behind Dad's voice. He says no. I ask him if there's anything of value in the pile that should be saved. He

goes over and pulls out a worm: Worms and bugs can turn the gar-
bage into earth. He suggests we pour kerosene over the pile to drive
them out before we light it.

Now comes Big Red. He says he isn't real, only a projection behind
which other parts were concealed. He pisses and spits on the pile.
Mom was a shit and it was too bad.

Little Red Painholder comes up. He's angry, but his anger turns to
disgust because he can't bring himself to hit a whining, whimpering
victim. Nan reminds him of the Watkins' idea of separating the emo-
tions and feeling each one. Little Red comes back to anger. He goes
over and hits her again. He has fishhooks in his flesh that Mom tried
to use to manipulate him. He rips them out contemptuously and
throws them on the pile. The pain helps the termination. Recurring
waves of anger surface. Little Red is angry that he wasn't protected:
"You could have saved me from the torture." He beats her head with a
baseball bat. He wants to keep his anger without bonding it to Mom.
He goes to the edge of the circle and removes his clothes. He washes,
smudges, throws the clothes and dirty water on the pile, and dresses
in clean clothes.

New Man, the part that brought the message of Mom's role, is next.
He hates her cunt for sucking him in. He might have forgiven her for
not protecting him from Dad on the grounds of weakness, victimhood
and insanity, but incest was not forgivable. Was she a victim of her
own horniness? Mom displays her cunt, holding it open: "You wanted
this. You raped me." New Man is upset. He is crying. Bob and Little
Red come and stand with him. They want to kill Mom, but New Man
says no. He holds a mirror up to her. Then he puts her in a straitjacket
and shoots her in the head. . . .

I see a bridge blowing up; it's the George Washington Bridge near
my New York City home. The last fragments of the bridge crumble
into the river and are washed away.

Tiny comes up carried by Big Honey. Or is it Dream Woman? He
tells Mom, "I learned to distrust and lie from you. I got really good at
it."

The two babies wave good-bye from their place in the circle.

Robert takes a piece of his heart from his chest and throws it on the
pile. "Let the love for her die," he says. Other things are thrown on:
dolls, baseball bats.

We pour kerosene over the pile and give the bugs and worms time to flee. Then we light it. It ignites with a roar. I feel afraid, but Big Honey gets a hose and wets down the surrounding area. Kaleidoscopic images. Little Red enjoys the heat and dancing flames. New Man is sad. Big Honey gathers all the insiders to one side and tells them she will tend the fire. They may leave or stay as they wish, but the fire will burn a long time.

Postscript

It has been many years now since I started therapy. My healing did not end with the pyre ceremony. It hasn't ended yet. I continue in therapy with Nan; I continue to attend workshops with Mariah Gladis and others. I continue my bodywork and my long daily walks. I continue my research. I'm "in recovery," as the twelve-steppers say, but I'm not recovered. Nevertheless, the pyre ceremony was a major turning point, a graduation ceremony. A commencement.

A few weeks after the ceremony, Mom moved out of the house I'd rented to her for years and into a retirement home. I felt gleeful to have her gone. She left a lot of stuff in the house for me. I sorted out what I felt I could safely take. It was important to me to save anything I could from my childhood that had beauty or value. The rest I burned in a large outdoor bonfire, a pleasing reenactment of the internal ritual.

I finally did decide to confront Mom again. It was a matter of leaving no stone unturned. My basic strategy was that my best chance of getting truth from her was to make the meeting safe for both of us. The way for me to do this was to keep the focus on healing, not on anger or retribution. Nan and I arranged to have the meeting at a psychiatrist's office so that Mom would have someone there to support her, and neither Nan nor I would get sucked into caretaking her.

I carefully told Mom that the meeting was for healing. I told her again what Dad and Hugh had done, but this time I added that she had been Dad's partner. She had known what was going on; she had sexually abused me too.

She denied everything. She even claimed that the only reason she drank was because Dad forced her to. This sad outcome was what I'd expected. I told her I would continue to administer her trust fund with absolute impartiality but would not interact with her again. I said good-bye with finality, and I have not spoken to her since.

I took some time after the pyre ceremony to enjoy the feeling of accomplishment, even a little quiet celebration; but I knew that a lot of healing tasks still lay ahead. Since then therapy has been less about what was done to me and more about me. My childhood had left me with severe developmental defects. It affected my ability to give and receive love, my spirituality, my psychological boundaries, my self-esteem, my social skills and my overall emotional maturity. Relationship issues, too, remain unresolved. I have had to heal the aftereffects of the abandonment and isolation I experienced as a child. This process has led to the emergence of additional insiders.

Little Honey, Big Honey, Frankie, Q, Grace, Robert, Bob, Rob, Bobby, Dream Woman, and Bear continue to be important functioning parts of my personality. The transformation of the punitive Dad introject into Frankie has remained solid. Frankie is a valued resource, and I have never again been bothered by intrusive images of my father or by his critical voice. Young One and Red don't appear much any more. They seem at least in part to have been projections behind which other insiders were concealed. Some insiders, such as Frozen and Waxy, are inactive. They had a specialized purpose; they contained the memories of extreme pain and the bizarre psychic states it engendered.

One insider, New Man, seems unique. He is the only one that I believe was created in my adulthood. Most therapists who deal with dissociative disorders consider it a bad sign if a client continues to create new ego states or alters while in therapy. It usually indicates that primitive dissociation is still the primary functioning defense. The case of New Man is different. He was created for the special purpose of finally getting it through my thick skull that Mom was an active abuser. Having him deliver the message saved the other insiders from risk: I might have found the message so abhorrent that I would shoot the messenger. Since he delivered the message so successfully, New Man has faded away and has not reappeared.

I have accomplished a great deal of healing. All the major parts that had been encapsulated and hidden away have been released. The entrenched civil wars among the insiders have ended. I have not achieved a state of perfect harmony and probably never will; but certain basic rules of civility are observed, even during conflict. Love and mutual respect prevail inside me. I will never close the door to memories, but no significant new memories of abuse have emerged.

Messages about clinical practice are inherent in my story. What follows is an explicit summary of some of these lessons.

Dissociation is a normal and valuable process. Individuals couldn't concentrate if they were unable to dissociate from distractions. Without dissociation they would be hard pressed to move between different social roles. Many theorists, especially Ernest Hilgard (1977), think that dissociation is the mechanism behind hypnosis. There is a continuum of dissociation from normal, dissociative skills and hypnotic responses through "child within" experiences and ego-state phenomena to dissociative identity disorder and polyfragmented chaotic personality systems. As John Watkins stated, a major goal of treatment is moving the client down the dissociative continuum into more normal ranges. The basic difficulty in treating dissociative clients centers around the question: How can the dissociated personality fragments be recognized and validated without increasing the dissociation and solidifying the ego states? The reader may have felt confused and frustrated by the way my ego states changed, split, and recombined, but this is actually a sign of health. More rigid and permanent delineations would indicate more severe dissociation.

A major lesson is that there are no enemies inside. Hug your demons; don't try to exorcise them. Even the most destructive fragments, the chronically suicidal, for example, need to be befriended, not annihilated. A positive intent exists in each ego state, and it needs to be found, joined, and strengthened. The internal civil wars must be stopped, not pursued with more force.

In direct contradiction to this dictum, the Russian sports psychologists working for the Olympic teams used hypnosis to identify ego states sabotaged athletic performance. Once they identified such an ego state, they would do whatever they could to weaken or destroy it. Of course, these sports psychologists were only concerned with short-term performance goals; the long-term well-being of the athletes was not a concern for them.

There are two other possible exceptions to the hug-your-demons rule. If you are treating a client where your goals are limited to support and containment, any accessing of hidden ego states may be contraindicated. The most interesting possible exception is Pia Mellody's concept of carried emotions. She believes that whenever a major caregiver is irresponsible with their emotions, the child sucks them up like a sponge and carries them. Pia feels that these emotions can not be processed or healed and must be symbolically returned to the caregiver or parent involved. This is sometimes appropriate, but since the natural tendency of the dissociative client is to disown difficult emotional states, every attempt to hug the demons should be explored first.

The relationships between the ego states and the adult self are crucial. They are probably more important than the recovery of memory. Force does not work. My initial attitude was that of a bulldozer. I just wanted to crash through. The more energy I put into this assault, the more energy went into my internal divisions and defenses. It's like those Chinese finger traps we played with as kids; the harder you pull, the more firmly you're trapped. The solution is a 180-degree change of direction: provide safety, support, and protection for the resistant, evasive ego states, and they will open and heal.

Many writers have developed classification systems for ego states. Transactional analysis used internal parent, adult, and child. Allison hypothesized an internal self-helper. Fritz Perls had his "top dog" and "underdog." Pia Mellody had her "wounded child" and "adult adapted wounded child." In *The Mosaic Mind,* Regina Goulding and Richard Schwartz discuss "Firefighters," "Managers," and "Exiled Child" parts. Many theorists discuss parental introjects. A book could be written describing and comparing these and other ego-state classifications. These theories are fascinating and sometimes helpful, but it is of paramount importance to recognize the individual ego states and not treat them as representations of a class. It is the Martin Buber I-thou relationship attitude on an intrapsychic level.

With almost all traumatized dissociative people some kind of biphasic response occurs: periods of intrusive emotion and memory alternating with periods of numbing. These responses occur both in short cycles—daily, hourly, or even minute by minute—and in long cycles of weeks and months and years. Periods of memory recall alternate with periods of denial. Flooding and shutdown, sobriety and relapse occur, causing frustration, but less so when it is planned for and expected.

The history of denial of child abuse in our culture recapitulates the cycles of denial in an individual. Roland Summit (1988), in a wonderful article, has shown how we have repeatedly discovered that child sexual abuse is prevalent and that it causes adult psychological dysfunction; and yet we have repeatedly buried and denied this knowledge when its painful implications become clear. I hope we won't bury it again. One of my major sources of hope is that we are becoming aware of the basic uniformity of response to all kinds of trauma. The patterns of post-traumatic stress disorder are similar in war veterans, sexually abused children, and adult victims of violence and rape. It would take massive denial to bury the voluminous evidence now available from many different populations.

I end this book with two passages that express my underlying attitudes:

THE GUEST HOUSE

This being human is a guest house.
Every morning a new arrival.

A joy, a depression, a meanness,
some momentary awareness comes
as an unexpected visitor.

Welcome and entertain them all!
Even if they're a crowd of sorrows,
who violently sweep your house
empty of its furniture,
still treat each guest honorably.
He may be clearing you out
for some new delight.

The dark thought, the shame, the malice,
meet them at the door laughing,
and invite them in.

Be grateful for whoever comes,
because each has been sent
as a guide from beyond.

Rumi

Through the gateway of feeling your weakness lies your strength; through the gateway of feeling your fear lies your security and safety; through the gateway of feeling your loneliness lies your capacity to have fulfillment, love and companionship; through the gateway of feeling your hate lies your capacity to love; through the gateway of feeling your hopelessness lies true and justified hope; through the gateway of accepting the lacks of your childhood lies your fulfillment now.

Eva Pierrakos and Donovan Thesenga
Fear No Evil (1993)

Bibliography

Barach, P. M. "Multiple personality disorder as an attachment disorder." In *Dissociation: Progress in the Dissociative Disorders, Vol. 4*, (pp. 117-123) 1991. Smyrna, GA: Ridgeview Institute.

Barrett, Deirdre (ed.). *Trauma and Dreams.* Cambridge, MA: Harvard University Press, 1996.

Bass, Ellen and Laura Davis. *The Courage to Heal: A Guide for Women Survivors of Child Sexual Abuse.* New York: Harper and Row, 1988.

Bateson, Gregory. *Mind and Nature: A Necessary Unity.* New York: Bantam, 1979.

Beahrs, John O. *Unity and Multiplicity: Multilevel Consciousness of Self in Hypnosis, Psychiatric Disorder, and Mental Health.* New York: Brunner/Mazel, 1982.

Bliss, Eugene L. *Multiple Personality, Allied Disorders, and Hypnosis.* Oxford: Oxford University Press, 1986.

Bollingen, William McGuire (Ed.). *The Freud/Jung Letters,* Series XCIV. Princeton: Princeton University Press, 1974.

Bolton, Frank G. Jr., Larry A. Morris, and Anne E. MacEachron. *Males at Risk: The Other Side of Child Sexual Abuse.* Newbury Park, CA: Sage, 1989.

Braddock, Carolyn J. *Body Voices: Using the Power of Breath, Sound, and Movement to Heal and Create New Boundaries.* Berkeley, CA: Page Mill Press, 1995.

Bradshaw, John. *Healing the Shame that Binds You.* Deerfield Beach, FL: Health Communications, 1988.

Bradshaw, John. *Homecoming: Reclaiming and Championing Your Inner Child.* New York: Bantam Books, 1990.

Braun, Bennett G. "The Bask Model of Dissociation." In *Dissociation: Progress in the Dissociative Disorders, Vol. 1* (pp 4-23), 1988. Georgia: Ridgeview Institute.

Briere, John. *Therapy for Adults Molested as Children: Beyond Survival.* New York: Springer Publishing Company, 1989.

Briere, John. *Child Abuse Trauma: Theory and Treatment of the Lasting Effects.* Newbury Park, CA: Sage, 1992.

Buber, Martin. *Tales of Hasidism: The Early Masters.* New York: Schocken Books, 1947.

Buber, Martin. *Tales of Hasidism: The Later Masters.* New York: Schocken Books, 1947.

Butler, Sandra. *Conspiracy of Silence: The Trauma of Incest.* San Francisco: Volcano Press, 1978.

Campbell, Joseph with Bill Moyers. *The Power of Myth.* New York: Doubleday, 1988.

Carnes, Patrick J. *The Betrayal Bond.* Deerfield Beach, FL: Health Communications, Inc., 1997.

Colegrave, Sukie. *By Way of Pain: A Passage into Self.* Rochester, VT: Park Street Press, 1988.

Courtois, Christine A. *Healing the Incest Wound: Adult Survivors in Therapy.* New York: Norton, 1988.

Donaldson, Mary Ann and Susan Cordes-Green. *Group Treatment of Adult Incest Survivors.* Thousand Oaks, CA: Sage, 1994.

Elliot, Michele (ed.). *Female Sexual Abuse of Children.* London: Guilford, 1993.

Engel, Beverly. *The Right to Innocence: Healing the Trauma of Childhood Sexual Abuse.* Los Angeles: Tarcher, 1989.

Evert, Kathy and Inie Bijkerk. *When You're Ready: A Woman's Healing from Childhood Physical and Sexual Abuse by Her Mother.* Walnut Creek, CA: Launch Press, 1987.

Farmer, Steven. *Adult Children of Abusive Parents: A Healing Program for Those Who Have Been Physically, Sexually, or Emotionally Abused.* Los Angeles: Lowell House, 1989.

Finkelhor, David with Araji, Sahron, Baron, Larry, Brown, Angela, Peters, Stephanie Doyle, and Wyatt, Gail Elizabeth. *A Sourcebook on Child Sexual Abuse.* Beverly Hills, CA: Sage, 1986.

Forward, Susan and Craig Buck. *Betrayal of Innocence: Incest and Its Devastation.* New York: Penguin, 1978.

Frankl, Viktor E. *Man's Search for Meaning: An Introduction to Logotherapy.* Boston: Beacon Press, 1963.

Fraser, Sylvia. *My Father's House: A Memoir of Incest and of Healing.* New York: Perennial Library, 1987.

Frederickson, Renee. *Repressed Memories: A Journey to Recovery from Sexual Abuse.* New York: Simon and Schuster, 1992.

Freud, Sigmund. "The Aetiology of Hysteria." In *Sigmund Freud Collected Papers,* Vol. 1 (Trans. Joan Riviere). New York: Basic Books, 1959.

Freyd, Jennifer J. *Betrayal Trauma: The Logic of Forgetting Childhood Abuse.* Cambridge, MA: Harvard University Press, 1996.

Friedrich, William N. (ed.). *Casebook of Sexual Abuse Treatment.* New York: W.W. Norton, 1991.

Gannon, J. Patrick. *Soul Survivors: A New Beginning for Adults Abused As Children.* New York: Prentice-Hall, 1989.

Gil, Eliana. *Outgrowing the Pain: A Book for and About Adults Abused as Children.* New York: Dell, 1983.

Gil, Eliana. *Treatment of Adult Survivors of Childhood Abuse.* Walnut Creek, CA: Launch Press, 1988.

Gil, Eliana. *Outgrowing the Pain Together: A Book for Spouses and Partners of Adults Abused as Children.* New York: Dell, 1992.

Goodwin, Jean M. (ed.). *Rediscovering Childhood Trauma: Historical Casebook and Clinical Applications.* Washington, DC: American Psychiatric Press, 1993.

Goulding, Regina A. and Richard C. Schwartz. *The Mosaic Mind.* New York: W.W. Norton and Co., 1995.

Graber, Ken. *Ghosts in the Bedroom: A Guide for Partners of Sexual Abuse Survivors.* Deerfield Beach, FL: Health Communications, 1991.

Haley, Jay (ed.). *Advanced Techniques of Hypnosis and Therapy: Selected Papers of Milton H. Erickson, MD.* Orlando, FL: Grune and Stratton, 1967.

Harlow, H. F. and Mehrs, C. *The Human Model: Primate Prespectives.* New York: John Wiley and Sons, 1979.

Havens, Ronald A. (ed.). *The Wisdom of Milton H. Erickson: Human Behavior and Psychotherapy.* New York: Irvington, 1989.

Herman, Judith Lewis. *Trauma and Recovery: The Aftermath of Violence from Domestic Abuse to Political Terror.* New York: Basic Books, 1992.

Hilgard, Ernest. *Divided Consciousness: Multiple Controls in Human Thought and Action.* New York: John Wiley and Sons, 1977.

Hunter, Mic. *Abused Boys: The Neglected Victims of Sexual Abuse.* Lexington, MA: Lexington Books, 1990.

Hunter, Mic (ed.). *The Sexually Abused Male: Vol I, Prevalence, Impact, and Treatment; Vol II, Application of Treatment Strategies.* Lexington, MA: Lexington Books, 1990.

Johnson, Robert. *Innerwork: Using Dreams and Active Imagination for Personal Growth.* San Francisco: Harper and Row, 1986.

Kane, Evangeline. *Recovering from Incest: Imagination and the Healing Process.* Boston: Sigo Press, 1989.

King, Neal. *Speaking Our Truth: Voices of Courage and Healing for Male Survivors of Childhood Sexual Abuse.* New York: Harper Perennial, 1995.

Kluft, Richard (ed.). *Incest Related Syndromes of Adult Psychopathology.* Washington, DC: American Psychiatric Press, 1990.

Kluft, Richard P. (ed.). *Childhood Antecedents of Multiple Personality.* Washington DC: American Psychiatric Press, 1985.

Lew, Mike. *Victims No Longer: Men Recovering from Incest and Other Sexual Child Abuse.* New York: Nevraumont, 1988.

Maltz, Wendy. *The Sexual Healing Journey: A Guide for Survivors of Sexual Abuse.* New York: HarperCollins, 1991.

Maltz, Wendy and Beverly Holman. *Incest and Sexuality: A Guide to Understanding and Healing.* Lexington, MA: Lexington Books, 1989.

Masson, Jeffrey Moussaieff. *The Assault on Truth: Freud's Suppression of the Seduction Theory.* New York: Penguin Books, 1985.

Mellody, Pia, Andrea Miller, and Keith Miller. *Facing Codependence: What It Is, Where It Comes From, How It Sabotages Our Lives.* New York: HarperCollins, 1989.

Middelton-Moz, Jane. *Children of Trauma: Rediscovering Your Discarded Self.* Deerfield Beach, FL: Health Communications, 1989.

Middelton-Moz, Jane. *Shame and Guilt: The Masters of Disguise.* Deerfield Beach, FL: Health Communications, 1990.

Miller, Alice. *Thou Shalt Not Be Aware: Society's Betrayal of the Child.* New York: New American Library, 1984.

Miller, Alice. *Banished Knowledge: Facing Childhood Injuries.* New York: Doubleday, 1985.

Miller, Alice. *The Untouched Key.* New York: Doubleday, 1988.

Mindell, Arnold. *Dreambody.* Boston: Sigo Press, 1982.

Mindell, Arnold. *Working with the Dreaming Body.* Boston: Routledge and Kegan Paul, 1985.

Mindell, Arnold. *The Dreambody in Relationships.* Boston: Routledge and Kegan Paul, 1987.

Peck, M. Scott. *The Road Less Traveled: A New Psychology of Love, Traditional Values and Spiritual Growth.* (pp. 44-46). New York: Simon and Schuster, 1978.

Peck, M. Scott. *People of the Lie.* New York: Simon and Schuster, Inc., 1983.

Pierrakos, Eva, and Donovan Thesenga. *Fear No Evil: The Pathwork Method of Transforming the Lower Self.* Madison, VA: Pathwork Press, 1993.

Poston, Carol and Karen Lison. *Reclaiming Our Lives: Hope for Adult Survivors of Incest.* Boston: Little, Brown, 1989.

Putnam, Frank W. *Diagnosis and Treatment of Multiple Personality Disorder.* New York: The Guilford Press, 1989.

Pynoos, Robert S. (Ed.). *Post Traumatic Stress Disorder: A Clinical Review.* Lutherville, MD: Sidran Press, 1994.

Rowan, John. *Subpersonalities: The People Inside Us.* London: Routledge, 1990.

Rumi. "The Guest House." In Coleman Barks (trans.) *The Essential Rumi* (p. 109). New York: HarperCollins, 1997.

Salter, Anna C. *Transforming Trauma: A Guide to Understanding and Treating Adult Survivors of Child Sexual Abuse.* Thousand Oaks, CA: Sage, 1995.

Sanders, Timothy L. *Male Survivors: 12-Step Recovery Program for Survivors of Childhood Sexual Abuse.* Freedom, CA: The Crossing Press, 1991.

Satir, Virginia. *Peoplemaking.* Palo Alto, CA: Science and Behavior Books, 1972.

Satir, Virgina, John Banmen, Jane Gerber, Maria Gomori. *The Satir Model: Family Therapy and Beyond.* Palo Alto, CA: Science and Behavior Books, 1991.

Shengold, Leonard. *Soul Murder: The Effects of Childhood Abuse and Deprivation.* New Haven: Yale University, 1989.

Spiegel, David (ed.). *Dissociation: Culture, Mind and Body.* Washington DC: American Psychiatric Press Inc., 1994.

Summit, R. C. Hidden Victims, Hidden Pain: Societal Avoidance of Child Sexual Abuse. In C. E. Wyatt and C. J. Powell (Eds.) *Lasting Effects of Child Sexual Abuse* (pp. 39-60). Newbury Park, CA: Sage, 1988.

Terr, Lenore. *Unchained Memories: True Stories of Traumatic Memories, Lost and Found*. New York: Basic Books, 1994.

van der Hart, Onno and Freidman, Barbara. A Reader's Guide to Pierre Janet on Dissociation: A Neglected Intellectual Heritage. *Dissociation* 2(1): 3-16. 1989.

Van der Kolk, Bessel A. *Psychological Trauma*. Washington, DC: American Psychiatric Press, 1987.

Van der Kolk, Bessel A., Alexander C. McFarlane, Lars Wiesaeth (eds.). *Traumatic Stress: The Effects of Overwhelming Experience on Mind, Body, and Society*. New York: Guilford, 1996.

Van Dusen, Wilson. *The Natural Depth in Man*. New York: Harper and Row, 1972.

Van Dusen, Wilson. *The Country of Spirit*. San Francisco: Appleseed and Company, 1992.

Watkins, John G. *Hypnotherapeutic Techniques*. New York: Irvington, 1987.

Watkins, John G. *Hypnoanalytic Techniques*. New York: Irvington, 1992.

Watkins, John G. and Helen H. Watkins. *Ego States: Theory and Therapy*. New York: Norton, 1997.

Whitfield, Charles L. *Healing the Child Within: Discovery and Recovery for Adult Children of Dysfunctional Families*. Deerfield Beach, FL: Health Communications, 1987.

Williams, Linda Meyer. Recovered Memories of Abuse in Women with Documented Child Sexual Victimization Histories. *Journal of Traumatic Stress 8:* 649-673. 1995.

Woititz, Janet G. *Struggle for Intimacy*. Deerfield Beach, FL: Health Communications, 1985.

Woititz, Janet G. *Healing Your Sexual Self*. Deerfield Beach, FL: Health Communications, 1989.

Zeig, Jeffery K. (ed.). *A Teaching Seminar with Milton H. Erickson*. New York: Brunner/Mazel, 1980.

THE HAWORTH MALTREATMENT AND TRAUMA PRESS®
Robert A. Geffner, PhD
Senior Editor

THE INSIDERS: A MAN'S RECOVERY FROM TRAUMATIC CHILDHOOD ABUSE by Robert Blackburn Knight. (2002). "An important book. . . . Fills a gap in the literature about healing from childhood sexual abuse by allowing us to hear, in undiluted terms, about one man's history and journey of recovery." *Amy Pine, MA, LMFT, psychotherapist and co-founder, Survivors Healing Center, Santa Cruz, California*

WE ARE NOT ALONE: A GUIDEBOOK FOR HELPING PROFESSIONALS AND PARENTS SUPPORTING ADOLESCENT VICTIMS OF SEXUAL ABUSE by Jade Christine Angelica. (2002). "Encourages victims and their families to participate in the system in an effort to heal from their victimization, seek justice, and hold offenders accountable for their crimes. An exceedingly vital training tool." *Janet Fine, MS, Director, Victim Witness Assistance Program and Children's Advocacy Center, Suffolk County District Attorney's Office, Boston*

WE ARE NOT ALONE: A TEENAGE GIRL'S PERSONAL ACCOUNT OF INCEST FROM DISCLOSURE THROUGH PROSECUTION AND TREATMENT by Jade Christine Angelica. (2002). "A valuable resource for teens who have been sexually abused and their parents. With compassion and eloquent prose, Angelica walks people through the criminal justice system—from disclosure to final outcome." *Kathleen Kendall-Tackett, PhD, Research Associate, Family Research Laboratory, University of New Hampshire, Durham*

WE ARE NOT ALONE: A TEENAGE BOY'S PERSONAL ACCOUNT OF CHILD SEXUAL ABUSE FROM DISCLOSURE THROUGH PROSECUTION AND TREATMENT by Jade Christine Angelica. (2002). "Inspires us to work harder to meet kids' needs, answer their questions, calm their fears, and protect them from their abusers and the system, which is often not designed to respond to them in a language they understand." *Kevin L. Ryle, JD, Assistant District Attorney, Middlesex, Massachusetts*

GROWING FREE: A MANUAL FOR SURVIVORS OF DOMESTIC VIOLENCE by Wendy Susan Deaton and Michael Hertica. (2001). "This is a necessary book for anyone who is scared and starting to think about what it would take to 'grow free.' . . . Very helpful for friends and relatives of a person in a domestic violence situation. I recommend it highly." *Colleen Friend, LCSW, Field Work Consultant, UCLA Department of Social Welfare, School of Public Policy & Social Research*

A THERAPIST'S GUIDE TO GROWING FREE: A MANUAL FOR SURVIVOR'S OF DOMESTIC VIOLENCE by Wendy Susan Deaton and Michael Hertica. (2001). "An excellent synopsis of the theories and research behind the manual." *Beatrice Crofts Yorker, RN, JD, Professor of Nursing, Georgia State University, Decatur*

PATTERNS OF CHILD ABUSE: HOW DYSFUNCTIONAL TRANSACTIONS ARE REPLICATED IN INDIVIDUALS, FAMILIES, AND THE CHILD WELFARE SYSTEM by Michael Karson. (2001). "No one interested in what may well be the major public health epidemic of our time in terms of its long-term consequences for our society can afford to pass up the opportunity to read this enlightening work." *Howard Wolowitz, PhD, Professor Emeritus, Psychology Department, University of Michigan, Ann Arbor*

IDENTIFYING CHILD MOLESTERS: PREVENTING CHILD SEXUAL ABUSE BY RECOGNIZING THE PATTERNS OF THE OFFENDERS by Carla van Dam. (2000). "The definitive work on the subject. . . . Provides parents and others with the tools to recognize when and how to intervene." *Roger W. Wolfe, MA, Co-Director, N. W. Treatment Associates, Seattle, Washington*

POLITICAL VIOLENCE AND THE PALESTINIAN FAMILY: IMPLICATIONS FOR MENTAL HEALTH AND WELL-BEING by Vivian Khamis. (2000). "A valuable book . . . a pioneering work that fills a glaring gap in the study of Palestinian society." *Elia Zureik, Professor of Sociology, Queens University, Kingston, Ontario, Canada*

STOPPING THE VIOLENCE: A GROUP MODEL TO CHANGE MEN'S ABUSIVE ATTITUDES AND BEHAVIORS by David J. Decker. (1999). "A concise and thorough manual to assist clinicians in learning the causes and dynamics of domestic violence." *Joanne Kittel, MSW, LICSW, Yachats, Oregon*

STOPPING THE VIOLENCE: A GROUP MODEL TO CHANGE MEN'S ABUSIVE ATTITUDES AND BEHAVIORS, THE CLIENT WORKBOOK by David J. Decker. (1999).

BREAKING THE SILENCE: GROUP THERAPY FOR CHILDHOOD SEXUAL ABUSE, A PRACTITIONER'S MANUAL by Judith A. Margolin. (1999). "This book is an extremely valuable and well-written resource for all therapists working with adult survivors of child sexual abuse." *Esther Deblinger, PhD, Associate Professor of Clinical Psychiatry, University of Medicine and Dentistry of New Jersey School of Osteopathic Medicine*

"I NEVER TOLD ANYONE THIS BEFORE": MANAGING THE INITIAL DISCLOSURE OF SEXUAL ABUSE RE-COLLECTIONS by Janice A. Gasker. (1999). "Discusses the elements needed to create a safe, therapeutic environment and offers the practitioner a number of useful strategies for responding appropriately to client disclosure." *Roberta G. Sands, PhD, Associate Professor, University of Pennsylvania School of Social Work*

FROM SURVIVING TO THRIVING: A THERAPIST'S GUIDE TO STAGE II RECOVERY FOR SURVIVORS OF CHILDHOOD ABUSE by Mary Bratton. (1999). "A must read for all, including survivors. Bratton takes a lifelong debilitating disorder and unravels its intricacies in concise, succinct, and understandable language." *Phillip A. Whitner, PhD, Sr. Staff Counselor, University Counseling Center, The University of Toledo, Ohio*

SIBLING ABUSE TRAUMA: ASSESSMENT AND INTERVENTION STRATEGIES FOR CHILDREN, FAMILIES, AND ADULTS by John V. Caffaro and Allison Conn-Caffaro. (1998). "One area that has almost consistently been ignored in the research and writing on child maltreatment is the area of sibling abuse. This book is a welcome and required addition to the developing literature on abuse." *Judith L. Alpert, PhD, Professor of Applied Psychology, New York University*

BEARING WITNESS: VIOLENCE AND COLLECTIVE RESPONSIBILITY by Sandra L. Bloom and Michael Reichert. (1998). "A totally convincing argument. . . . Demands careful study by all elected representatives, the clergy, the mental health and medical professions, representatives of the media, and all those unwittingly involved in this repressive perpetuation and catastrophic global problem." *Harold I. Eist, MD, Past President, American Psychiatric Association*

TREATING CHILDREN WITH SEXUALLY ABUSIVE BEHAVIOR PROBLEMS: GUIDELINES FOR CHILD AND PARENT INTERVENTION by Jan Ellen Burton, Lucinda A. Rasmussen, Julie Bradshaw, Barbara J. Christopherson, and Steven C. Huke. (1998). "An extremely readable book that is well-documented and a mine of valuable 'hands on' information. . . . This is a book that all those who work with sexually abusive children or want to work with them must read." *Sharon K. Araji, PhD, Professor of Sociology, University of Alaska, Anchorage*

THE LEARNING ABOUT MYSELF (LAMS) PROGRAM FOR AT-RISK PARENTS: LEARNING FROM THE PAST—CHANGING THE FUTURE by Verna Rickard. (1998). "This program should be a part of the resource materials of every mental health professional trusted with the responsibility of working with 'at-risk' parents." *Terry King, PhD, Clinical Psychologist, Federal Bureau of Prisons, Catlettsburg, Kentucky*

THE LEARNING ABOUT MYSELF (LAMS) PROGRAM FOR AT-RISK PARENTS: HANDBOOK FOR GROUP PARTICIPANTS by Verna Rickard. (1998). "Not only is the LAMS program designed to be educational and build skills for future use, it is also fun!" *Martha Morrison Dore, PhD, Associate Professor of Social Work, Columbia University, New York, New York*

BRIDGING WORLDS: UNDERSTANDING AND FACILITATING ADOLESCENT RECOVERY FROM THE TRAUMA OF ABUSE by Joycee Kennedy and Carol McCarthy. (1998). "An extraordinary survey of the history of child neglect and abuse in America. . . . A wonderful teaching tool at the university level, but should be required reading in high schools as well." *Florabel Kinsler, PhD, BCD, LCSW, Licensed Clinical Social Worker, Los Angeles, California*

CEDAR HOUSE: A MODEL CHILD ABUSE TREATMENT PROGRAM by Bobbi Kendig with Clara Lowry. (1998). "Kendig and Lowry truly . . . realize the saying that we are our brothers' keepers. Their spirit permeates this volume, and that spirit of caring is what always makes the difference for people in painful situations." *Hershel K. Swinger, PhD, Clinical Director, Children's Institute International, Los Angeles, California*

SEXUAL, PHYSICAL, AND EMOTIONAL ABUSE IN OUT-OF-HOME CARE: PREVENTION SKILLS FOR AT-RISK CHILDREN by Toni Cavanagh Johnson and Associates. (1997). "Professionals who make dispositional decisions or who are related to out-of-home care for children could benefit from reading and following the curriculum of this book with children in placements." *Issues in Child Abuse Accusations*